A Parisian's Paris

Philippe Meyer

A Parisian's Paris

Chronicle for the millennium

Flammarion

For Olimpia and Paul-Annick, who warm the heart of Paris and the hearts of certain Parisians—including my own.

Introduction in the Guise
of a Foreword and a Wish

A few years ago I traveled the length and breadth of France, and then recounted my experiences in a book. Its title was lifted from the second half of a line by Aragon: "In a land so strange, *In My Very Own Land....*" In making the various stages of that journey, and in drafting the chapters of that book, I realized that my tour of France would never be complete if I failed to "do" Paris. That is not only because the capital is everpresent in the life and minds of provincials (whether they mock, damn, envy, or long for it); nor is it because there's an old love story between me and Paris (and, often enough, between Paris and me); it's also because nothing is more tempting or more intimidating than to crisscross Paris in an attempt to describe and understand—like countless writers before me—this city composed of so many varied villages, this city adopted by so many people seeking to become free agents again, to escape life's laws of gravity.

I'm immoderately fond of that special variety and freedom, which is what I wanted to recount in such length and breadth. This book is therefore not by an aspiring urban scientist (even supposing such a thing existed) nor even by a sociologist, but simply by a Parisian, a citizen of Paris who embarked on the exploration of his own city armed with his own questions, which he hopes are shared by others.

As the next century, indeed millennium, approaches, I want to see if Paris has remained a kind of New World where

9

everyone can hope to make a fresh start in life, choose a new path, discover new tastes, find whatever new energy, shelter, or consolation that seems needed. To see if Paris is really a city where people escape the eyes and judgment of man's natural enemy—neighbors. If it's a capital where so many nationalities, cultures, habits, and lifestyles from so many different places meet and procreate. A city rich with life as varied as its *quartiers*, its buildings, its populations.

Does Paris still merit the affection and disgust it has sparked for so many centuries now? Can it still live up to its myth? *That's* what I want to find out.

This book doesn't pretend to be a tourist guide to Paris any more than it claims to be a sociological treatise. However, should it fall into the hands of someone who has never set foot in our fair city, or someone who'd like to renew an acquaintance with her (or him—Paris permits gender switch), I'd like to offer not advice, but a wish: that such visitors do so during the most propitious season. Which is not winter (Paris being too stony, and often gray), nor summer (mercury too high, too many tourists at the sights and in the streets). Spring, too, is misleading; you might think it would do fine, but spring agitates Parisians, making them more inhospitable than ever. Which leaves the fall. But autumn is also the time when the countryside is at its best, when mountains are bathed in gentle light, when the seaside is mild and beaches rid of clamorous crowds and showoffs.

The season that most suits the capital is a fifth season, one that exists only in Paris. It lasts an unpredictable length of time. I've seen it last ten full days—a banner year. And I've seen it vanish within forty-eight hours, banished by ill winds, a low-pressure weather system, or some undefinable event. Sometimes the season never comes. It can't be identified in terms of temperature, quality of light, length of days, or hours of sunshine (which nevertheless play a role), but rather through myriad subtle, unexpected changes. For example:

10

If a pedestrian hasn't yet reached the other side of the street as the light turns green, drivers won't hit the accelerator just as the pedestrian passes in front of their car;

If a traveler tries to get out of a Metro car, people on the platform step aside before trying to climb aboard;

If someone runs toward a bus stop just as the bus is leaving, the driver waits and reopens the door;

If people are walking on the sidewalk after a rainstorm, cars avoid speeding along the gutter for the fun of splashing shoes and trousers;

If, during rush hour you ask a taxi driver to take you from Place d'Italie to Butte Montmartre, you receive neither reprimand nor commentary on the difficulty of accomplishing such an exploit in anything less than half a day. (And, if asked politely, the driver will even turn down the bawling, insipid radio drumming on your ears);

If, in a café, you dare to order a *fine à l'eau* rather than the standard whiskey and soda, the waiter, instead of acting aggrieved, will display a thoroughly Parisian sign of satisfaction in dealing with a connoisseur (or, if he's not sure how to mix the brandy and water—alas, an all-too-frequent occurrence—he'll inquire of the customer with authentic and friendly curiosity);

If you accost a resident in order to ask the way, he or she will flash a smile and will take the time to make sure you've understood.

This fifth season is called *la rentrée*. It begins when Parisians, most of whom migrate out of town for the summer, return home. It ends without warning. It's a time when Parisians reclaim possession and awareness of their city, once again struck by a beauty they had managed to overlook, by the realization that Paris is still a miracle. Filled with pleasure and pride, Parisians delight in sharing their contentment. They know full well they couldn't live anywhere else. That's the time to visit the capital, because it's the one moment when Paris and Parisians show themselves at their best.

11

Ich Bin Ein Pariser

I don't mean to brag, but I can't think of anyone who could claim to be more Parisian than me. (I was going to write "zan me," but it's hard to pen Maurice Chevalier's drawling accent.) Admittedly, I'm not Parisian by birthright, since I wasn't even born in France—I first saw the light of day in Germany, where my noble progenitor was serving his country at the time. Nor can I claim Parisian ancestry, my mother having been born in Nice and my father in Valence, neither of them having had ancestors who so much as sojourned in the capital. At the very most I might suggest that my two grandmothers genetically programmed me to settle down on the banks of the Seine some day, since both of *them* were from Aveyron. Indeed, Paris could be described as a prize city conquered by Aveyroners, although this fact is not widely known.

The *département* of Aveyron, not averse to occasionally using its ancient name of Rouergue, now boasts more descendants in Paris (around a quarter million) than within its own borders, which are marked by the towns of Saint-Affrique, Laguiole, Decazeville, and Millau. Aveyron immigrants were the ones that native-born Parisians, who remain ignorant of everything beyond the city's outer boulevards, once contemptuously dubbed bougnats, thereby mentally confusing them with Auvergnats, that is to say people from

Auvergne. This is roughly comparable to confusing Danes with Swedes, Turks with Greeks, Chileans with Argentineans, or Vietnamese with Cambodians. Even those Aveyroners who come from the northern fringes of the *département* remain true southerners, whereas an Auvergnat is just plain Auvergnat (or, if you will, merely Auvergnat).

I should point out that Aveyron has supplied everything to Paris, at least the Paris of today, the one that postdates Baron Haussmann's nineteenth-century urban renewal. Aveyroners first labored up the stairs of Paris buildings to deliver water and wood, then coal (the French for coal merchant, charbonnier, deformed by provincial accent into *charbougna*, led to the epithet *bougnat*). All the across the capital, Aveyroners set up the bistros that for so long were the life and soul of every *quartier*. Aveyron begat the Saint-Germain-des-Prés neighborhood, insofar as Brasserie Lipp is the work of an Aveyroner, and the famous cafés Flore and Deux Magots were also owned and run by Aveyroners until recently (everything's going to the dogs). Aveyron supplied Montparnasse with two of its "in" spots—or rather, institutions—La Coupole (recently gutted and rebuilt "the same," that is to say, in soulless imitation) and Le Dôme, which is one of the capital's fine fish restaurants (despite the fact that Aveyron, like Bolivia, is unjustly landlocked). Aveyroners also monitor Paris's thirst—two of its descendants control delivery of beer, coffee, fruit juice, and soda to every one of the capital's cafés.

Nor do I underestimate Aveyron's spiritual contribution to Paris. Countless priests from the ranks of what were once called "southern *Chouans* " (Catholic royalists) came up to the capital from the province to baptize, marry, confess, administer, and bury Parisians, producing archbishops whose memories linger on: Monseigneur Affre, who died on the barricades in June 1848 while calling for an end to the violence; Cardinal Verdier, during the 1930s; then Cardinal Marty, who was welcomed in Paris with another bout of barricades—those of

May 1968—yet is remembered as a good country priest serenely standing up to Parisian agitation, attempting to infuse it with a little evangelical gentleness and, above all, modesty. It was reportedly Marty who, on meeting the Prince of Wales during an official ceremony at the presidential palace, asked, after customary greetings, "So how are Mom and Dad?" (Thus are Aveyroners made—institutional grandeur doesn't turn their heads; for that matter, they rarely stray into politics). Finally, the current cardinal and archbishop of Paris, Jean-Marie Lustiger, although born a Jew in Paris of Polish immigrant parents, spent his childhood during World War II at Aubin, in Aveyron's coal basin, and is quick to commend the friendliness of a *département* where he likes to return as an adopted son.

Once you realize that the bistro owners' children have gone to the city's best colleges to become teachers, engineers, and university professors (ENA, the elite grad school that produces all the country's leading politicians, being the choice of the less talented among them), you can see why the Aveyroners who control the real city (the one that eats and drinks) and whose offspring have infiltrated the very heart of the symbolic city (the one that thinks, teaches, researches, and administers) can assert with a straight face that Paris is little more than a colony, or distant possession, of Aveyron.

I myself raise these facts about Aveyron not to support that hypothesis but merely to point out, right from the start, that Parisians inevitably prove their superiority and Parisianness by invoking their provincial roots. Even Paris-born Parisians (barely one-third of the population) display this trait—all of them can tell you where their parents, grandparents, or great-grandparents hailed from (and all of them, in one way or another, brag about it).

It is nevertheless not on the basis of my Aveyron chromosomes that I lay claim to Parisianness of the highest order. Nor on the basis of my childhood or adolescence, since I grew

up in Versailles, a town which, although just eight miles outside of Paris, must be the city in France the farthest removed
from the capital.

Versailles has turned its back on Paris, which represents everything God should never have tolerated—railroads, riots,
revolutions, proletarians, workshops, factories, houses of ill
repute, women of easy virtue, students, cafés, tuberculosis,
priests in civilian dress, alcohol, sodomites, shameful diseases,
atheism, Freemasonry, wealth, theaters, nightclubs, Roth-
schilds and other Jews, stateless persons, foreigners, divorce,
teenage mothers, abortion, universal suffrage (that is, the abolition of property requirements), women's suffrage, the aban-
donment of Saint Pius V's rites, reds, communards,
Dreyfusards, pacifists, anarchist thugs (Bonnot, Ravachol,
Landru... Cohn-Bendit), short skirts, women who go out
without a hat, men without gloves, the Edict of Nantes, the
abolition of the death penalty, marriage outside one's own
social group, paid holidays, the abolition of third-class train
tickets (and first-class Metro carriages), the birth-control pill,
condoms, the banning of corporal punishment, the end of the
draft, military courts and military prisons, the closing of
forced labor camps in the colonies, songs by Georges Brassens,
songs by Jacques Brel, songs by Léo Ferré, and, globally, any
songs after *Aux Marches du Palais* (even those by Père Duval
and Sœur Sourire), black music, living together in sin, idle-
ness, "evilmindedness," the loss of the West African colonies,
the independence of Algeria, the advent of the French republic, and even the movies.

I'm referring here to the Versailles of my teenage years, but
I have excellent reasons for believing that the town has with-
stood the march of time. In 1995, one of my childhood
friends, a native of Versailles who, out of laziness, took over
his father's medical practice there, said to me: "Did you know
that this city dœsn't have a single AIDS patient or victim?"
When I expressed astonishment at this quirk, unable to bring

16

myself to believe that municipal chastity was so thoroughly impregnable, he continued, "That's because the word is never uttered. Knowing how fond you are of your native language, I suggest you come back here long enough to compile a glossary of all the circumlocutions employed when mentioning the unmentionable."

Fortunately, my tender years were spared scourges of this type. Yet one of my friends, in his senior year at *lycée*, having finally glimpsed his chance and hoping to prevent the misfortune that precipitously led one of our buddies to the altar, went into a drugstore to procure a pack a condoms. I waited on the sidewalk outside, keeping a lookout for the possible approach of his parents or one of his countless aunts. Nervously (it was going to be his baptism of fire), he asked the druggist for a "contraceptive." Said druggist assumed a semi-indignant, semi-ignorant tone, claiming he didn't understand exactly what was desired. Then, when the impatient virgin corrected his error by asking for a condom (reddening to a shade of crimson), the druggist withdrew to the back room, returned with a packet already wrapped in a brown paper bag, and rang up the sale, all the while implying that my friend was mighty young. It was four o'clock in the afternoon, a time when we correctly gauged that stores in Versailles would be devoid of customers (every one of whom was a potential spy). At 7:00 P.M. the druggist, having obtained heaven knows how the name of the purchaser of the condoms, telephoned his parents; at 7:30, the young fiend was summoned before his old man; by 8:00, he was confined to his room, deprived of supper. His longed-for ecstasy came close to being replaced by flagellation. The rod was rarely spared in his (sizable) family. (But then, they were all sizable.)

Just to situate this anecdote in the minds of readers who may think I was born during the Victorian era, I might point out that this tale of a tattling druggist occurred the year the Beatles took the world by storm. That very same year our history teacher, discussing American civilization, suggested that we devote two hours of our weekend to seeing a Raoul Walsh film, *The Enforcers*, thinking that we would benefit from lively artistic stimulation as well as from a great deal of information on life in the United States. The movie was playing at the town's art-house cinema (called *La Tannerie* in order to convey, like everything else in Versailles, a whiff of La Varende's swashbuckling Catholic novels), whose artistic pretensions confirmed the educational soundness of our teacher's recommendation. But a few clods in the class asked their parents' permission to follow his advice, upon which said parents called each other up, formed a committee, and sent a delegation. They informed the principal that any teacher who advised his pupils to go to the movies as a type of homework—a cops-and-robbers film, to boot—could hardly expect to enjoy the confidence of decent families. The teacher was young, having just finished his military service, and was performing his first gainful employment. He was placed on "probation" for the rest of the school year. Having taken the full measure of the weirdness of planet Versailles, he managed to obtain a transfer the following fall. Today he's one of the top ten historians in France.

If I add to the preceding two tales the fact that I spent part of my Versailles youth at a Catholic boarding school, and that I regularly transfered from the public lycée to the boarding school and just as regularly back to the lycée, in the hope that unhappy memories of my previous stay would have faded with each new move (I owed my readmission to public school to a high civil servant—and lyricist—who was a friend of the family, and my acceptance by the private school to a well-placed ecclesiastical uncle); and if you realize that, coming from an anticolonialist left-wing milieu, I was largely surrounded by partisans of right-wing figures such as Tixier-Vignancour and General Salan; and if I inform you that on the anniversary of the death of Louis XVI, a mass was said at the academy and boys were advised to wear a black tie (this is the mid 1960s, remember, just a quarter of an hour from Paris); and if you realize that fistfights still broke out among my school chums between backers of the comte de Paris, supporters of the Spanish house of Bourbon, and zealous Carlists of the Bourbon-Parma clan (when, that is, they weren't endlessly arguing over the comte de Chambord's decision to refuse the French throne if it meant accepting the tricolor flag); when you think that after the putsch by French generals in Algiers two of my schoolmates explained in the cafeteria why the country needed to dump de Gaulle and call on General Weygand (a ninety-year-old, Vichy-backing Colonel Blimp); if you realize that the timetable of the girls' school across the way was carefully calculated to be out of sync with ours so that the probability of chance encounters was practically nil; if I tell you that during school plays by Corneille and Racine the female roles were played by boys whose voices hadn't yet broken and who placed a pair of ski socks under the rented costume in order to represent what we all dreamed of (a travesty that should have led us all astray—straight into British public-school morals); in short, once you appreciate that my childhood and teenage years were the most provincially provincial possible anywhere in France, then you'll understand why I feel entitled to write that no one can claim to be more Parisian than me. Because, although untold numbers of boys and girls my age may have yearned for Paris as much as I did, not a single one craved it more. And Paris is above all a city for which you enlist. A city viewed as a place to start over, a New World. A city that makes a break with provincial life as described by Mauriac: "wilderness without the solitude." A promised land just a train ride away—and in my case, a mere commuter train.

I'm not trying to mythicize Paris, or present it as a remedy for unhappiness. I don't even think it's a question of whether I was unhappy in Versailles. (For that matter, I took much delight—both bitter and sweet—in holding out against the city, whether privately or through "sallies" more or less borrowed from Cyrano de Bergerac and his famous "*Non, merci.*") The problem with Versailles wasn't happiness or unhappiness. The problem was Versailles. It drained the flavor from everything. Nothing was allowed to have its own savor or original taste. It was like a family tomb where nothing was supposed to upset the timeless arrangement of things, where the concept of noise began at just a few decibels. Universal disapproval was invisibly present in the air, ready to suddenly precipitate and rain down on any transgressor. This freezing of lifestyle and thought patterns, of language, habits, values, and hierarchies, surely represents the secret aspiration of much of the provincial middle classes (and, in those days, *all* of them) yet none had achieved it as fully as Versailles, itself a living wax museum (Opening times: 9 A.M. to 1 P.M. and 3 P.M. to 8 P.M.; closed Sundays once mass is over).

So at the age of seventeen, armed with my university ID (in those days a passport for independence), I had a room in Paris and three or four favorite movie theaters. A couscous restaurant on rue Xavier-Privas, near the church of Saint-Séverin, provided hearty repasts—cheap Algerian wine included—for barely four times the cost of a meal ticket at the university cafeteria. And when my friends and I decided to really splash out, we'd have a meal at a place on rue de Grenelle which had a generous fixed-price menu with unlimited wine. The lady who owned it was loudmouthed, and never missed a chance to harass us by calling us bourgeois spongers, layabouts, spoiled brats, names we wouldn't have tolerated from the mouth of anyone else but which, from hers, might be interpreted as terms of affection. (Or at least that's what we liked to think. With hindsight, I think she held her prices down to attract customers on whom she could vent all her spleen and resentment, but in our delight with our newfound freedom and our fledgling status as Parisians, we assumed that everyone wished us well.)

That's all I asked of Paris: no one to keep an eye on me or tell me what to do, a few friends scattered across town, non-stop cinema (in Versailles, of course, the first show wasn't till 8:00 P.M.), theaters, cheap opera seats, ploys for getting into orchestra rehearsals, restaurants that matched my fluctuating pocketbook and my unflagging appetite, and, in order to benefit from all of the above, part-time work that was relatively well paid and above all not too demanding. In general, students found work at the fruit and vegetable market in Les Halles, where several of my friends learned just how varied humanity can be. As for myself, a lycée buddy had an aunt who was a Communist (back in Versailles, he hadn't mentioned her to a soul), and this Communist aunt was a town councilor in the nearby working-class suburb of Saint-Ouen, which in turn was the headquarters of Bull General Electric, whose employee committee was dominated by the Communist CGT labor union. They were seeking a German teacher for evening classes twice a week—which nicely suited my financial needs. The CGT deserves credit for being a good employer, and for paying "intellectual workers" handsomely.

When you get down to it, all I ever asked of Paris (like so many others before me, I think) was simply the right to be there. To have a place there. To be able to proclaim my self-declared citizenship without having to pass a test, undergo examination, submit to selection. It wasn't a question of hitching up with the capital (an ambition Balzac had Rastignac express with the cry, "You and me together!") so much as the city—*the* city—which prompted Restif de la Bretonne to exclaim, "Oh Paris, you magnify me in my own sight!"

One afternoon, while hanging around the Latin Quarter, I was taken with the urge to have a beer at the Balzar on rue des Ecoles (which still serves some of the best beer in Paris) and to see what was playing at the Champollion (where neither screen, seats, nor copies of films had yet been restored). As I sauntered along the sidewalk on the even-numbered (north) side of the street, I noticed for the first time that the statue in front of the university administration building was of Montaigne. On the base was a quotation from that masterful author who wrote in "leaps and bounds": "Paris has had my heart since childhood.... I am a Frenchmen only by this great city... above all great and incomparable in variety and diversity of the good things of life; the glory of France and one of the noblest ornaments of the world."

I suddenly realized that you don't have to know Paris to yearn for it, that its incomparable variety was simultaneously a legacy and a promise that every generation in turn had to extract from the city, and that, for whatever reason you came to be there, truly belonging to Paris was a question of deliberate choice. Since this occurred not long after John F. Kennedy's historic trip to Berlin, symbolizing the struggle for the right to come and go freely, I murmured my decision out loud, solemnly swearing allegiance in the most unexpected of languages: "*Ich bin ein Pariser.*"

Thirty years later, roaming Paris with my head up and a pen and notebook in my pocket, I encountered all kinds of young men and women who might tell a similar tale, adapting it to the times. Student jobs are a lot harder to find. The market at Les Halles no longer exists. But getting by still means getting by, in similar ways. The only difference—a big one—is that this relative bohemia, this escape from convention so typical of student life in Paris thirty years ago, now extends to other age groups and social categories, and threatens to last forever. Whatever the case, Paris continues to be a city inhabited by anonymous narratives, all of which recount the first discovery and possession of the capital.

Crystelle—a name she chose upon arriving in Paris, in preference to Sandrine, the one her parents gave her—must be about thirty-five years old. At Valenciennes, in northern France, she'd had a job as a cashier in a do-it-yourself mart. A desire to see the world spurred her to leave for the nearby city of Lille. One evening, as she was getting ready to sleep outdoors, she met a group of people, mostly Belgian and Dutch, who offered her a place in their squat, near the new courthouse. She stayed with them for eighteen months. They sometimes sold jackets, vests, and tunics on college campuses or at street markets. Crystelle picked up some cutting and stitching skills. When the squat was cleared by the police, the group broke up, having stuck together mostly out of habit. Crystelle caught a train for Paris, and decided to become a fashion designer. Which she is.

Not many people know it, but Crystelle *is* a fashion designer. Has been for over ten years now. She didn't get into any of the leading schools of fashion design, and the others were too lightweight and too expensive. The fashion houses she's applied to have never offered her much more than menial work, but at least she's managed to learn some tricks of the trade and to become part of the scene she so craves. She lives in the 17th arrondissement—in what real-estate agents call the "downmarket" 17th, near La Fourche. One room with shower, kitchenette, and saniflush toilet that constantly breaks and floods the downstairs neighbor. Her neighbors on the same floor seem to come from all corners of the earth. In her room, Crystelle designs and makes the clothes she wears and that she occasionally sells to friends or friends of friends. She also swaps them for things like metal jewelry (made by a woman originally from Ariège who now lives near Place des Fêtes), a chair (designed and executed by a skinny curly-haired man who immigrated from the suburbs and for whom Crystelle cut a cloak from an army blanket), and an electric hotplate and a hairdryer (from a couple of women who, having decided to move in together, were getting rid of everything in duplicate).

Except when a fashion workshop needs extra hands during a rush job, Crystelle lives on the minimum welfare payment. Since that can't satisfy her needs, and since she swaps her "creations" more often than she sells them, she does countless microjobs on the side. She lists them carefully, trying not to forget a single one (clearly an impossible task): nursing, dog walking, cat and bird feeding, babysitting, errand running, cleaning and painting, darning and patching, ironing, helping with street market sales, replacing switchboard operators, and so on. Some years are better than others, but Crystelle claims she lacks nothing. She clings to the fringes of the world she dreams about and, whether the world recognizes it or not, she's a fashion designer.

Thomas, meanwhile, left Alsace for Paris soon after completing his army service. Having just barely obtained his *baccalauréat*, or high-school certificate, he ostensibly came to Paris to register in the humanities department of the university. His retired parents didn't try to keep him home; he's the youngest of five children, and anyway they didn't have anything better to offer or recommend. Thomas found an acting school through the Minitel (electronic yellow pages), and attended the admissions audition. He flunked, yet met a girl who also failed but mentioned another school, less well known but easier to get into. They were both accepted and soon decided to share an apartment in order to save money. The school wasn't cheap, but Thomas managed to make ends meet by working as a night watchman in a hotel, and occasionally driving a truck for a piano-moving firm (having earned his license in the army). A chance encounter in a bistro put him onto the "extras" network—regular work as an extra on TV dramas made an appreciable difference to his income and enabled him, above all, to qualify for the "part-time Equity guild" which entitles him to certain unemployment benefits during slack periods. With Elodie, his roommate, and other friends from acting school, he founded a theatrical troupe, La Compagnie du Vert Bois (named after rue du Vert Bois in the 3rd arrondissement, where they found an old storage shed for rehearsals). They produced a three-character

24

Chekhov play, *The Bear*, recommended by one of their teachers (not a major play, but it included the role of a fickle woman which Elodie liked a lot). A friend's brother, with connections in the arrondissement administration, booked them into a charity hall run by a rather dormant association. They built a set based on black drapes and gave eight performances to an audience of more-or-less direct acquaintances and fellow students. The audience never numbered more than eighteen, never fewer than six. The Compagnie du Vert Bois hopes to assemble enough cash to rent an "off" theater at next year's Avignon Theater Festival—they're sticking to Chekhov, rehearsing *The Cherry Orchard*. Thomas plays Trofimov.

No one's as good as Thomas at thriving in Paris on next to nothing. Through his connections as a movie "extra," Thomas managed to get onto several industry PR lists, so he now gets invited to preview screenings. If not invited himself, he can slip in with a friend who hosts a nightly radio program on a local station. And since most legit theaters in Paris have difficulty selling all their seats, they avoid presenting their shows before half-empty houses by distributing courtesy tickets— "freebies"—to certain circuits. It's all a question of being in the know. Back in Alsace, Thomas didn't know anybody; here in Paris, he often manages to find himself at the private opening of a major museum exhibition, or at a gallery reception, a rock concert, or a soprano's recital of heaven-knows-what repertoire. In this town, everyone has a dodge and willingly shares it, if only to feel important. Meanwhile, it costs next to nothing to borrow as many books as you want from municipal libraries, or CDs from the record library at Les Halles. And for a modest subscription the Videothèque de Paris offers citizens more films than they could ever watch. After a patient search, Thomas even found a gym he could join for just a third of the annual fee. He's not had many girlfriends in the five years, but he's lived in Paris. With two of the girls it was basically a question of keeping each other warm and feeling good; things inevitably cooled off, and when the time came it was easy to ring down the curtain while still remaining friends. With the third, things were more serious. Which Thomas liked, except that she wanted too much. Not marriage, but a commitment. It was a pretty wrenching affair ("that's good for an actor, you have to experience life"). For the moment, Thomas is on his own. He hasn't gone back to Alsace so much as once in five years. His mother, who calls from time to time, doesn't even ask him to. The link hasn't been broken, Paris has just melted it. Thomas the actor has no moorings.

So does he have a destination in mind? Probably—to earn a living as an actor. Or some related profession. If he doesn't make it as an actor, he at least wants to work on the production, technical, or PR side. At any rate, he never *ever* wants to enter the world of offices, working hours, rules, routine.

As Thomas talks on, I'm struck by his modesty. He's never imagined becoming a star. He knows he's handsome, thinks he's fairly talented, but realizes that getting to the top implies an aggressiveness—or, at the very least, competitiveness—foreign to him. The phrase "making it" is not part of his vocabulary. It's more a question of *s'éclater*—"having a blast." The French term might seem to suggest explosive thrill. In fact, it's more synonymous with *s'épanouir*—"blossoming"—in the sense of "fulfillment," like a flower that slowly opens thanks to the sunshine of good luck and the rain of Equity unemployment benefits. Nor does Thomas speak disparagingly of the universe of work, offices, factories, trade, and parents, referring neither to alienation nor exploitation. He's aware that such a galaxy exists, and that people like him live out there. It's just that he's never thought of making the trip, and he hopes to keep the relationship just what it is today—friendly but distant.

Although I earlier referred to Paris as a New World, for Crystelle and Thomas it more closely resembles a bubble. A world protected from society, like those sterile environments designed for children lacking immune systems. Or like a kind of self-run orphanage, a children's home where you can stay to a ripe old age. Perhaps even till death. Residents of this orphanage can be seen all over late twentieth-century Paris. They belong to a generation born into a world where unemployment is normal and commonplace. They grew up trapped between two kinds of institutions—those that seemed outdated and addressed them in meaningless terms, and those that, like school, constantly gave them the feeling of having to apologize for existing, for having no role or usefulness. As the years went by, they came to the conclusion that they had to live only for themselves. It was therefore logical to drop out, leaving behind a world that imposed, even lackadaisically, pressures to which they had never been given either the means or desire to conform. Only in a universe of total indifference could they "have a blast." And if you're going to live off the fat of society, you may as well go where it's most varied and abundant—to the capital city.

"New World" more closely describes Song's Paris. Song arrived in the city at age twenty-five, via a network he prefers not to describe because it is still in use (or may someday be used again). He was welcomed by "uncles" who had already been in France for a decade or so. For two years Song worked in one of their restaurants, doing every job from bottlewasher to waiter. For 25,000 francs ($4,500), he bought an authentic passport from an Asian country whose nationals were granted the status of political refugees by the French government. From that point onward, things moved quickly. Song's "uncles" located a bistro for sale in northern Paris. They lent him the 1,5 million francs needed to buy both the premises and the business (the latter not worth much), and to convert the bistro into a "Chinese-Vietnamese" restaurant. Song was given ten years to pay them back, but thinks he'll manage sooner. Although the prices at his restaurant are very low, his profit margins are substantial (another subject he dœsn't wish to expound on). Two of them run the show: Song and a fiftyish Chinese cook who remains in the kitchen, speaks barely fifty words of French, and lives in a highrise apartment block near Porte de la Chapelle, on the northern edge of town. Song, meanwhile, sleeps in a small upstairs room that came with the restaurant. He works fourteen or fifteen hours a day, and turns in only after having spent at least an hour improving his French by listening to a language course on cassettes. He'll apply for French nationality as soon as possible. His regular customers include an inspector from police headquarters, who has said she'll help. During lunch hours, Song can be seen moving from table to table with unflagging amiability. The place is more than clean: it sparkles. It's decorated with colorful Chinese baubles that Song bought—along with furniture, crockery, cutlery, tablecloths, napkins, and curtains—from a Chinese wholesaler on the southern outskirts of Paris. Every Monday, when the restaurant is closed, Song receives a visit from an accountant sent by his "uncles," who dœs the books and, above all, wades through the swamp of employer's health contributions, taxes, trading licenses, etc.

In two or three years, Song hopes to get married. A love match? If it so happens. If not, the "uncles" will act as matchmakers. Song spends most of the little free time he has with them, gambling and watching television (to improve his French as much as for entertainment). He dœsn't understand French politics. Everyone insults everybody else and says abstract things. None of it seems very responsible to him, and he has realized, to his lasting astonishment, that in France politicians are neither respected (as befits everyone from whom favors flow) nor feared. He also finds them young (he dœsn't say "too" young, but it's easy to see that's what he's thinking).

Sometimes Song wanders through Paris alone. He is struck by the number of old houses and buildings here. The fact that the French have managed to build modern neighborhoods without demolishing the old has given him food for thought. The Saint-Paul and Île Saint-Louis quarters never fail to impress him, but what really knocks him out is Avenue Henri-Martin. He's not at all embarrassed to admit that what delights him are the signs of wealth. When there's so much money around, business must have a fine future.

Among the aspects of the city that Song mentions with strong approval are cleanliness and the Metro. He's bowled over by the clean streets, even though they give rise to a total mystery: how can Paris spend so much money cleaning streets, gutters, and sidewalks, and then let dogs crap everywhere? When Song first arrived, he thought—having heard that Indians worship cows—that dogs, without being gods strictly speaking, had acquired divine status over here. Now disabused, Song remains completely baffled. As to the Metro, he would almost take it for fun, if he had time for fun—except for the Clignancourt-Orléans line, where he was jostled and had his wallet picked (fortunately containing little cash, but money is money). By Arabs. It had to be Arabs. He didn't actually see them in action, of course, but there were lots of them—two pretended to get into a fight to create a diversion, and it must have been at just that moment that he was relieved of his wallet. At any rate, Arabs, blacks, it's better to leave them out of the conversation.

Song is serenely racist. It would never occur to him to make things hard for blacks or North Africans because of their origins, but he can't imagine placing them on the same shelf as Chinese and Europeans. A shelf which would also exclude Koreans and Cambodians, whom he'd place above Arabs and blacks but who are really made for menial and obscure tasks.

Whereas the universe in which Crystelle, Thomas, and their ilk exist has neither past, future, nor (practically any) signposts, Song's is peaceful and ordered. Elders are respected and obeyed, men take precedence over women, life is made for work, work for money, and money is primarily made for scientifically measuring the power of various individuals (hierarchies need fine tuning, like an engine). Secondly, money is made for gambling. Thirdly and potentially, money is made for becoming French should official channels become bottlenecked or blocked. (Any request for further details on this point would be idiotic, and in poor taste.) Song intends to spend the rest of his life in Paris, and to beget little French citizens. The thought that his grandchildren might bring mixed marriages into the family provokes neither alarm nor displeasure in Song. The main thing is that, from one generation to the next, traditional values survive. Which will surely be the case. Some of his "uncles" have been in France for more than thirty years, and Song has noted that nothing essential has been lost in their community, that even grandchildren who haven't been taught Chinese behave according to the rules.

Here, Paris doesn't make a dent on essentials. But what if the Chinese in Paris modify the essentials in question as the city steadily encroaches on their ways of thinking, provoking more and more confrontations with other ways of viewing and experiencing things? Whatever the case, as long as the Chinese community is able to find work for all its offspring, it will control the strings attaching them, thereby making them Chinese in Paris rather than Parisians of Chinese stock. Those ties will last as long as they don't represent a major constraint, and as long as the constraint is accompanied by an incomparable network of support in a city which otherwise offers almost none.

David, for instance, has seen what the Chinese can do. In the garment district known as Le Sentier, they have already swallowed up half the firms and triggered tough restructuring among "Sephs." David is a Sephardic Jew through his mother. His father is Ashkenazi. Such a match is neither common nor

30

rare in Paris; the antagonism between North African Jews and Central European Jews began fading fast once the numerical preponderance of the former became overwhelming, following the French decolonization of North Africa. At which point the community's main gathering spots, both religious and secular, suddenly changed, spreading more evenly throughout the capital. At the same time, rivalries became more subtle, setting Tunisians against Moroccans and Algerians, Algerians against "Tunes" and Moroccans, and Moroccans against the other two. The main verbal jousts concern the quality of couscous. Even after it has been established that Jewish couscous is far superior to the Arab version, there is still plenty of room for disputing which variety is absolutely perfect. At any rate, David employs countless criteria for distinguishing—and potentially ranking—the subgroups within his Jewish community. Algerians are the most intellectual (those from Tlemcen, at least). Tunisians display the greatest solidarity, but are less enterprising, whereas Moroccans are the most ambitious. Unless it's the other way around. In any event, all three groups agree that Ashkenazim are more hidebound and more religious. ("We, on the other hand, are mainly traditionalists. We always get together for a meal on the Sabbath, but when it comes to going to the synagogue....") Not to mention the fact that Sephs like to party and adore spending money, whereas Ashkenazim are cheapskates. "They're the real Jews," David asserts with a wholehearted laugh, while his two Seph buddies, Rudy and André-Marc, give him a dig with their elbows even as they suppress their own laughter.

It was probably the Sephs' penchant for partying that made David lean toward his maternal roots. After rudimentary schooling, he went into his father's business, selling men's clothing under various brand names, all well established. David is a regular at two or three discotheques on the Champs-Elysées, whose customers are almost all members of the Jewish community. On the first Saturday in September, they and their parents all used to meet at the Renault pub on "the Champs." These days, the rendezvous has shifted to a Häagen-Dazs ice-cream parlor (also on the Champs). When he says, "the Champs-Elysées is ours," he doesn't mean "it belongs to us," but rather, "that's where we meet." There, or over in the Bonne-Nouvelle quarter around Faubourg Montmartre and rue Richer, with its well kosher Chinese and Italian restaurants. Or in a tearoom, where elegant ladies gather in the afternoon to gossip, recreating the very universe of all those jokes that Jews so enjoy telling about their mothers. And in fact, even without lending an ear you can overhear them all, talking (but not listening) about the wonderful son they've brought into the world. You should always watch out for clichés and commonplaces—they usually turn out to be true.

Recently, two or three movies have been set in Paris's Jewish community, mainly the Sephardic community. Which produced moving and perfectly accurate clichés. David describes himself as "a great joker who doesn't kid with tradition." You can rely on him to endlessly mock the younger generation, listing the ways his Sentier colleagues show off. "They're all straight out of some boy band—tight jeans, close-fitting tee-shirt, super-coifed hair, sunbed tan, and dark glasses perched on top of the head. Everything with the labels showing." Nevertheless, those are the guys, along with their big brothers, that David meets in nightclubs. And at the synagogue, when he goes. "It's mainly to be seen and to chat with the guys. Christians have no idea what a bordello a synagogue can be. A Seph synagogue, at any rate." David's conscience isn't completely clear when it comes to religion. He was much more conscientious as a boy. Then, in his teenage years, he started to become a "Kippur" Jew—an occasional, seasonal attendee. Now aged twenty-five, he keeps his distance, although he never goes out without a yarmulke in his pocket. (Which he showed me, for that matter, pointing out that its fancy fabric signified his support of Israel.) Whatever, he knows he'll return to the fold later. When he has children of his own, he'll tell them the history of their people, take them to synagogue.

"How do you know you'll take your kids to synagogue? Are you sure they'll be Jews? You're sure you'll marry a Jew?" David bursts into laughter that temporarily startles the other customers in the former baths on rue des Rosiers, now converted into a fashionable Jewish café.

"You crazy or what?! My mother'd kill me!" And he laughs again all the louder, mocking both the incongruousness of my question and corniness of his reply. He's a member of the community, period. On nights when a soccer match is particularly important or it looks like the score will be particularly tight, he'll go to a *brasserie* in the 17th arrondissement—all the way across town from where he lives—to watch it on television surrounded by a clientele that is 95 percent Sephardic.

I had difficulty grasping the name of the organization that spawned and nurtured this sense of belonging. David was always referring to the "E.I.s". Rudy and André-Marc, too. "That's where we met, in fact." At the E.I.s. The what? The E.I.s, the *Eclaireurs Israélites*, that is to say the Jewish scout movement. Three thousand boys and girls in Paris are scouts. It's not a very religious organization, and the kids stick with it until they're relatively old, assuming more-or-less supervisory responsibilities. The organization encourages mixing through games, outings, and camps, as well as discussions on Israel and the history of persecution. "It's one of the best marriage bureaus in Paris," adds David with another laugh. "Rivaled only by the *Union des Etudiants Juifs de France*, the Jewish students' union, though there's no real competition since all the UEJF leaders are former E.I.s." For that matter, the Jayesse and his supervisory role in the organization provided David with an excuse for leaving the French Riviera, where his family lives, and moving to Paris, where he can breathe more freely. Not that he has the least complaint about his parents. Not a day goes by that he doesn't talk to them on the phone. Not a month goes by without a visit to them. But it's easier to appreciate them if you're not on top of them all the time. And in Paris, you're always being spurred, pushed, driven, rushed.

"So do you do things here that you didn't do on the Riviera?" Come to think of it, no. Less sport, more nightclubs, maybe. But what counts is that you're not always running into the same people, and even if you almost always go to the same places, at the first sign of overdose you only need to go next door for a complete change of scenery, or simply to be on your own, someplace where you're a complete stranger even though you're right near home.

Cozy anonymity only comes in a crowd. Or at the very least, in being surrounded by clusters of people, men or women, young or old, locals or visitors. Their role is to cushion us, but from a decent distance, entertaining us with their noises, with whatever we hear, grasp, or intuit from their conversations, from the way they hold themselves, the way they're dressed, from what we see of the newspaper they're reading, from what we imagine them to be, from their movements and the regular turnover of their numbers. They form a sea of faces, sounds, and existence on which we can drift safely, floating along on thoughts that may be glum, moody, pleasant, or simply vague.

Parisians maintain a contradictory relationship with the café or bistro where they seek this amniotic sea of humanity. On the one hand, they don't want anyone to interrupt their temporary retreat, but on the other hand they expect a bistro to be a great place for surprise (and welcome) encounters. On the one hand, they go into a café to be Mr. or Mrs. Average, on the other they appreciate not being taken for just any old customer. This contradiction can be resolved, but it requires exceptional tact. Assiah and Dermott both possess that quality to a high degree.

Assiah's father was a *harki*, that is to say an Algerian who fought for the French during the Algerian war; so although she was born in Algeria, as an infant Assiah was shipped to a "temporary" camp in Marseille (which still exists nearly forty years later). Encouraged by a school principal who had herself emigrated from Algeria, Assiah obtained a degree in accounting.

Dermott, a native of Galway in western Ireland, came to Paris on vacation at the age of twenty, and decided to stay. Several months later, he joined the ground staff of an airline company, where he worked for twelve years before becoming a shipping agent for an American employer, later continuing on a self-employed basis.

For fifteen years, Assiah drank her morning coffee in the same bistro, run by an elderly couple. The husband fell ill. Assiah began giving the wife a hand and then, without really thinking about it, offered to manage the place for them. Today she owns it.

Dermott, meanwhile, was a regular at all five of the Irish pubs in Paris, at least until 1988. That was when he decided to open a sixth, since none of the others really suited him. After hunting for two months, he located a working-class restaurant with two rooms, one wide and shallow, the other long and deep. Since the restaurant's clientele was shrinking as neighborhood workshops closed, Dermott and the owner came to a quick and reasonable agreement.

Assiah's regular customers included a young accordionist. She suggested that he play one Saturday afternoon. His repertoire ranged from prewar ballads to jazz. The variety was a hit. The accordionist had buddies who were equally eclectic and equally young. They began gathering once a week, then twice a week, creating an easygoing atmosphere, playing tunes on request every now and then. The musicians' various qualities provided a basis for conversation between Assiah and her customers. "When will that guy be back?" "Couldn't that one do us an evening of dancehall tunes?" "Dœsn't one of them know somebody who plays the squeezebox?" Talking about music brought people closer to Assiah. Then someone might confide in her. She became a friend. Assiah played along, being careful never to solicit confessions or approach even the most regular customers unless they took the first step—it was as though permission for intimacy had to be renewed every day. Despite their air of aloofness, two-thirds of the customers wound up baring their souls to Assiah. Her tact, patience, clever advice, and thoughtfulness created an atmosphere of trust. A good number of the previous owners' customers, who had changed cafés to avoid frequenting a joint owned by an Arab, noticed that something was happening back there and wound up returning to their old ways. They were delighted to discover that in their absence the clientele had become younger, delighted with the accordion even if they complained about its being used to play jazz (or, worse, "thrash music"), and delighted when one of the new crowd offered a greeting or when Paul, a prankster who worked for a local architect, honored them with a nickname and started making cracks about them, thereby triggering a verbal joust in which everyone played their role to the hilt—ignorant youth on one side and old Parisian sticks-in-the-mud on the other—with Assiah awarding, at the end of the tournament, compliments and prizes to the winning side, all the while making sure that no one went so far as to spoil all the fun. As the years went by, Assiah managed to create a café so Parisian—the place now has a terrace—that it seems straight out of a Robert Doisneau photo, with its mix of customers and its 1950s decor (just freshened up a bit). You wouldn't know, but Assiah now makes a tidy living. She's initiating thirty-year-old Yasmine, a young Frenchwoman of Arab stock who started out as a customer, into the fine art of running a café. Assiah will let Yasmine manage the place in five years or so, when she intends to retire down south where she's bought a small farm with René, a teacher (and former customer). Together they'll make a shared dream come true—raising horses. "And maybe I'll take in a few paying guests, some of the regulars here may want to take a vacation in the country every now and then."

Dermott worked on his own at first. In addition to the Irish who followed him, and other countrymen who happened to live in the neighborhood (part of the fifteen thousand Irish in Paris), who came over as soon as they saw a pub sign (the way snails are drawn to a field of lettuce), Dermott's modest clientele was initially made up of students and teachers, who were still numerous in that part of the 5th arrondissement. Then, in the early 1990s, Ireland became fashionable. Its image as a rugged country, not terribly rich nor endowed with much sunshine but populated by poetic madmen, drunken mystics, and boxing priests, created a pleasant contrast with the international uniformity of financial whiz kids sipping Perrier. People were beginning to tire of high-tech bars and postmodern cafés all made of glass, metal, and halogen lamps. Ireland was a purported land of "authenticity," whose exoticism made its archaic Catholicism bearable, making it an antidote to scandal-ridden Italy, scandal-ridden Spain, and scandal-ridden France (just as the notoriously tightlipped Quiet Man provided a counterexample to the communicative superficiality that emerged with President Giscard d'Estaing and blossomed under Mitterand). This infatuation had an impact on all pubs marked with a cloverleaf—in the past ten years, thirty-five have opened in Paris. Of those thirty-five, three or four were former bistros whose *bougnat* owners reckoned that total conversion would retain (and maybe even swell) an increasingly fickle customer base. These converters were assisted in their metamorphosis by a major brand of Irish beer which, wagering that the infatuation with Ireland would last, offered Parisian café-owners five models of Dublin-style pubs, all ready to go and all the more "authentic" for being equipped with used furnishings.

Dermott reacts to "Ireland in a kit" with a mixture of ridicule and rage. What makes an Irish pub Irish is the Irishman, not walls hung with a dartboard and—even less—stuffed salmon and photos of Connemara, James Joyce, Oscar Wilde, Samuel Beckett, or even Charlotte Rampling in *Un Taxi Mauve*. The Irishman stays behind the bar. Customers place their orders directly, without passing via a waiter. Inevitably, people wind up saying a little more than "*Bonjour*, a pint of Guinness, please." Especially since the draft beer has to be pulled in two stages, with a pause while the head forms a thick white blanket, providing time to exchange a few words. An Irish publican is like a ship's captain, responsible for the atmosphere on board. He's also a little like a missionary or ambassador, quickly becoming nostalgic. "We all want to promote Irish culture." So, once or twice a week, musicians and singers from back home occupy a corner of the pub, just like in Clifden or Bantry. Or else someone will launch into a poetry reading. There's even a theatrical troupe that specializes in presenting short plays with just a few characters.

Irish music pulls the city's Bretons into the pubs. (Always this need of Parisians to cultivate the roots from which they have been untimely ripped.) Rugby, meanwhile, draws southern Frenchmen. Games are watched in the back room and, when one of the Five Nations Tournament matches is to be played in Paris, Dermott buys seats for anyone interested and they all go to the stadium together. The same goes for soccer, but at a more modest level, while an even smaller group—practically a cult—gets together for competitions of Gaelic sports, each of whose rules are more complicated than the other.

Unlike French bistros, Irish pubs are not haughty and aloof. People pool their resources so that the cost of entertainment is as cheap as possible, and they organize friendly competitions. Dermott makes sure that everyone knows it was his pub's team that won the latest darts tournament. The team is captained by a shy, almost antisocial Tunisian, who long sat alone meticulously sipping his beer until one day somebody (nobody remembers who) convinced him to have a go at darts, for which he turned out to have a mysterious gift. He led his gang to victory, beating a team of dyed-in-the-wool Irishmen that is now plotting its revenge over these multinational upstarts.

Dermott has quietly prospered. There must be an Irish equivalent to the French phrase, *bonne renommée vaut mieux que ceinture dorée* (a good name is worth more than great wealth), but instead of "worth more" it probably runs "brings in." The owners of "good old Parisian bistros," meanwhile, get together only in order to grumble in unison. Business plummets if a bistro is not located right in the path of traffic flow—train stations, tourist sites, major cultural institutions. A growing number of owners go bust every year. So what's the government going to do about it, they ask indignantly. Quick—grants, subsidies, tax breaks! Don't bother pointing out to them that they offer their 1999 customers the same facilities as they did in 1950. Don't try to establish how many of them still feature—like some "historic monument" with heaven only knows what aura—repulsive Turkish toilets lit with a chintzy timed lightswitch that regulates a bulb worthy of World War II. (In one of these infamous places, a jesting hand has written, among the usual obscenities, "Pull the flush-chain carefully. Or equip yourself with flippers.") Don't bring up the tastelessness of the bread in their sandwiches, or the extra two francs they charge for pickles (perhaps the most striking example of cheapskate *à la française*). Nor how expensive their coffee is, nor the hostile looks they give anyone considered to have lingered at a table longer than the modestness of their custom would authorize according to the unofficial chart of bistro hospitality.

Don't bother pointing out that a small number of them do now manage to present a less clutzy, stereotyped decor, provide comfortable furnishings with clean lines, arrange tables so that people aren't breathing down each other's necks (rather than try to profit from every square inch of space), and offer service which doesn't seem to charge by the minute and doesn't take orders with a disapproving air. In short, offer a welcoming atmosphere that humors its clientele to just the right degree—isn't humoring an art that every accomplished manager should master? Today's clientele no longer resembles—whether you miss it or not—the one described in Georges Simenon's crime novels. It no longer accepts the clutter, the filth, the noise, and the loudmouthed tyrant behind the bar hollering at his waiters; it wants to feel young, relaxed, friendly, in the know.

So don't take traditional owners to Dermott the Irishman or Assiah the Arab. It just might just turn out (may the shades of Inspectors Maigret and Janvier forgive us!) that the friendly, good-natured spirit of bistros has found asylum or reincarnation there.

No decent transition is possible from the bar of a bistro—not even an Irish, and therefore Catholic, one—to the private cemetery in the Picpus neighborhood of Paris. Least of all on this very day, a Friday evening in June when Xavier and Isabelle—who, although only thirty years old, are the comte and comtesse de V.—attend mass in the company of Isabelle's parents, the baron and baronne de C. de T. Mass you say, on a Friday evening? Yessiree. A mass jointly celebrated by a sitting bishop, a canon with a noble particle, and a reverend father who also boasts a particle. To be followed by a ceremony presided by a duke and a count. Protected by the high, sturdy walls behind which white-garbed nuns of the Congregation of the Sacred Hearts of Jesus and Mary and of the Perpetual Adoration of the Holy Sacrament quietly conduct their daily devotions, in a convent lacking grace but not charm (with its squat chapel and surprising garden). The atmosphere is that of languid, melancholy sweetness, like the one Rostand envisaged for the last act of *Cyrano de Bergerac* : "Let them go pray, since their bell is tolling."

From inside the compound, you feel like you're still in the village of Piquepusse in the days when Henry IV had a hunting lodge there, when the canonesses regular of Saint-Augustin organized an annual procession, as stipulated by their constitution, every October 7th, to celebrate the victory of Don John of Austria over the Turks at Lepanto, or when Ninon de Lenclos retired nearby to correspond with Saint-Evremond and to receive learned Epicureans, or when the marquis de Sévigné fought his fatal duel, or when Queen Christina... but I'm straying from my subject, the (blue) blood must be going to my head.

The village is no longer, Piquepusse is no longer, and there are no longer very many nuns in the Congregation of the Sacred Hearts of Jesus and Mary and of the Perpetual Adoration of the Holy Sacrament. The youngest are in their seventies. To the south of their 12th-arrondissement convent is the Rothschild Hospital, while to the north are highrise apartments whose balconies have a wonderful view of their garden and cemetery. The Little Sisters are no longer to scale. Which perhaps makes what they do within the walls that no longer cloister them doubly incomprehensible—day and night, they pray. What's more, ever since 1805 they've been praying for the eternal rest of victims of the "Great Terror," guillotined between 14 June and 27 July 1794 (and praying for God's mercy to extend to the victims' executioners).

The nearby Place de la Nation, formerly Place du Trône, was dubbed "Place of the Overturned Throne" during the French Revolution. Due to the stench and constant noise of cartloads of corpses, the guillotine, no longer welcome in its original setting (now Place de la Concorde) was moved to the city gate just beyond Place du Trône (now Cours de Vincennes). It then got down to work, fast. That's where execu-

41

tioner Henri Sanson established his all-time personal record—fifty-four beheadings in only twenty-four minutes. Twenty-six and a half seconds per head, from start to finish: strap victim to platform, swing platform down, chop, drop into wicker basket. The fifty-four included at least five youths aged between sixteen and eighteen.

A memorial plaque still indicates the wooden lintel under which "the guillotine's bloody tumbrels" rolled, because the garden of what was then the nursing home of a Dr. Coignard was partly requisitioned for the digging of two mass graves. Next to the coach gate, "the gravediggers set up their office [in a former oratory], where they divvied up the garments stripped from their victims." The bodies of 1,306 people were dumped in those two mass graves, one forty square meters and the other sixty, both six and a half meters deep. The heads were thrown into the gaps. One hundred and ninety-seven were women: seven Parisian nuns, fifty-one former noblewomen, 123 commoners (do they teach that at school, how the Terror was so unsparing with the lives of the "common people"?), and sixteen Carmelites from Compiègne. The very ones described in Bernanos's powerful and disturbing *Carmelites* ("It is not the rule that keeps us, we keep the rule."). The ones who sang as they mounted the steps of the guillotine until only the voice of the prioress, who climbed last, could be heard.

The men numbered 1,094: 178 members of the ancient nobility, 130 members of the administrative nobility, 108 ecclesiastics, 108 former noblemen, 570 commoners. During those six weeks, the executioner had to rise early, for he had a full day's work ahead of him. In forty days at the gate of the *Trône-Renversé*, he relieved as many people of their heads as during the previous thirteen months back at Place de la Concorde (called, at the time, Place de la Revolution). In memory of those victims, every year in June a mass is held, the very one attended by Xavier and Isabelle, comte and comtesse de

V., accompanied by none other than yours truly. To be honest, it's mainly the aristocrats who are being commemorated here. Firstly because almost all of the 123 female and 570 male commoners tossed into the graves were merely counted, not identified, by their gravediggers. Secondly because once the families of guillotined nobles learned where the graves of their forebears were located, they formed an association which bought Dr. Coignard's nursing home and transformed part of the grounds into a private cemetery for descendants of the victims, next to which they established the convent and chapel of the Sisters of the Sacred Hearts.

Here lie some of the best names from France's noble houses—Lévis, Montmorency, Biron, Noailles, La Rochefoucauld, Luynes, Nicolaï, and General Lafayette (who died in his bed in 1834, but was the son-in-law of the duchesse d'Ayen, guillotined in June 1794). No one is entitled to eternal rest in Picpus if he or she can't prove a noble lineage. Except for Théodore Gosselin. Gosselin published, under the pen-name of G. Lenotre, *Vieilles Maisons, Vieux Papiers* (Old Houses, Old Papers), and *Captivité et Mort de Marie-Antoinette* (The Imprisonment and Death of Marie-Antoinette), both of which were bestsellers in the early twentieth century and helped to console the victims' descendants.

Dozens of candles have been set on the ground between the chapel door and the mass graves, tracing a path through the cemetery. As the service draws to an end, Xavier and Isabelle and three other young couples go out and light them all, each armed with a blowtorch connected to a gas canister (wonders never cease). Along this lighted pathway the two hundred or so descendants of guillotined victims then proceed toward the graves, either reciting the rosary ("for the sick," "for those without hope"), or softly singing (*Ave Maria, Regina Cœli,* or *Salve Regina*—"Eia ergo, advocata nostra, illos tuos misericordes oculos ad nos converte"). A nasty smell, sugary and chemical, wafts over the procession, which I have joined.

How can that be? Here we are outdoors, in a garden, on a spring evening. Maybe the nearby hospital is discharging the odor? Not at all. The smell is coming from the glowing candles on the ground—it turns out they're scented, anti-mosquito models, sold in jars designed to protect the flame from sudden gusts of wind. There must be three or four hundred of them stretching along the path, every meter or so. And they're all giving off a "fragrance" typical of air fresheners, sickening enough when there's only one candle. So, multiplied by four hundred....

The balconies of the surrounding highrises—each ritzier than the next—are peopled with small clusters of human beings (even though this is prime time movie hour) who watch the parade without audible comment or bustle. What's going through their minds? Maybe they're used to this annual event. They probably think it's just another religious ceremony, unaware that the crowd beneath their balconies frequents the Jockey Club more often than the 12th arrondissement (whose mayor has joined the procession). Nothing, for that matter, clearly distinguishes these two hundred pilgrims from the rest of humanity. The man over there, though, could certainly play the role of an old aristocrat in a movie—posture stiff and straight, nose a little long but fine and firm, gaze blasé to just the right degree, nice hands, a dark gray suit into which he seems to have been born, a sure and steady gait. His wife, unfortunately stuffed into a dress that shows every bulge, is carrying a handbag with a (chic) label visible at a hundred paces, plus a hat like those that protect mules in Provence from the scorching heat. Three rows behind that couple comes a pair who clearly like the good life, whose hefty figures and ruddy complexions suggest that they own a country chateau—in fact, you might mistake them for successful butchers. Their children, who are just negotiating the threshold of adolescence, pay little attention to the ceremony, whispering heaven knows what, earning angry looks from the man just behind who is overdoing the blue-blood thing at every level. He looks like Noël Roquevert (I'm sure he cultivates this resemblance to an actor who specializes in harrumphing characters), wears his beard and mustache *à l'impériale* (with a little tuft below the lip), and swells his chest (covered in a black vest dotted with gray). The only thing he lacks is a monocle. (I'd love to hear a street brat from one of the surrounding highrises bait him with one of the cracks that have made Parisian wit famous. But it seems highly unlikely.)

Some of the younger people make an effort to "rise to the occasion." One man over there is playing the dandy—bronze trousers, mustard jacket, brown vest, black tie, longish hair. Clearly a Romantic in an eruptive phase. The vacant gazes and weak chins of some of the others perhaps indicate too much interbreeding in the past. On the whole, however, the sole feature that might set this group apart is the military bearing of a remarkable proportion of the gentlemen, combined with the modesty—not to say dullness—of the ladies' attire. (True enough, this is a memorial service, not a fashion show.) And then there's all that short hair on the boys and the hairbands on the girls.

The necropolis has been traversed at last—an attentive eye could read tributes to the sacrifices made during the World Wars I and II by descendants of guillotined aristocrats. We have now arrived at the mass graves, simply covered with grass. In its naked simplicity, this is most moving spot in the cemetery. The bishop blesses the site, and then everyone present. That is when I notice on the wall separating the mass graves and the cemetery a plaque in memory of "André Chénier, son of Greece and France [who] served the muses, loved wisdom, and died for truth. 1762-1794."

I wouldn't swear that Chénier's *Iambes*, composed during his final hours of imprisonment in the Conciergerie—despite being a partisan of the Revolution, he was executed for condemning its slide into freedom-killing Terror—is part of the high-school syllabus in France today.

45

Comme un dernier rayon, comme un dernier zéphyre
Animent la fin d'un beau jour
Au pied de l'échafaud j'essaye encore ma lyre.
Peut-être est-ce bientôt mon tour;...
Quoi! nul ne resterai pour attendrir l'histoire
Sur tant de justes massacrés;
Pour consoler leur fils, leurs veuves, leur mémoire;
Pour que des brigands abhorrés
Frémissent au portraits noirs de leur resemblance;
Pour descendre jusqu'aux enfers
Chercher le triple fouet, le fouet de la vengeance,
Déjà levé sur ces pervers;
Pour cracher sur leurs noms, pour chanter leur supplice!
Allons, étouffe tes clameurs;
Souffre, ô cœur gros de haine, affamé de justice.
Toi, Vertu, pleure si je meurs.

Just as the sun's last gleam, or the zephyr's last sigh,
brings life to the close of day,
so awaiting the scaffold I pick up my lyre.
My turn, perhaps, is on its way;...
What! none will remain to mortify History
over the slaughter of so many righteous;
To comfort their sons, widows, and memory;
To draw, furthermore, so black a likeness
that the loathèd brigands quail;
To venture deep down into hell
and seize the scourge, the triple flail
already raised over those devils;
To spit on their names, laud their tortured fate!
No, no, stifle your outcry
and suffer, O heart, pierced by injustice and hate.
But you, Virtue, weep if I die.

No, I doubt those lines are very well known. Literature
courses are not supposed to contradict history courses, which

have been totally dominated—even today, to an unknown extent—by the decree that "the Revolution has to be taken *en bloc*." We constantly proclaim our obeisance to the imperative "duty to remember" the victims of dictatorships, tyranny, and totalitarianism. But we still look the other way when it comes to the prisons of 1794, filled with people arrested on the basis of simple denunciation, deprived of all rights by terrorists who invoked human rights yet sent them to their deaths without a trial, whether aged fifteen or eighty-five, male or female, cartload after cartload subjected to the howls of the worst kind of mob, one fueled by resentment, drowning its cowardice in numbers, drunk on the realization that a spineless world would give it free rein.

It is nevertheless amazing that the only people who actually fulfill this duty of "remembering" are the ones at the mass and ceremony this evening, even if for most of them it's mainly a question (and perhaps only a question) of a caste ritual; many of them would be shocked if their distinguished ancestors were mentioned in the same breath as the children of Polish immigrants corralled by Nazis into the Vélodrome in Paris, or the pathetic prisoners in the Soviet Union's labor camps.

The last members of the procession have now fulfilled their obligations. Xavier and Isabelle, along with several friends, begin to pick up the candles marking the pathway across the convent garden. Elsewhere, back patting and news swapping goes on. A number of viscounts greet other viscounts. They tell the usual stories. The comte de G., who heads the association that has organized the ceremony, receives compliments. To which I add my own, expressing surprise that on a warm, sunny Friday evening in June so many people volunteer to preserve a memory so faded that it is nearly blank. "Yes, there must be between a third and a half of our six hundred members here tonight."

"Six hundred members? Heavens, that's a lot!"

"Yes," replied the count, "in the past few years our numbers have grown significantly. The bicentennial of the Revolu-

47

tion helped a good deal." (The ways of the Lord are certainly mysterious.) "This evening," continued the aristocratic president, "was a complete success. It's only unfortunate that Philippe de M."—the duke listed on the program as copresident of the ceremony—"didn't make it. I can't understand what became of him." The count seemed to be expecting an explanation from me. But before I had the time to express my own perplexity at the absence of the nobleman in question, the cemetery caretaker stepped forward to enlighten us.

"The duke telephoned, your lordship. He was stuck in dreadful traffic jams. Rather than arrive late, he preferred to turn back. He called from his car. He was furious. Positively furious."

I adopted an air that I hope was suited to the occasion and, in a reassuring tone, confided to the caretaker. "Don't you worry about that, old boy. A duke should always be furious!" As the caretaker stood there speechless, I slipped out the back way.

Parisians always like to have the last word. It gives them the illusion that they run the show. And, as I've already pointed out, *Ich bin ein Pariser.*

La Jungle d'Asphalte

Paris is made for cycling. I'd even go so far as to say eminently
made for cycling. That, moreover, is one of its mysteries, since
its slopes are nothing short of discouraging. With the exception of two narrow strips of land flanking the Seine (widening
into the Marais on the Right Bank, swelling at Champ-de-
Mars on the Left), Parisian thoroughfares are hilly. Cyclists
know this better than anybody, at their own cost. Starting
from Saint-Augustin, the plain of Monceau has to be earned;
l'Etoile must be conquered from whatever angle it is attacked;
you have to pump hard on the pedals to get from Île de la
Cité to Place d'Italie. And don't think you can coast from
Opéra to the Saint-Martin Canal. Climbing rue des Martyrs
can be torture. Going from the cemetery at Charonne to the
one in Belleville is like an act of penitence—it puts you in a
sweat. Even getting to Montparnasse makes you huff. Meanwhile, the long but steady slope from Place de la République
to Nation may seem gentle, but don't be fooled, it's deceptive.
As to reaching the top of Butte Montmartre, don't even
attempt it unless you've eaten a hearty ration of carbo-
hydrates. Sunday cyclists don't care how long a trip takes and
don't mind reaching their goal all sweaty, but people who
adopt a bike as an everyday means of transportation have to
put up with an unpleasant feeling of dampness wherever they
go; the jacket and tie sometimes required by their job or an

important appointment lends them an appearance of dignity that belies the way they feel inside.

Every time a cyclist reaches a desired goal and then manages to return home safe and sound, a few minutes of thanks to the relevant patron saint are in order. Cyclists' associations have calculated that *Homo velocipedis* in Paris is the victim of a serious accident every five hundred hours. This figure seems extremely low to anyone who has ever used a bike in town, even once. It's an understatement to assert that cyclists are surrounded by enemies here—their lives are under constant threat from predators. Bicycle thieves are hardly worth mentioning; one risks falling prey to them once a year, on average. At least this results in (temporarily) saving the victim from the dangers of traffic, although not from the shame of having to take the Metro again, nor from the rage of discovering that nothing is safe from anyone in this town.

In addition to thieves—whose ingenuity, industry, and nerve get the better of the best safeguards—cyclists have to beware of just about everything. Starting with two-wheeled vehicles like motorcycles, scooters, and mopeds. The power of the engine doesn't make much difference (except, perhaps, at the moment of impact) since all these vehicles generally travel at the same speed on city streets (only their top speeds differ). And all of them specialize in overtaking cyclists from behind—from both sides, right or left—in such a way as to make the pedalist feel not only the closeness of the call but especially the humiliation of being an entity that doesn't count, that barely exists (except as a persistent pain in the neck, like some insect). Everything in the behavior of couriers and pizza deliverers suggests that they've been recruited at the exits of juvenile court and that they undergo sophisticated training until they attain the condition of human cannonball. No obstacle can stay them from their course. Nothing slows them. Traffic lights are not even worthy of their attention. Sometimes they leap off the sidewalk, sometimes cut abruptly across the street in order to mount the curb. The law forbidding them to use designated cycle paths acts like a powerful stimulant, spurring repeated violation. They learn the one-way system by heart in order to be able to zip down a one-way street the wrong way anytime it saves them a bit of time. They also delight in going the wrong way around traffic circles. They're totally unpredictable because even behavior that places them at serious risk has no effect on their comportment. At least when the next war breaks out, they'll provide battalions of kamikazes.

If couriers and other deliverers don't even fear things that might do them harm, you can see why they barely bat an eyelid when it comes to bicycles. They've all adopted a non-negotiable attitude: "Cyclists just have to watch out." Believe me, cyclists watch out. That's about all they do. But dodging a Pizza Speed scooter often means finding oneself, willy nilly, in the path of a Presto Delivery motorbike, which can only be avoided by grazing an Eole Plus motorcycle (painted in raging colors) or sidling up to a black Vespa whose saddlebags indicate that it is ridden by a cossack from Chrono Plus. (Parisian delivery services rarely adopt names that might suggest a pacific approach to the trade. "Messages," "Mr. Courier," and "The Musketeers" are exceptions, while "Icarus," "Pegasus," and "Meteor" might claim the benefit of doubt; but when it comes to "Extreme," "Max Speed," "Drakkar," "MPH," "Target Express," and "Boomerang," only two hypotheses are possible: either these firms are militating for delivery races to be included in the Olympic Games—contact sport division—or else they are secret organizations preparing for the urban civil war that certain futuristic films present as the inevitable outcome of modern civilization. Should the latter hypothesis prove correct, I wouldn't be surprised if delivery companies trained their personnel in Bogota, a city where people clash over a trifle and gun themselves down over two.)

Real bikers—by which I mean riders of large, powerful motorcycles—are less fearsome than the human bullets described above, yet they still constitute a threat to cyclists. Parisian bikers suffer from constant frustration. Except between the hours of 10 P.M. and 6 A.M., and apart from the river expressways and the beltway, they rarely find an occasion to shift into third gear and maintain a speed justifying that shift. Since frequent intersections and dense traffic jams make it impossible to employ (and, coincidentally, display) the power throbbing between their thighs, they tend to compensate by overestimating the maneuverability of their machines, exaggerating their ability to thread in and out of the least crevice in traffic.

Yet it is precisely there—in the pockets between two lanes of cars, in narrow furrows between bus and sidewalk, in the inexplicable and unpredictable hollows that form in the maelstrom of metal—that cyclists gently glide in the hope of silently accomplishing their modest business of locomotion. Their mere presence can disrupt the snaky progress of a biker, often forcing that latter-day Mameluke to undergo the ultimate humiliation: putting a foot on the ground. The biker then growls.

"Sire," pleads the bicycle, "do not be angry with me, but rather reflect that I move infinitely slower than Your Majesty, and that, consequently, I can in no way hinder your progress."

"You're hindering it!" roars the biker, and flashes ahead of the bicycle with an incremental twist on the accelerator, leaving a thick cloud of exhaust in the cyclist's face.

And that's just the most polite case, not the most common. Usually, bikers who discover a cyclist in the region they aim to conquer or traverse ostentatiously run the latter down, making it clear they feel (often correctly) that in the asphalt jungle small critters would be wise to keep clean away from the big game.

Apart from these twin categories of two-wheel motor vehicles, cyclists need only fear—dread might be a more appropriate term—cars, trucks, pickups, postal vans (all of which veer left and right at whim, stopping and opening their doors at random), city buses (which not only stink but enjoy nothing more than overtaking a bicycle just before arriving at a bus stop, where they then crowd the curb), police cars, police vans, police motorcycles (sometimes even mounted police), delivery vehicles, moving taxis, parked taxis, taxis hailed from a distant sidewalk by an invisible pedestrian, and irate taxi drivers who feel that the authorization granted bicycles to use bus-and-taxi lanes constitutes: firstly a personal affront; secondly an unmistakable sign of the end of Western civilization, the advent of the reign of "couldn't-give-a-damnism," and France's irreplaceable loss upon the death of de Gaulle (who at any rate, though it is better to refrain from mentioning it, would be 107 years old at the time of writing). The foregoing considerations, taken collectively, induce said taxi driver to squeeze cyclists against the sidewalk all the while tossing them regular looks to indicate that the maneuver has nothing to do with inattention, and will end only once the cyclist has fallen. Having attained this end, the irate taxi driver scoots off to radio his buddies with the news that another kill has been chalked up. (Rest assured, dear readers, that the words you have just read are the fruit of long personal experience and observation, backed by the testimony of other survivors.)

During the high season—May to October—it is wise to remain wary of the moods of tour-bus drivers. I won't dwell on the differences between vehicles owned and driven by French nationals and buses that come from the countries of the tourists they carry (Poland, Czechoslovakia, or, if you really hit the jackpot, Romania). Suffice it to say that the main drawbacks of the former are the way they crush cyclists, park where cyclists usually take refuge, and then suddenly release a plethora of disoriented humans (like goat droppings) who clutter the street and suddenly scatter in all directions. The second category of tourist bus can be criticized for the same things. To which could be added frequent hesitations over the route to take, leading to looping maneuvers that require cyclists to concentrate like fighter pilots. Which is all the more difficult since the exhaust issuing from those mastodons is toxic after only one breath, and since the vehicles seem so rickety and fragile that they spur fears of spontaneous disintegration into sharp, rusty pieces, one of which will almost certainly hit the cyclist right in the kisser. The final—and most attractive—drawback of this second category of omnibus is that it is full of people for whom poverty is a recent memory, travel a recent privilege, and Paris a magic name. Since they are not yet blasé, they openly demonstrate their joy on arrival and their goodwill toward Parisians by offering a greeting or wave that they legitimately hope will be returned. For some reason unknown to me—perhaps cyclists back there enjoy a different status than we do here—bicycles attract special attention from tourists of the second type, who direct most of their enthusiastic waves at us. But relinquishing the handlebars, even with a single hand, constitutes what is now generally known as an "unnecessary risk." Personally, the thought of seeing a Pizza Speed delivery boy or a Chrono Plus courier surge forth at the very moment I might make such a gesture has always induced me to maintain a certain reserve toward foreign bus tourists in Paris. I deal with my guilt by religiously offering affectionate waves when, standing on a bridge or quay, I see them gliding down the Seine in a *bateau-mouche*. Unfortunately, I don't think they're ever the same tourists.

What else do Parisian velocipedists dread? Little else. Rollerskaters, perhaps, now called *rollers* in Franglais, perhaps in tribute to their spectacular improvement in performance. So spectacular that skates have changed in nature; whereas they were once an item of play or promenade, rollers are now a ballistic device belonging to the bobsled family. While it is rare to see a bicycle on a "bob" run, it has become frequent for *rollers* to challenge cyclists to their traffic lane. And even though *rollers* can now expect to reach the cruising speed of a South African springbok (roughly fifty-five miles an hour), they still move like crabs, lurching from left to right. The path of their trajectory thereby acquires a breadth that enhances their ability to mow down everything in their way. Technical advances have rendered skates almost silent yet not equipped them with horn or bell, requiring cyclists to pay exhausting attention if they wish to avoid discovering what mass multiplied by the square of speed yields in terms of energy.

Cyclists must display the same vigilance toward pedestrians. Pedestrians comprise an urban species that is particularly dangerous in Paris. They consider a cyclist to be an apostate, indeed a Judas. In the best of cases, pedestrians punish a cyclist through contempt, totally ignoring him or her. This means that while waiting for the light to change at an intersection, they edge into the road where cycles normally pass. Just as Parisian bikers detest putting a foot on the ground, so Parisian pedestrians refuse to step back onto the sidewalk. They prefer to adopt a bold, icy attitude toward bicycles, similar to the one that delights fans of bullfighter Jesulin de Ubrique who, even as a novillero, was famous for his phlegmatic stance toward a charging bull—straight, motionless, drawing the beast as close to his body as possible, seemingly concerned only with keeping his "suit of light" impeccable despite all the dust raised by the animal's attack.

Confronted with an adversary of this class, the cyclist begins to feel like a beast, almost brutish. The shrill, silly tinkle of a bell has no positive effect on pedestrians. To the contrary, it merely increases their disdain, leading them to stiffen their posture, assert their stance. That's why said cyclist tried equipping his vehicle with a horn-and-rubber-ball, thinking that a loud "honk" reminiscent of farcical clowns would lighten the tone and send bipeds a subliminal message, simultaneously offering apologies for the inconvenience caused, asking that the passage be cleared, and imparting a knowing wink which means, "All the same, there's more in common between you and me than between me and a car." This message rarely comes across, even when accompanied by a forced, phony smile designed to stress the cyclist's good intentions. So the only thing to do is to aim between the pedestrians and the cars, hoping that the former won't inch forward and the latter won't turn right. (It should be noted that the most dangerous of all the various types of pedestrian is, beyond all dispute, the one pushing a stroller. Crossing against the light, far from a crosswalk, these pedestrians look straight ahead in a way that seems to say to cyclists: "I dare you to exercise your right of way at the expense of a helpless child." This tactic of the human shield—rarely employed when it comes to cars or motorcycles—is a heavy blow to the cyclist's moral. Accustomed as he is to being a potential victim, rehearsed in the reflexes of the prey, he suddenly finds himself tarred as the aggressor, the barbarian, the Hun.)

Bicycles are faced with yet another danger—other bicycles. It must be admitted, regardless of the consequences, that Parisian cyclists go through red lights whenever possible, in order to avoid the fatigue of frequent halts and to take advantage of momentum. They also go the wrong way up one-way streets, leap onto sidewalks, zigzag between cars, bolt out from behind trucks, turn without signaling, suddenly attain speeds that force other cyclists to move out of the way or, to the contrary, adopt a stately pose and pace that oblige overtaking cyclists to risk moving into the "motorized" lane. In short, unpredictability and irresponsibility are not only the wellsprings of cycle traffic but also the twin foundations of the chronic insecurity of cyclists, whose accidents, it should be remembered, are almost always serious.

Several factors promote such accidents. Few people appreciate, for instance, how windy Paris is, or how often that wind blows in gusts. Cyclists are often blown off course through no fault of their own and with no malicious intent. Furthermore, the capital's pavement is often covered in oil leaked from various "motor vehicles," not to mention shards of glass from some collision. Some streets—rue Tiquetonne, rue Montorgueil, and also Place Vendôme—have recently been resurfaced in small cobbles made from some bizarre stone. Originally pale gray, they quickly turn a shade of dirty gray that no cleaning seems to remove. They also seem to retain canine excrement, thereby increasing the skid factor. Furthermore, these cobbles often come loose, ultimately forming small craters or enormous potholes that the city street department never manages to fill. Apparently the only way to repair the modest damage once one of these newfangled cobblestones has left its bed is to entirely rip up and recobble the street. The cost of such an operation—and the frequency with which it would have to be conducted—has led municipal authorities instead to just plug the hole with loose cobbles that either form a rut lethal to bike tires or a tiny hillock of stones featuring two or three jutting cobbles that aggravate the effects of the aforementioned rut. In rainy weather, you can cycle on such pavement only if you're absolutely positive you won't need to brake.

In the spring of 1996 the city government spontaneously decided—independent of any electoral pressure—to address the problem of bicycle traffic in the capital. (Many Parisians, true enough, had brought their bikes out of the cellar during a very trying public transportation strike in the winter of 1995.) This led to the establishment of bike lanes. Elaborated with all the refinements beloved by the bureaucratic mentality cultivated in Paris ever since the city has been a capital, this innovation was initially interpreted as an attempt to protect and safeguard cyclists. Once in place, however, even the dullest of minds realized their mistake. In fact, the system was designed to solve the problem of bike traffic by exterminating cyclists through the judicious establishment of "death corridors." In a

57

worthy cost-cutting effort, this system obviated the need for municipal exterminators by relying solely on ordinary (non-cycling) users of the city's streets, avenues, and boulevards, that is to say simple taxpayers who demanded no special remuneration for participating in mass cyclicide.

Just picture a strip some four feet wide bounded on the right by the curb and on the left by a series of rubber sausages some fifteen inches long and four inches wide, set roughly one yard apart, as well as by semihard plastic thingamajigs some two feet high, stuck upright at the entry and exit of this strip as well as everywhere the municipal services thought they should be erected, without any intelligible principle behind their implantation being discernible.

Cyclists are henceforth expected to keep to these lanes wherever they exist. As soon as the very first corridors of death were installed, police officers courageously demonstrated their preference for fining every *Homo velocipedis* in violation of this new rule rather than collaring all the motorcyclists who run red lights in order to deliver pizzas in less than thirty minutes. (A fine costs 250 francs—$45 at current rates—which represents 10 percent of the price of a good street bike. The equivalent, for the owner of the average car, would be 10,000 francs. Note that said car owner would have to run over a pedestrian in order to face so serious a fine—and even at that, probably only if it wasn't a first offense.)

The rubber sausages are too high for a cyclist to cross without damage or danger, and much too low to offer any protection whatsoever from other vehicles. These latter, for that matter, couldn't give a fig. Whether two-wheeled or four-wheeled, private or public, motor vehicles jauntily cross them, often without even noticing, and bear down on cyclists like a lioness after a gazelle. (Division of labor among the king of beasts, of course, attributes hunting to the lioness whereas the lion is in charge of taking siestas.)

Yet it's well known that, in the savannah, a gazelle stands a fighting chance. Assuming, that is, that another lioness doesn't surge forth every twenty yards or so, which is what happens in the corridors of death, thereby reducing a cyclist's chances of survival almost to zero, especially since the semihard vertical thingamajig, supple enough to bend under the impact of a car or motorcycle and then right itself, is too hard to behave the same way when hit by a cyclist, whom it resists just as a low wall would do (being about the same height). Motorists can therefore take advantage of cyclists' forced concentration within their corridor to run them down directly or, for the playfulminded, to squeeze them steadily until they either slam into the vertical thingamajig or lose their balance by hitting the curb, or else go into a terminal zigzag following one or several encounters with the rubber sausages (which, on wet days, are slick as ice).

Note that pedestrians are invited to play their part in this tale of suspense. They need merely occupy—unexpectedly, if possible—part of the bike lane for a cyclist to be obliged either to collide with a semihard vertical thingamajig or to deal with a series of slick rubber sausages, unless said cyclist prefers (and can manage, by slipping between two of the sausages) to regain the portion of the road reserved for motorists all the more oblivious in that they're convinced that bicycles are now restricted to their own reserve. That's why the sudden appearance of a cyclist outside the reserve triggers in relatively short order exactly what's been triggered by every unexpected exit from a reserve ever since the concept of reserve was invented—an unfortunate accident.

At the time of writing, statistics on Parisian cyclicide have not yet been established. But based on the results of my own personal observations, as well as on accounts straight from the mouths of reliable witnesses and survivors, I feel I can only assert that anyone who persists in cycling through Paris after the invention of bike lines displays as much reason as, say, someone who, in the aftermath of the Saint Bartholomew's Day massacre, stopped one of the duc de Guise's henchmen in the street in order to ask the way to a Protestant church.

Any one of the aforementioned reasons why cyclists should fear for their safety is more than sufficient cause to give up riding a bike in Paris. And yet, as I stated at the outset, Paris is eminently made for cycling, as anyone who has crossed it astride a bicycle will long remain convinced. Pedaling is the best way to discover the city and appreciate the diversity of its *quartiers*. Drivers are blind—they have eyes only for their watch and their destination. They listen to the radio. They make phone calls. They're interested only in themselves, except when, on one of the two riverside expressways that blight the Seine, the beauty of the river or the elegance of Île Saint-Louis strikes them with the same force as the first time they set eyes on it. In no other part of the city has anyone ever claimed to have gone for "a little outing in the car." Cars are made to keep moving, and when you keep moving there's nothing to see.

Pedestrians, meanwhile, stroll, inhale, explore, and see. They're a little like divers who swim in and out of a coral reef. Every dive provides a chance to discover a new feature of this object of affectionate curiosity. Repetition is not a source of monotony—*au contraire*, it is the cause and very basis of re-newed wonder. One day, a stroller pushes open a door (one not shut with a coded lock) only to discover a droll courtyard featuring a valiant if skinny tree, a dashing if unpretentious inner staircase, and a former concierge's hut like the ones seen in black-and-white movies (the door of this one moreover has a haughty sign worthy of a mean old lady: "No noise in the courtyard. Keep children under control.") The next day, said stroller extends his exploration as far as the intersection where, on raising his head, he notes a tastefully planted if tiny terrace on the sixth floor of an otherwise ordinary edifice, giving a lively air to the surrounding buildings. And some day he'll delight in a facade or a storefront, in the twist of an alleyway or the liveliness of a street market. Pedestrians are gourmets of their *quartier*. Or rather a fragment of their *quartier*. They cultivate details, deepening their knowledge, sometimes getting bogged down. (I'm referring here, of course, to strollers, and not to people who mechanically walk the same path every day to reach the bus or Metro stop.)

Cyclists are much more superficial. They don't set off on expeditions, they let themselves be drawn by the city. They pass from one universe to another. From the Bastille, via rue Saint-Antoine, a cyclist will suddenly arrive at Marché-Sainte-Catherine, which is the liver or spleen (if not exactly the heart) of the touristy Marais district. A stone's throw away, on rue de Turenne, you can still see traces of the elegant Marais alongside the working-class Marais which huddled there before the war. Angling up rue de Saintonge you reach Boulevard du Temple which—unlike Saint-Martin, Bonne-Nouvelle, and Poissonnière—has not lost all its character and originality. Without straining the imagination, it's easy to picture how lively it once was, with its promenades, its trees (and suppose we replanted them?), its theaters, its stalls (for crêpe sellers, snake swallowers, flea circuses, and rabbit trainers), its cafés, kiosks, and houses of ill repute. The boulevard flows into Place de la République, which looks like a terminus. It does have its bright side, but what can be expected of a square where a Second-Empire barrack occupies 115 yards of the facade fronting it? And yet you only need to snub the barrack and continue obliviously along the north side until, twenty pumps of the pedals later, you enter the realm of the Saint-Martin Canal. Water, as ever, calls for a change of pace. Sometimes even for a halt, for contemplation. Then you can placidly follow the canal up Quai de Jemmapes, whose slope requires a certain effort. On the right is a strangely wide and short street. This squat street has been promoted to the rank of avenue, a distinction it has difficulty meriting since it measures only 120 yards long. Never mind—its very strangeness is inviting, and you'd be well advised to succumb to its appeal. For at the end of Avenue Richerand is one of the most discreet marvels in Paris, namely the Saint-Louis Hospital with its Henry IV courtyard (even more charming than Place des Vosges, which has the same warm brown brick, soft whiteness of decorative dressed stone, attractive proportions, gentle spareness, and sheltered location). A few patients are taking their first steps toward recovery there. Mothers sit on the benches, reading about the latest adultery scandal rocking the House of Monaco as their children run about. Lovers dream of being able to make love there. But all these people together still make for a small population. The courtyard of the hospital is off the beaten track and is intended to remain so. It's one of those totally "different worlds" hidden within Paris. (There's even a different world within this different world— the *Musée de la Dermatologie*, where over four thousand casts, drawings, sketches, and so on provide a glimpse of the less repulsive skin disorders. A waxworks of horrors. Absolutely delightful. And there's no one to bother you.)

The architectural elements of Saint-Louis Hospital blend as smoothly as the ingredients of a pound cake—Henry IV-style architecture folds into Louis XVIII, which melds into Third Republic and the resolutely late twentieth-century additions. The transition is so steady that you return to the teeming, bustling city without being traumatized. On the way out, given that ever since the days of saintly King Louis this hospital has treated and studied every kind of skin disorder, you pass a fin-de-siècle school established for certain young patients, with the appealing name of "School for Scabby Children." Just think of being awarded an honorary degree from such a school!

In Saint-Louis, you advance on foot. That's the advantage of being a cyclist in Paris. Whenever you feel like it, provided you manage to find something to which you can hitch your steed, you can delve deeper into impressions gleaned on two wheels. Steeped in the pleasant sensations of the Saint-Louis courtyard, the cyclist mounts once more and returns to the real world, climbing rue Sainte-Marthe. The wrong way up a one-way street. But there's never much traffic on it. For that matter, the city authorities who determined the one-way flow within the quadrilateral formed by rue du Faubourg-du-Temple, Boulevard de la Villette, rue de la Grange-aux-Belles, and rue Saint-Maur must have been in the throes of an epileptic fit. To get from one street to the other—if you obeyed their decrees—you'd have to beat around the bush so long you'd wear your tires out. Rue Sainte-Marthe is narrow, poor, and somewhat dilapidated. There's no extra flesh on the architecture. Behind these walls, it's easy to picture working-class masses like the ones that manned barricades in the past. When the street widens, toward the top, and becomes a square without frills but not without charm, you encounter all kinds of natives who, almost completely cut off from cars, take advantage of their isolation. Kids play soccer on a field reduced to minuscule dimensions, old folks sit on a bench waiting for prime time, a group of North African men stand and palaver incomprehensibly, while a more "in" crowd (steadily becoming the standard population in the neighborhood's renovated apartments) offers their custom to the wine bar and the little restaurant on the square.

It's hard to describe the modest appeal of Sainte-Marthe. Like many nooks hiding behind Haussmann's broad boulevards, it's a place without pretensions. No architectural pretensions. No pretension of enjoying any status whatsoever. Ordinary—*perfectly* ordinary. You can appreciate these little uninspired buildings the way you appreciate a fisherman's lodge on the coast of Brittany, or a tile-roofed shepherd's hut in the hills of Aubrac, or a train station in a small town in the Ardennes. No art historian will come along to explain what's so nice about these buildings, all built to be cheap and useful. Quality materials weren't employed or, if they were, it was just a stroke of luck. Design was based solely on function.

Neither the person who commissioned it nor the one who built it (assuming they're not one and the same) seems to have felt, even deep down, the least aesthetic urge. And yet their buildings are handsome. Or rather, have what is called—for lack of a better term—an undeniable handsomeness. But they're so ordinary we don't notice it, much less dwell on it. It's just like baked potatoes, which no would dream of citing as an example of haute cuisine, nor rank with hare *à la royale* or broccoli mousse, yet which provide great contentment. The same could be said of certain everyday clothes. Neither their cut, fabric, or color merits attention; they're unworthy of certain occasions; you're not affronted or surprised when no one complements you on them. And yet, although it's hard to say why, you're sure those clothes are just right for you.

If Place Sainte-Marthe had to be defended—and it did have to be defended, along with the surrounding streets—the only thing you could say in the end is this: it's a nice spot. Which was enough to convince the developers to go develop someplace else—the stubborn resistance of a residents' association saw to that. Developers and promoters of ZACs (special development zones) have won so many victories in Paris that they can easily afford this small setback.

A hundred pumps of the pedals later, the cyclist reaches Boulevard de la Villette. From here you might tack over to Belleville, but you suddenly decide to dismount. You find yourself in Place du Colonel-Fabien, where a curved building designed by Oscar Niemeyer is proof that Paris sometimes manages to combine periods and styles to everyone's benefit. But this city square is really an urban traffic circle, since cars stream into it from seven streets, boulevards, and avenues. So there's no incentive to linger at a sidewalk café or *brasserie*. May as well head back down to the canal, coasting as far as Square Villemin, another spot saved by stubborn neighborhood activists from the lazy shortsightedness of city "decisionmakers" and greedy promoters. From Square Villemin, if you have the energy, you can head over to Boulevard de Magenta, which itself lacks character but offers a good view of one of the finest train stations in Paris, the Gare de l'Est. Journalist Yvan Audouard has described its noxious appeal in the following way: "There are days when you feel so bad you want to go to the Gare de l'Est to see if war has been declared...."

Across rue du Paradis and down Faubourg-Poissonnière and you're already on the outskirts of Le Sentier, or garment district, where trucks park any old how, two-wheeled dollies are so overloaded that you can only see a little tip of the porter, shouts ring loudly from courtyards, and figures pace back and forth (one hand clapping a cellular phone to the ear while the other hand argues in an endless succession of gestures invisible to the person on the other end of the line). This ant-hill gets denser, its Brownian motion increasing, once you cross the boulevard—passing that dinosaur of a movie theater known as the Rex—and enter the sacred heart of the garment district itself. Here, taking a look around is as sure a way of being flattened as taking your hands off the handlebar. Porters dart everywhere—Arabs, Chinese, whites, a few blacks. They follow completely unpredictable paths, calculated to cut things as close as possible, abruptly changing course to accommodate the stop or start of a truck, the sudden appearance of another dolly, an encounter with a swarm of carts, or the sudden halt of a column of boxes crushing a sweaty porter weary of having to navigate by dead reckoning. Everyone in Paris—everyone in France, probably—knows you can't drive through the Sentier, but between people obliged to deliver something to rue d'Aboukir or rue de Cléry and people who enjoy tempting fate, it's possible to witness a textbook traffic jam—a total freeze-up—every single working day from 9 A.M. to 7 P.M. Even on a bike you have to ski your way through, using hip-work, constantly targeting fleeting gaps, and inhaling huge clouds of black exhaust. If you want to appreciate the neo-Egyptian facades of the buildings on Place du Caire, come back on a Sunday, when the whole place will be deserted (except maybe for an old Arab in a phone booth, calling home, shouting the way rural folk used to do while fearfully clutching the black ebonite device).

If you manage to reach rue Réaumur, you're justified in thinking you've made it. Carry on to rue du Mail, where you may—you must—have a look around (don't worry, the couriers streaming out of the Figaro building are gentlemen who don't stoop to the level of running cyclists down), because the seventeenth century—France's *grand siècle*—begins to enter the picture. Just take a good look at the church of Notre-Dame-des-Victoires, and you'll realize that Place des Petits-Pères is four hundred yards and four hundred years removed from the Sentier. This Louis XIII church faces the fading vestiges of a convent that once stood there—the only reminder is a store selling religious items such as statues of major saints, prayerbooks, videocassettes of papal voyages, rosaries, candles, holy pictures, biographies of great mystics, nativity-scene figurines, and crucifixes. The proud display window seems unaware of the snide looks it often draws, but maybe it should meditate on the fate of its neighbor, another religious shop called La Maison Bleue, which was bought up by an Italian garment merchant who transformed it into a sportswear boutique dubbed with an English-sounding name. The Historic Monuments Commission obliged the new owner to preserve the statue of the Virgin atop the facade, which had been the ensign of his predecessor. But an Italian would consider this obligation an advantage.

I mentioned that the *grand siècle* begins to enter the picture on rue du Mail. It has fully arrived at Place des Victoires. Cyclists circle the equestrian statue of Louis XIV in the center, noting that whereas a square (like Place Vendôme or Place des Vosges) always supposes a certain idea of order (if gentle and harmonious) and encourages people to assemble, a circle suggests instead playfulness, movement, indeed fun. Or at any rate, gaiety. This inorganic circle—half of whose facades are impostors and pastiches that postdate Second-Empire demolitions—always seems ready for the entrance of one of Molière's comic characters: Scapin mulling over one of his tricks, Arnolphe ruminating over his cuckold's horns, Pourceaugnac seeking someplace to flee, Valère cooing with Marianne, or Dorine chatting with some gossip or other. It's hard to take a circle seriously.

Place des Victoires is one of the best places to appreciate (or deprecate) the accomplishments of Baron Haussmann's nineteenth-century town planning. The circle has been gutted to the east by rue Etienne-Marcel, wide enough for four lanes of cars, scarring its harmony but making traffic flow smoother. If mechanical means had permitted (and if the Franco-Prussian war of 1870 hadn't brought work to a halt), rue des Petits-Champs to the west would have been doubled in width, and the two residences along it would now just be ghosts on old engravings. Better still, rue Etienne-Marcel would have been pushed as far east as Boulevard Beaumarchais, hemorrhaging the heart of the Marais and leveling dozens of mansions dating from the *grand siècle*. Rue des Petits-Champs, meanwhile, after cutting across Avenue de l'Opéra (at the expense of symmetrical damage—adieu, hôtel de Lully), would have reached Place de la Madeleine. Oh, what a wonderful town for military maneuvers Paris would have been!

When returning to the Bastille, cyclists encounter the usual problem, namely the problem of having to choose. Let's say you save the descent from Place des Victoires to Beaubourg for another day (here, too, you see that highly different architectural styles can be happily combined, and that boldness pays, as also demonstrated by the Institut du Monde Arabe on Quai Saint-Bernard). Suppose you decide not to cross the Marais via rue Rambuteau, Place des Vosges, and a short stretch (not the best) of Boulevard Beaumarchais. We'll assume you don't consider heading down rue Réaumur to Carreau du Temple, and from there to Filles-du-Calvaire, past Saint-Sébastien and Chemin-Vert toward the tall column rising in the middle of Place de la Bastille. Let's just assume that you finally decide to follow the Seine, which you reach between Pont des Arts and Pont-Neuf, after having flitted past the colonnade of the Louvre and the church of Saint-Germain-l'Auxerrois. Yet more than one dilemma remains to be resolved: will you roll along the quayside avenues—Quai de la Mégisserie, Quai de l'Hôtel de Ville, Quai des Célestins—as far as Boulevard Henri IV? Or you will play a little hooky by skipping across the Pont-Neuf to Île de la Cité, with a nod to Inspector Maigret (and to Simone Signoret) as you pass Quai des Orfèvres, then slip behind Notre-Dame Cathedral to hop islands by crossing over to Île Saint-Louis, which can be traversed by following rue Saint-Louis (unless, of course, you prefer to savor the facades along Quai d'Orléans and Quai de Béthune), finally taking Pont de Sully to Boulevard Henri IV, which leads straight to the elephantine building designed by Carlos Ott as a new opera house for the Bastille.

Clearly, a cyclist's life is a series of choices. Outings on a bike become something like a board game where the dice are rolled by the marker itself. You can suddenly go from one little world to another, crossing the borders established by broad avenues and wide boulevards, flushing out all the irregular, unusual, unique features that hide behind those thoroughfares. Because Paris, such as Haussmann left it, is in fact the product of a mania for alignment that applied solely to the new, wide streets. Although the facades of buildings that went up along these new or renovated avenues were strictly monitored, no one paid the least attention to what remained invisible, such as inner courtyards; similarly, the people who laid out these boulevards and avenues (which meant, first of all, long demolition operations—it took fifteen years to cut and complete Avenue de l'Opéra) couldn't have cared less about

68

what remained or went up in the hinterland. Abandon Boulevard Auguste-Blanqui by rolling down little rue Corvisart for barely two hundred yards and you'll find a change of period, pace, atmosphere, attitude. A park, low houses, gently rolling street—it's a vacation from the city in the city. Leave Boulevard Barbès or Boulevard de la Chapelle and tell me where you are, when a few hundred paces away you find yourself in front of the church of Saint-Bernard. Still in Paris? On the outskirts already? In some provincial town? None of the above. You're in a square as comfortable as a minor administrative town, as muffled as a middle-class suburb. Within Paris, this peacefulness generates a feeling of calm or respite, whereas in a provincial town it might connote stasis, indeed stagnation. Within Paris, its sleepiness means serenity, because everyone knows that boulevards roar a stone's throw away, and that a three-minute stroll down rue des Poissonniers will plunge you into a teeming African market that overflows the sidewalks and invades most of the street.

In the 16th arrondissement, quit Avenue Paul-Doumer and head down rue de Passy. In less than three hundred yards you go from this opulent district's stiff facades to a tiny square with a "dish-of-the-day-plus-house-wine" bistro. The waiter may not give a whistle or a sexy pat to his many female—and mostly white-haired—customers, but he'll joke with them and ask after their grandchildren in a way rarely seen in Parisian establishments today. That's because, although within hailing distance of "the avenue," we're no longer in a kingdom where people live on the interest generated by the interest on their capital. This is a republic of widows on pensions, ladies free from want—but no more—who might bargain at a local shop and who don't think the most delightful pleasures are necessarily the most costly. I once saw a small squadron of them at tea time, having a muffin party at a fast-food joint on Passy— they looked like college girls who had sneaked out of their dorms.

The path of a bike can weave these worlds together. You can flee any one of them as soon as you weary of it. Or you can collect all their scents, atmospheres, personality traits. You can do whatever you want with them, whenever you want (except, perhaps, when it rains too hard for too long—on such days, stay at home and read a book). It's these thousand and one cities within the city that make every reason to give up cycling in Paris vanish with the first stroke of the pedals. Parisian individualism finds its freest, easiest, most joyful and fulfilling expression in the use of a motorless two-wheeled vehicle, and so a bicycle in Paris—even more than elsewhere—is a symbol of lightness, of youth recovered at will, of well-tempered frivolity, of the spirit of liberty.

Everyday Jobs in Paris

Where can you meet Parisians? I mean, where can you go to observe the city's human tide in all its diversity, to appreciate its differences—indeed, divergences—to savor its heady admixture? On the Champs-Elysées some Sunday afternoon? Hardly—all you'll see there are suburbanites, provincial hicks, and foreigners. On the *grands boulevards*, some Saturday night? Not much livelier than Bagneux cemetery, with the exception perhaps of Boulevard des Italiens, where a dense concentration of movie theaters creates snaking lines (whose surplus agitation is absorbed by more-or-less exotic restaurants—ranging from lousy to appalling—which divvy up the sidewalks). At Les Halles, on a weekday? Maybe, if you like watching ants scurry, or enjoy wondering if they know where they're coming from, where they're going, and why on earth they bother. But Les Halles is hardly where people stroll, either at street level or below ground in the train and Metro station. For that matter, Les Halles is no longer part of Paris, having turned itself into a suburban ghetto in the center of town.

No, Parisians can no longer be found on any of their former parade grounds, nor in the big music halls (*what* music halls?), nor in any new area of promenade and display that late twentieth-century Paris might have devised, nor in or around some amusement center or attraction where social

71

classes and generations mix. In order to observe Parisians, you now have to flush them out. Fortunately, just as there exist certain watering holes were you can be sure various wild beasts will gather (each at an appointed hour, or all together), so in the capital there are certain shared places—shared by all social groups—where, with a little patience, you can observe something of the private life and habits of *Homo parisiensis*.

Take the post office, for example. Sooner or later, everyone has to go there, whether rushed or relaxed, whether worried by the enigmatic slip announcing a registered letter (with return receipt requested), or excited by the issue of a new stamp, or, more generally, obliged to perform an operation or administrative formality that can be accomplished nowhere else. A striking reversal of perspective on these things can be had if you manage to convince the Postal Administration, in its benevolence, to allow you to sit behind the counter for a while. For instance, there are very few "slow periods" in a Paris post office, and the almost constant flow of men and women leaves an observer with one overriding impression: Parisians—male and female—are in a hurry.

When entering the building, a Parisian's first task is to ascertain which of the many lines is advancing the quickest. For some people, this operation requires reflection; it's not only a question of assessing the number of people in line, but estimating the amount of time each person will monopolize the postal clerk. In one line there may be just three customers, but two of them are carrying parcels. Which have to be weighed and stamped one by one. Risky! Better to join the line with five people, though with apparently lighter loads. Other users size up the situation in a flash, deciding instantly. Still others, not sure which window handles their business, or wanting to obtain a form not displayed on the counter, boldly ignore the line and go smack up to the dividing glass, right next to the person being served, in order to question the clerk through the window and thereby avoid lining up twice. This maneuver triggers a complex exchange of glances. The interloper stares at the postal employee in the hope of attracting his or her attention, head held as though wearing blinders, pretending to be oblivious to the sharp looks unleashed by people waiting their turn according to the rules. Such a posture is wise, because these looks are heavy with threats, disapproval, annoyance, rage. They express everyone's vigilance concerning respect for rightful order, and warn of the possibility of a sudden outbreak to reestablish that order. (In fact, it's not the perpetrator who bears the brunt of the storm, should it break, but the clerk, who is reproached for falling down on the job should the violator's request require anything more than the briefest of exchanges). Sometimes, the second person in line, just behind the customer being served and the most immediately affected by the intrusion of this cad, begins subtly shifting position to get closer to the coveted window and to place himself between the person in front and the intruder, toward whom he slowly turns his back. At the same time he slides one leg forward, barring the troublemaker's route and forcing the current customer, once business is completed, to depart by the opposite side. In this case, the intruder has only one option left: plaster himself to the glass partition, lean forward, and nervously await the brief interval in which he can make his request, still pretending he doesn't see anybody.

On the other side of the fence, the employee's safety rule is to concentrate on the operation at hand, totally ignoring anyone other than the person with whom he's dealing. Depending on his assessment of the level of tension on the other side of the window, he may decide to listen to the unsolicited request or to feign deafness (displaying total indifference in order to discourage any idea of a second try). In the latter case, a wave begins to ripple down the line, from one person to another. It conveys personal and collective triumph, which reaches a paroxysm when the pathetic reject abandons his station to attempt the same maneuver at another window—or, if his failure has drained all self-confidence, to join the end of another line, turning his back on the one that bested him.

The relaxed atmosphere produced by this victory is usually shortlived. A man may have chosen window number three, for example, on the assumption it was moving fastest, only to discover that his predictions are being trounced. Two places ahead, a lady inquires about the guaranteed delivery times for various postal rates—standard "Letter" versus "Chronopost" versus "Colissimo." The object she wants to send is not exactly a letter, nor exactly a parcel. It's a padded envelope eight inches by twelve, some three inches thick. Apparently it contains—"here comes the whole story," groans the failed forecaster—a file which has to reach the south of France tomorrow, but the last time the woman tried to send a similar document by Chronopost, she was sorely disappointed because instead of the advertised twenty-four hours it took three days to arrive.

Thus begins a dialog characterized by absurdity cloaked in diplomacy. Diplomacy because the lady, who hopes to be relieved of her anxiety even as she places the blame for the shoddy performance on the postal clerk, does her best to remain impersonal in her criticisms and polite in asking for help. It's a question of making the person behind the window feel duty-bound toward her, and therefore guilty about the firm's poor showing. But this guilt must be sparked and fueled without uttering a single insulting word, which would give the employee room to put an end to the discussion by insisting that the customer hurry up and make a decision on her own (*"I'm sorry, but people behind you are waiting... "*).

The postal employee, meanwhile, remains alert for any faux pas. It's not that he doesn't want to be helpful, but experience has taught him that there's no answer to the question being asked. On paper, it can always be argued that a certain rate corresponds to a certain delivery time, but in practice what is presented as a certainty is really only a greater or lesser degree of probability. Since it's impossible to admit this to customers, the clerk waits until his adversary provides an opening.

For the moment, the adversary has instead decided to complicate matters by multiplying her queries. (Two places behind, the failed forecaster fidgets, shifting from one foot to the other; he looks to see if it's worth changing lines, decides it isn't, drums fortissimo on the envelope he has come to send, and emits loud sostenuto sighs through his nostrils in order to simultaneously shame the lady and hurry things along. From the other side of the glass partition, the observer notes not only the extent to which Parisians are, by nature, in a hurry, but also how resourceful they can be when it comes to nonverbal communication.) Finally, the customer, irritated by the postal clerk's tactics, mutters, "In any case, say whatever you like..." which provides the awaited *faux pas* and creates an opening. "If you think I'm making it up as I go along, Madame, there's no point in asking me any questions."

"I didn't say 'making it up,' (she tries to recover lost ground, but knows the jig is up) I said 'say whatever you like.'"

"Seems the same to me, Madame. At any rate"—in an exaggeratedly courteous tone and haughty gaze—"I'll have to ask you to make your mind up. *I'm sorry, but people behind you are waiting.*"

The lady makes up her mind. Against all logic, she opts for Chronopost again. The failed forecaster shifts from sharp nasal sighs to a long oral exhalation designed to inform the lady that her behavior has put a serious brake on terrestrial motion. Luckily, the person in front of him remains at the window for just a few seconds (merely wanting confirmation that a letter didn't weigh more than twenty grams); the forecaster therefore feels reconciled with *La Poste* and opens with a declaration to the clerk: "Customers like that need a special window for the handicapped." He's barely finished this quip when one of the employee's colleagues passes by and asks about lunch plans. It turns out that their schedules differ by half an hour; the former normally wouldn't mind waiting for the latter but has promised his wife to do some errands, so the two employees decide not to lunch together. The forecaster's fondness for the postal service melts like butter in a frying pan; although the exchange between the two postal clerks lasted less than a minute, it constitutes a high crime. To indicate the extent of his wrath, the forecaster, as he hands over a form for a registered letter with return receipt, turns his gaze on me (seated somewhat behind, scribbling away) and, addressing no one in particular, says in what he feels to be a haughty tone: "As to that one there, he must be too dumb to even be assigned a window of his own."

Too dumb, perhaps. And most certainly lacking the requisite self-control. While observing Parisian post office workers do their job, I imagined inventing a device to measure the dose of aggressiveness to which human beings are exposed. As soon as a customer sets foot in the post office—this is more true of men than women, but not by much and, according to postal employees, less and less so—it's apparent that he's driven by warlike intentions seeking an outlet. The post office is the place *par excellence* for Parisians, irascible by nature, to find somebody to lay into. And not just any old body, but an individual who, when being told off, represents a telling-off of the Government, the Civil Service, and moribund Public Spirit all in one.

People can't go into a police station and give officers a dressing down. And opportunities for telling employees of the National Health Service what you think of them are few and far between. Meanwhile, the occasions on which you encounter firemen, ambulance drivers, hospital doctors, and nurses almost always place you in a position of inferiority. And the less you see Internal Revenue employees the better, especially since encounters organized at their behest are hardly condu-

76

cive to an aggressive attitude. Most of us have little contact
with judges (and when we do, we either hope they'll award us
something or dread they'll inflict something on us; neither
instance represents an appropriate moment to go into a long
harangue on the legal system's slowness, haphazardness, and
inequality). When it comes to the army, the draft provided
the only occasion for late-twentieth-century males to have any
contact with that institution, but draftees are never in a position to make their comments heard. In fact, schoolteachers
are the only national civil servants who have to put up with
insolence or unpleasantness, although no one really expects
them to carry the can for the whole government, or even the
ministry of education. So teachers pay solely for their own
shortcomings.

Thus, to my knowledge, only Parisian postal clerks are
expected to foot the bill for every charge. I wouldn't say provincial customers never behave likewise, but they're not subject to temptation as often as the capital's residents. They lack
the irritability and the somewhat explosive atmosphere that
constantly ticks in Paris (both within and without), they lack
the feeling of being unique that goes with urban solitude and
incites Parisians to treat any dysfunction as a personal offense.
Provincials don't experience frequent, entirely one-sided tell-
ings-off from various people on both banks of the Seine (a po-
liceman who must be heard deferentially, a taxi driver who
rolls up his window after having called you libelous names, a
motorbiker who heaves out of sight after having compared
you, in a screaming voice, to the dregs of humanity). This all
provokes in Parisians a swollen mass of internalized invective
just waiting to get out. Finally, provincials can't get into a
public spat without everyone ultimately hearing about it.
Their reputation might suffer, especially if the outburst
recurs. Parisians couldn't care less about their neighbors,
whom they usually don't even know, shielded as they are by
armor-plated anonymity. Half-blusterers, half-doomsayers,

Parisians can tilt at windmills as often as they like, at no risk whatsœver. They risk looking foolish, you might suggest. Perhaps, but in Paris, foolishness neither wounds nor kills. It's often a sign of life—or at least of existence.

So from the other side of a post-office window, what you see are faces marked by a bad temper that has been thwarted, or at least contained, all day long. But you also see a host of people who have no seat on the capital's merry-go-round, who live life at another pace, another level. At 11:00 A.M., an elderly lady straight out of a Sempé cartoon (wrapped in an ageless coat, carrying a dirty blue cloth shopping bag, her thinning hair neither very neat nor very coifed) gets in the "All Transactions" line. When her turn arrives, she greets the postal clerk—which is not all that common even though the clerk makes a point of saying hello to every customer—and holds out her post office savings book, asking to withdraw ten francs (barely $2.00). The postal clerk, who knows her well, marks the withdrawal on her account book with a pleasant joke: "So, Madame Brossard, playing the lottery today?"

"I'd sure like to, I'd treat myself to a vacation," answers the little lady as she picks up the coin and departs. Half an hour later she's back, wordlessly placing her bank book and five francs on the counter. The clerk credits her deposit and politely wishes her an enjoyable meal. "She went to buy her lunch," he explains. "She dœs it every day. One day when I had a little time, I got her to talk. I gathered that a church organization gives her food parcels. She fills them out with whatever she can. With bread, I think. Just now there was a little under 180 francs in her account. Sometimes she gœs into the red. Obviously, we give her ten francs anyway. Yesterday, some guy in a hurry, waiting behind her, laid into me, saying that if I wanted to do charity work I should become a monk. All I could do was shrug my shoulders. If I answer back in the same tone, I'm in the wrong."

It's usually at night that the needy head for the post office. And there's only one post office open all night in Paris—or in all of France for that matter, and even all of Europe—the post office on rue du Louvre. The five windows usually open on an average night act as emergency banks for holders of post office savings accounts (those people who have lost or have never had the right to a bank card). Up to 1,000 francs ($180) can be withdrawn at a time, if the account can cover it. Between 10 P.M. and 2 A.M., only one client requested such a sum; the dozens of other customers asked for 100 to 400 francs. A fiftyish woman wanted to withdraw 520 francs, but since this special withdrawal service works only in multiples of 100, she had to chose between 500 and 600. She wavered. Five hundred.

People receiving the minimum welfare grant (*revenu minimal d'insertion*, or RMI), come twice a month to claim their payments, which creates traffic jams at the counters on the first and fifteenth of every month. Why do people come late at night or in the early morning hours which, in the latter case, means arriving on foot since the Metro has stopped? Because they sleep any old where, because they don't want to run into "normal" daytime customers, because it's at night that they feel most at a loss (and a trip to the post office gives them something to do), because Les Halles is just a stone's throw away (where a few bistros are open nonstop), because on cold nights they can sit for a while in the post office before and after having claimed their money. For a long time a few of them obstinately tried to sleep there. The postal clerks had to go wake them and explain that, really, they couldn't turn the place into a shelter.

Clerks who work the counters while the city sleeps display a perceptible fellowship and mood all their own, based on casual and chatty friendliness. All of them lead somewhat special lives, prompting them to volunteer for this shift, which brings in a very small pay bonus but a great deal of extra vacation time. One woman employee lives in the Limoges region, a few hours away, where her boyfriend has started an "organic" farm; she's able to help out during much of the month. Another clerk is crazy about Brazil, where he manages to spend four or five months a year by working nights and weekends whenever he's back in Paris. Yet another devotes his extra time to a small political party. A fourth chose this lifestyle in order to spend more time with his small daughter after his girlfriend ran off. A fifth does it for no particular reason: "Because it lends a certain spice to my job, the atmosphere between us is good, management is a lot less oppressive, we're given more autonomy and responsibility...."

Certain nights, indeed, abound in lively scenes. Nights when the moon is full are thought to top the list, but no one has established solid statistics because no one wants to risk demolishing a belief that fuels so many conversations and animates a coffee-room controversy as endless as the one over the chicken or the egg. Does the moon affect behavior (as advocated by the clerk with the "organic" boyfriend, who supplies countless examples drawn from observations of both animals and people)? Or do people, attached to the idea that a heavenly body that governs the tides can also induce special behavior, behave differently when they know the moon is full (the opinion of the political activist, himself attached to the idea that any hint of irrationality is the opium of the people)?

Whatever the case, the night of 15 June is always one of those special nights. Midnight on the 15th is not only the deadline for submitting special wealth-tax declarations, but also the deadline for requesting a transfer within the clubs of the French Football Federation. There's a constant mob at all five windows: welfare recipients, young soccer players, and wealthy taxpayers are sandwiched like layers of tutti-frutti ice cream. More than ever, the other side of the post-office window offers a good seat for watching the world go by.

One guy wants to withdraw 100 francs. The only ID he can offer is a shredded driver's license with an illegible address that no longer seems to be the right one anyway. The clerk tries to obtain a more recent address. The photo on the license—valid for life—is too old to insure that it belongs to the holder of the card. The guy launches into a complicated explanation of his current situation, spinning a zigzagging yarn that gœs back to the end of his army days. The clerk grumbles, cuts the story short, and hands over the requested sum—at least ten people await their turn, and the night is still young and full of promise.

The young woman must be between twenty and twenty-five. She hands over her savings book and asks what the balance is. The clerk queries the computer: five francs. But since he pronounces *cinq* (five) as *cin*, she adopts a delighted expression which baffles me until she declares: *Cent* (100) francs? I'll withdraw it all."

"Not 100, five: *cin-QUE*."

"Oh." Her expression changes, and she leaves without a word. (Not long afterward a confident-looking fortyish man with briefcase would also ask for a statement: "Balance on hand, twelve francs." He left it intact, and departed without betraying how he felt about the information he'd just received.)

A man wants to mail his wealth-tax declaration. On the way, however, the envelope fell and is now somewhat soiled. Can the clerk sell him a clean one? He can. The man is relieved. On departing, he left ten francs on the counter. Which looked for all the world like a tip.

Another man wanted a stamp that was issued that morning, which he hadn't managed to buy. He needs to complete his collection. "Come back tomorrow," says the clerk, "there's no philatelic service at this time of night." The man tries to palaver—it's clear he'll have a tough night if he dœsn't return home with the object of his desire (which he'll be able to buy in unlimited quantities in a matter of hours). He finally concedes, but only after the clerk repeatedly insists that special issues are kept in a safe to which he has no key.

Then there are three of them—a black, an Arab, and a white, like the three Wise Men. Except that their ages, all together, wouldn't add up to sixty. They want to leave their soccer team. According to regulations, they have to send one registered letter (with return receipt) to the Federation and another to the team they want to leave. The clerk handles all six registration forms at the same time. On reaching the fifth, he pauses and raises his eyebrows, asking, "Who's So-and-So?"

"I am, why?" answers the white kid in a nasty voice, frowning, chin thrust forward.

"You filled it in backwards. You put your name down as addressee and the Federation as the sender." The kid takes the news badly.

"What ya talkin' 'bout? What the hell did I do to your fuckin' form?" His two friends laugh and mock him. Since he addressed the clerk in the familiar *tu* form, the clerk replies in like manner.

"You gotta fill in two more forms." He hands them over. "Relax, no sweat, happens to everyone." But his buddies suggest, to the contrary, that it only happens to him and that, at any rate, he's a jerk both on and off the soccer field. The kid is cut to the quick. And implodes. In an astonishingly powerful voice, he shouts that he never went to school, he couldn't give a fuck about all this bureaucratic crap used by guys like the clerk to hassle people, that nobody's gonna take advantage of him and that they'd better send off his transfer request because if it doesn't get sent right now he'll fucking bust the place up. When he stops to catch his breath—as his buddies, suddenly serious, try to calm him down, while people in the various lines stare at floor or ceiling—the clerk hands two blank slips to the black guy and asks him to go quietly fill them out with his buddy. "You don't have to get back in line, I'll keep your letters here at the window," he adds as a final peace offering. Ten minutes later, the three Wise Men reappear, relaxed and joking. The clerk performs his duty and, as he finishes, the white kid leans toward the window. "Sorry about earlier, I thought ya didn't wanta send my transfer request...."

Up comes a woman straight out of a 1940s flick. Bobbed hair, print dress cut like the one worn by Danielle Darrieux in *Battements de Cœur*, high-waisted belt. I'm almost tempted to stand up to see if her shoes have wooden soles. She wants to send a fax. The clerk takes the document and goes to the fax machine. He returns and announces that the number is busy. But the machine will automatically redial until the connection is made. For a full hour, he goes every five minutes to see if it has been sent. The lady remains glued to the glass partition, never taking her eyes off the clerk as he deals with subsequent customers. She almost seems to suspect him of something. The number is still busy, the fax still bottled up. She finally decides to send it as a registered letter. When he hands her the receipt, she ostentatiously takes time to study it, then declares, "You haven't stamped the date on it."

"There's no point, Madame, the computer automatically prints the day and time of dispatch. See, it's on the right there. That's what constitutes the postmark now."

"I'd rather you stamp it."

The clerk acquiesces. A hundred times that night—without exaggeration—he'll hear the same request. He'll offer the same explanation but everyone, without exception—soccer players, wealthy taxpayers, senders of legal documents or architectural drawings—everyone wants him to stamp it anyway.

A fellow reporter who is a distant acquaintance of mine appears at one of the windows. He stares at me through the partition. At first he doesn't seem to see me, despite the stare. (Rarely have I seen a finer illustration of the phrase "couldn't believe his eyes.") Suddenly the realization hit. "Say, what the hell are *you* doing here?"

I hold up pad and pencil: "I've come to make a list of all the reporters who have to file the wealth tax." An expression of confusion and anxiety clouds his face for three seconds, then he holds up a brown envelope.

"No, no, not me, this is for my landlord."

A (real) filer of the wealth tax is worried about when her form will arrive. She is assured that it's the date of the postmark that counts. Yes, but if she opts for a registered letter with return receipt, won't that slow down delivery? Not at all? For sure? OK, and how much does it cost? Twenty-six francs fifty. She nods in a way that suggests she finds the price reasonable.

A forty-something couple wants to send a package to their son, who's studying English in England. What's the fastest way? The package contains crackers—can they be sure they won't arrive too broken? "You see," says the wife, "it's the first time he's been away from home alone."

The next man's been drinking. No—he's drunk. He wants to withdraw five hundred francs, to which he is perfectly entitled. He strikes up a conversation with the clerk, asking if there's a cheap hotel in the neighborhood. He won't go away. The employee has to call the night manager, who goes to the other side of the partition and draws the drunk away from the counter, finally helping him to sit down at the other end of the post office, where the windows are closed. He'll let him steep in his juices for an hour or two. As soon as he's seated, the man sinks into an agitated sleep punctuated by starts and loud groans.

A Japanese customer wants to send something express— photos. He's told it will cost 280 francs ($50). You're on....

As midnight approaches, the flood of rich taxpayers and soccer players swells. As does tension in the lines. Everyone worries about not making it to the window in time. The clerk steps up the pace. I reckon he takes a minute and a half to complete an operation that would require five if he took his time. His rhythm is broken by a fiftyish lady in a panic. She sent a registered letter earlier that afternoon in which she mistakenly slipped a document that she *ab-so-lute-ly* must recover. She wants her letter back. The clerk tries to cut her short since it is physically (and administratively) *im-poss-i-ble*. She hangs in there, against all logic. "But it's *my* letter." A wealthy gentlemen behind her addresses the clerk over her head. "That'll do. We're all waiting. You can see she's just being stubborn." The clerk asks him not to complicate things, which sparks the retort, "Pathetic. You're being totally pathetic."

The employee says nothing. Once the night manager has relieved him of the lady who continues to plead her case (sometimes in a plaintive tone, sometimes in an imperious one), it's the insulting gentleman's turn. The clerk, with somewhat emphatic movements, gets up and gœs to a cupboard just behind him, where he finds a bottle of mineral water. He takes a long swig. Then he returns to his seat and accomplishes his duty wordlessly. Meanwhile, the man opposite clenches his teeth and glares with a hatred so palpable you could seize it with your hands.

Nighttime is less and less a world of its own. There's hardly any difference any more. Those working the night shift the longest say that only fifteen years or so ago, until the early 1980s, the start of the night brigade's shift corresponded to the arrival, on the other side of the partition, of a population distinctly different from day customers. Of people who were chattier and more relaxed. "Characters" who liked witty comments and all kinds of jokes. People for whom the rue du Louvre post office represented a landmark, an institution within the nocturnal universe. They would fill it slowly, first making sure that daytimers had abandoned it, that the post office no longer looked so much like a post office. Much of that crowd came from Les Halles with its market workers and night revelers. They continued to flow in for ten or fifteen years after the old market was demolished. Then the flow steadily dried up, until it became just a memory. These days, the night shift is no longer another universe. It's a convenience. People come to conduct operations they didn't have time to do during the day. They come because they know the lines are shorter than during normal office hours. Or to extend the working day—at 2:00 A.M., a thirtyish guy came in to buy some shares in the post office's mutual fund. There's no more mountain ridge between day and night.

Come the day, when backstage characters don't go to the post office, the post office goes backstage. At around eight in the morning, mail delivery squads pile into minivans that then take each deliverer to an operations zone, which corresponds to half an administrative *quartier*. Of the ten that I interviewed, all ten expressed their amazement on discovering, when they first began, the difference between the facades of buildings and their interiors, between outside behavior and indoor habits, between how they'd imagined the capital's residents and what they found. Examples of such discrepancies flew thick and fast around the table where my interviewees were having lunch, making it difficult to grasp which surprise had been the greatest—the filthiness of many apartments, perhaps, regardless of *quartier*. Filthiness and smelliness. It seems most windows are never opened. A great number of buildings therefore give off a strong odor. Almost every one has its special odor, but all are strong. Anyone who claims there's an "odor problem" in the African ghetto known as the Goutte-d'Or should climb the staircases of buildings on streets like middle-class rue de Bagnolet, trendy rue de l'Epée-de-Bois, or bourgeois rue de Gergovie. The fragrances may not be the same, but they cling. One apartment smells of mothballs, as though the occupants had turned it into a napthalene factory. Another emits stratified cooking smells in which the various components, mainly greasy, can no longer be identified. Elsewhere, the smell is "scented"—the air is sugary from regular use of aerosols designed to "purify" the atmosphere. And there are many other smells: sour, tart, spicy, or heavy, not to mention the smell of dust. You'd think Parisians remain constantly leery of city air, or that they feel they can protect themselves from pollution by keeping their windows shut 365 days a year. Or that they need to make their home a lair, marking their territory like any other animal. Some buildings have new storm windows with plasticized metal frames, a fashion that is spreading fast because it cuts down significantly on noise from the outside (which thereby makes sounds from neighboring apartments, notably TVs, seem louder). But they also significantly reduce the arrival of air from outside. Domestic scents thrive vigorously behind these new windows.

Even when mailmen remain on the surface—I mean when no special letter obliges them to plunge upstairs—they frequently have to deal with a concierge or custodian. (A concierge is a concierge twenty-four hours a day; a custodian has a nine-to-five job.) Topping the deliverers' charts are Portuguese concierges and custodians, who win praise for friendliness (a smile and a cup of coffee for the mail lady) and conscientiousness. At the bottom come Yugoslavs: said to be not polite, not reliable, not there; or always delegating the task to interchangeable cousins; rarely sticking to the job for long; not knowing who lives in the building; keeping deliverers waiting at the doorstep, giving the impression that, behind the door, they're secretly building an atomic bomb.

In the periods when notices of corporate tax and social security payments are sent out, deliverers observe that the mailboxes of many small boutiques and companies vanish for two weeks or so. All this paperwork and all these payment notices then have to be returned to the sender, stamped with "Not known at this address." Postal employees are forbidden to leave the mail anywhere other than in a box with the addressee's name on it.

Of course, most of the people mailmen meet during their rounds, the people to whom they hand registered letters or parcels, have one thing in common: they're at home in the morning because they don't work. Many live alone (over half the apartments in Paris are occupied by a single resident) and a significant part of them are elderly or nearly so. Mail deliverers therefore deal with customers who often perceive their arrival as a high point of the day. They are sometimes the object of kind gestures—a cup of coffee, cookies—designed to make them stay a little longer, to chat a while. They listen to details of the neighbor's latest turpitudes, to complaints about the concierge, and to queries about an expected letter (or postcard or catalog) that was certainly mailed a while ago (the conclusive argument being that Madame So-and-So has already received the postcard her grandchildren sent during the Easter vacation). Or about the Damart catalog (featuring warm underwear favored by the elderly), which had already arrived by this time last year, so that it could be leisurely perused during the gap between the 3:00 P.M. soap opera and the one just before the evening news. "In Paris," joke the postal workers, "everyone's expecting an important letter every day." It's not unusual for someone who didn't see the mailwoman or who didn't manage to collar her in the hallway or stairway to call the post office and ask if a letter or parcel has arrived—and if not, why not.

Elderly people living alone, whether affluent or having difficulty making ends meet, make a great many mail-order purchases. Marketing people claim it's because they're put off by the crush of people at department stores, because they like taking their time to choose, and because they don't like leaving the neighborhood where they do their everyday shopping. But postal workers know it's really because they want to see the mailman. Who else is there to tell about the children's divorce, or the grandchildren's exams, the "crowd" the grandkids hang out with, and the worry they cause? Who else is there to listen to the way things used to be, to tales about the "dear departed husband" who, ever since his death, grows more handsome, good, and wise with each passing year? Who else will discuss the (dreadful) news seen on the TV last night? Who else will do a favor if you're feeling unwell? Indeed, Parisian mailmen and women occasionally head back into the street to buy bread or fill a prescription. Nor—to put suspicious minds at rest—are such favors done out of self-interest: a law forbids mail deliverers from ever inheriting anything from, or exercising a power of attorney for, anyone on their route.

The mailman is the only young person with whom some people have regular contact. In Paris, the average age of deliverers is among the youngest of any profession. Women are increasingly numerous; many of them, initially disappointed at "finding nothing better" after anywhere from two to five years of higher education, eventually come to appreciate an occupation they wouldn't trade for a better-paid office job. Despite the loonies and the disappointments.

The loonies—"it seems like there's more and more of them every year"—are always in the midst of a dispute, and expect you to take their side. "I know you give the mail to the custodian, but he doesn't bring it upstairs. He gives it to his dog, who eats it. You're the only one who can do anything about it. The police will believe *you*." The disappointments come in countless varieties. There's the TV celebrity living in a duplex-with-terrace in one of the buildings on your route; he takes a registered letter without a glance, muttering that there's always somebody making trouble. Then there's the movie star you always thought of as a grand lady—she has a hard time opening the door, so drunk is she, wrapped in a bathrobe splattered with various leftovers; and once when you handed her a parcel, she burst into tears and fell flat on her back (a disappointment, maybe, but it still makes a good story). Or the apparently classy gentleman who took liberties—swiftly halted—on the person of a young mailman who had no intention of performing that kind of service; furious at

89

this rejection, the gentleman delivered threats and insults, then wrote to the post office asking that the route be given to someone less insolent, with better breeding. "Fortunately, I'd already recounted the incident to the gang, so no one was fooled. But I was still the butt of jokes for the next three months. After each morning's round, they'd ask, 'So—raped how many times today?' When there was a registered letter for the guy that harassed me, I never went upstairs to see if he was in, I always slipped a notice in his mailbox. And you know what, he wrote a letter of complaint! When I went back home to the Jura Mountains, I told my parents all about it. My father wanted to write to his representative, in order to alert the government to our working conditions. Of course, he's an old union activist, my father. I managed to dissuade him. He halfheartedly allowed himself to be convinced, but said to me, 'Be careful. People live like animals in Paris. And the danger is that you get used to it.' Whereas I think that in Paris, even if everything seems more expensive, tense, tougher, there are so many possibilities that it's still the best place to live. Sometimes, on Sundays, I go back to the *quartier* where I have my route, just to stroll around and have a closer look at some of the buildings. I take my girlfriend. She's a secretary in a skyscraper in the La Défense business district on the outskirts of town, and she says I'm really lucky. We live at Porte d'Orléans, but we're looking for something more central, in the 10th or 11th arrondissement. All I know is, after all I've seen, when you're no longer in the race there's no point living in Paris. It's too tough. But you know, just the other day I said the same thing to an old couple when I handed them a package. They complain about everything—noise from jackhammers, high prices in stores, children who only live half an hour away by Metro but don't come to visit much. So I said, 'But why don't you move to your family's country house, in Berry?' They were taken aback. First of all, it seems that when they go there, all the people they went to school with more or

90

less refuse to talk to them. Out of jealousy because they didn't dare leave themselves, and also because the guy had a pretty good career. So this couple gets bored after two weeks there. And in the end, as the old guy says, 'All this brouhaha in Paris doesn't have only a bad side. It also makes you feel alive.' His comment struck me as funny. Because it's the same for us young guys. Here you're always making plans."

Like the lame devil in Lesage's eighteenth-century novel, who lifted rooftops to allow the insatiably curious student Cléophas to peer in, mailmen can play a revelatory role for someone wanting the inside story on Paris. But Paris firemen play it even better. Firemen, called *sapeurs-pompiers*, are a part of a military organization that historically performs civilian rescue as well as fire extinction. They're called into the streets of Paris nearly 200,000 times a year—that is to say, over 500 times per day—of these calls, scarcely 6,000 are related to fires, which may range from a kitchen flare-up (frequent) to the conflagration of the huge headquarters of Crédit Lyonnais (rare)—fires represent only 34 percent of the calls answered by *sapeurs-pompiers*. (In their jargon, a call is a *décalage*, which means "unblocking the wheels," in reference to the days of horsedrawn fire engines.) That's barely twice the number of calls prompted by the threatened collapse of a cornice of a building, or a leak in a domestic oil or gas tank. And only half the number of calls due to burst water pipes or the smell of gas (real or imagined), one-third the number of traffic accidents, and not much more than the number of false alarms, which account for 2 percent of the sallies executed by the *Brigade des Sapeurs-Pompiers de Paris* (BSPP).

Let's face it: Paris isn't burning. Or doesn't burn anymore. Most fires break out not in private homes but in factories and warehouses (though few remain) and in workshops (which are fewer and fewer). If the BSPP's only role were to put out fires, as is the case with its counterparts in London, New York, and most other major cities, it would be scandalously overstaffed.

91

But, even though each "barracks" begins every day with stiff physical exercise, training maneuvers, and meticulous maintenance of vehicles and equipment, and even though every fireman dreams of fires (while those who have fought serious ones recount their war stories over and over again), Parisian firemen are first and foremost social workers. Not as a sideline, like postal workers. Social work takes up fully 75 percent of their time, under the potentially misleading labels of "aid" and "rescue."

True enough, these statistical categories include a significant number of urgent calls involving real tragedies—poisonings from gas, medication, or drugs (6,500 per year), knife wounds (1,200), heart attacks (2,200), traffic accidents (13,000, of which fifty-two are fatal and 500 "serious" or "very serious"). Under the same labels, however, firemen answer tens of thousands of calls that amount to next to nothing. Or seem like nothing. But, as recounted below, certain seemingly innocuous interventions by firemen play a key role in the daily life of the capital, and can only be carried out by them—not because they're the only ones technically able to do so, but because it's the *pompiers* that Parisians want to see. Their presence is required to a degree I would never have imagined possible had I not been allowed to follow the *décalages* of two companies, one in the north and the other in the west.

Farewell, then, to the traditional calendar image of intrepid troopers fighting flames or diving into dark, icy waters to save some desperate soul. One hundred drowning victims are pulled from the river every year—sixty of them still alive—which might be described as a leap into the Seine every three and a half days. Which seems pretty frequent. But for the BSPP, it's six times less common than the elimination or capture of animals (removal of wasps' nests alone represents two hundred calls annually).

Above all, Paris firemen are all-purpose fixers of unexpected problems and soothers of life's unbearable tensions whenever those tensions exceed a critical—if often low—threshold. Fixing unexpected problems means shoring a tree about to topple, anchoring equipment before it falls; unclogging a sewer main; cutting off a gas leak (and airing out the premises); halting a flood; dissuading a person about to leap into the void and convincing him to come back inside; rescuing another person trapped in an elevator; cleaning up acids, hydrocarbons, or dangerous products spilled on city streets; assisting a woman in childbirth; getting a drunk back on his feet; freeing someone locked inside an apartment due to a scatterbrained spouse or a child who took the keys and shot the bolt; breaking open the door of someone whom worried neighbors in the building haven't seen for some time. (Pursuant to which, let us put to rest the myth that Paris is full of corpses waiting to reach an advanced state of decomposition before the neighbors notice anything. Although it would be unfortunate, and perhaps even wrong, to deprive Parisians and provincials of the delightful *frisson* they get every time this subject comes up—with its attendant, remorseful comments on the solitude of big cities and the dehumanization of metropolises, etc.—the *pompiers* found only ninety-one bodies behind the doors they broke down last year. Given that nearly two-thirds of these deaths were due to suicide or drug overdose, the figure drops to thirty people—out of a population of two million—who abandoned this vale of tears in a "natural" manner without anyone worrying or even noticing.)

Unbearable tension, meanwhile, refers to what we French call, for want of a better term, a "fit of hysterics" on the part of a coworker, a neighbor, a friend. A calming effect is provided by the uniform, which represents authority, and the red emergency van with its ambulancelike siren, which conveys security. A fit may be triggered by a child who hasn't come home from school, an elderly mother who left to "do some errands" and still hasn't returned, a husband or wife who stormed out of the house after a pretty sharp exchange ("but (s)he didn't take anything, and couldn't have gone far. It's just that maybe (s)he's had an accident, but it's not really worth contacting the police yet"). Or it may refer to an elegant, indeed very elegant, lady whose costly ring—both a precious gem and a priceless memento—fell, following a false move, into a hole, a sewer, or the Seine. Quick! Call a diver, or a spelunker (the BSPP has both). Or maybe a gentlemen calls because the elevator is making funny jerking movements and the maintenance company doesn't answer; can the fire brigade shut it down? Or someone is going crazy because the alarm in the store downstairs has been howling nonstop (and for no reason) for three-quarters of an hour, and it's past midnight, you see, and he has to get up at 6:00 A.M. Or a woman calls because her fridge gave off a blue spark and "zapped" her, and now she's paralytically afraid to unplug it and only her husband, who's away on a business trip, knows where the fuse box is. Could a fireman come over and turn the thing off?

Always prepared (like boy scouts), the firemen always can. Unless they're already someplace else. And assuming that the request for help remains within the realm of the reasonable. When a Parisian dials "18," a switchboard takes the call, screens it, and dispatches it to the local company. Roughly one-third of the calls are eliminated. Once through the filter, a call sets in motion a mechanism whose every movement is noted, filed, computerized. An alarm suddenly sounds in the courtyard of a company in north Paris. The number of blasts indicates the type of call. In this case things aren't too clear—apparently someone has been hurt. The police are already on the scene, downstairs. Upstairs, a West Indian from Martinique, going through withdrawal symptoms, has stabbed himself with a knife. Says he's HIV positive, wants to contaminate his son with his blood. His girlfriend—big and nasty—is shouting at no one in particular and threatening to take revenge on whœver called the cops. She cools down a little when the firemen turn up. A boy of seven or eight, sitting on

94

the floor, stares at the man (his father?) sitting on the edge of the bed in undershorts, bleeding. The man lets one of the firemen approach, indicating that he no longer has the knife. Cleaned, bandaged, calmed, and dressed, he lets himself be taken to the hospital. There are traces of blood all over the apartment walls. One of the firemen gives rubber gloves to the large lady, who continues to glower in rage. "Put these on when cleaning up, and don't let the kid touch it."

"That bastard of an addict can clean it up himself," she snaps. She must have had a terrible fright.

The next *décalage* takes us to the rotunda in the Villette quarter. Someone's hurt. A call came from a phone booth. Once on the spot, the master sergeant sees a group of bums waving to the van. One of them is sitting on the ground. Young. (Later, he'll state his age as thirty. The fire brigade, after answering a call, always asks for age and name, but never demands ID, unlike the police. Yet another reason they're appreciated.) He can't walk. It's his ankle. It has swollen to the size of a softball. A *sapeur-pompier* takes off the shœ and removes the sock. (Show me another foot like that and I guarantee it'll make anybody retch.) "They'll clean this up at the hospital," says the fireman, who grimaces, then smiles as he begins to apply a restraining bandage, "unless they decide to dip it in acid." The bum and his buddies laugh. "Can't beat the fire brigade," one of them proclaims. Under the layers of filth on the ankle, snatches of tattooing can be glimpsed. Back to the hospital, where the nurses jest with the firefighters. "You might at least bring flowers."

"No need," comes the reply, "this one smells like roses."

Before the van even returns to the station, a radio call sends it elsewhere. A little girl has been knocked down by a motorcycle. She's shaken up but dœsn't seem to be injured. She's taken to a different hospital with her mother just to be sure. A local optician and custodian step forward as witnesses. The police are on their way. But they don't show up for another twenty-five minutes, on scooters. By which time the witnesses have gone home.

The next call comes, of all places, from a neighborhood police station. A meter maid has sprained her ankle; while bedecking illegally parked cars with her tickets, she fell from the curb. "Could you stop by the police station on your way to the hospital? That's where all her things are." Off they go; I return to the fire station on foot, just in case a fire has broken out anywhere. It turns out there's no smoke, but someone has alerted them to a gas leak. There's a great deal of commotion—the *décalage* no longer concerns just the first-aid van, but a big engine with ladder, hoses, the whole works. Hooray! The firemen have donned their leather suits, slipped their balaclavas over their heads and around their necks, and grabbed their silvery Darth Vader helmets. They finish dressing in the truck. You can feel the adrenaline flowing. When the truck pulls up at the address indicated, they leap to the sidewalk, helmets in hand. (They never wear them in the street, it upsets people.) They only put them on in the stairwell, while climbing the four floors.

A woman waits on the landing. She's fortyish, skinny, skittish, bleak. She leads the *pompiers* to her kitchen, where she noticed a funny smell "coming from the pipes." No one smells anything. For two minutes, everyone sniffs. Nope. No suspicious odor. "Dunno. I smelled it just a while ago," insists the woman, who then goes to shut the door on the landing before she explains. "It's the upstairs neighbors. The concierge, she's just bought the apartment. They're constantly doing renovation work, any which way. I don't even know if they have the right. It's awful. I'm always afraid. I've told them to stop. They just brush me off. Couldn't you go check upstairs? Tell them to stop?" She bursts into tears, shaking from head to foot. The sergeant calmly explains that no, they can't go investigate the neighbors' apartment. "But I went to the police. They say they can't do anything. Can't you file a report?

Then they'd have to come." No, the fire brigade dœsn't file reports and, anyway, about what? All they can do is note that they were called out. The sergeant takes his time. The woman calms down. She says she's a teacher. The firemen make to leave.

On opening the door, they find the concierge on the landing. She's the same age as the tenant, but otherwise is just the opposite: plump figure, dynamic air, sharp eye. She explodes: "She only did that to bug us! She can't stand the fact we've bought the apartment. She's jealous. It kills her to see we've made it!" From the upstairs landing a male voice—that of the concierge's husband, presumably—chimes in. "Bitch! When will you stop hassling us, bitch? You think we'll let you bug us forever, bitch?" The sergeant takes three steps upward and glares at the man. "That's enough, sir. You don't need to insult people."

The voice retreats, dropping two notches. "Yeah, well, she is a bitch."

"That's enough, I said. Go back inside." He asks the concierge to go downstairs, and waits for a moment until calm has momentarily returned. To the teacher, he says, "OK, Madame, try to work things out." She nods and gœs inside, crushed. The truck, the ladder, the whole works return to base. The firemen remove their leather suits, take off their balaclavas, and store their helmets. "Another life saved!" quips one of them, grinning.

The next call only concerns the regular van. An old lady has fallen unwell in her apartment. A small two-room apartment on the top floor, laden with overly large furniture covered with printed fabrics that compete with one another. On top of a large TV is one of those dolls in traditional Breton dress. On the walls are three crucifixes, two Virgins, engravings from the *Moniteur des Modes*, and a print of The *Oath of the Horatii*. The lady is lying in bed, wearing a bathrobe. Although pale, she speaks without difficulty. "I'm ninety-one years old," she states straight off.

"And I'm eighty-four," echœs her husband.

It seems they had gone to take a little stroll on Buttes-Chaumont, "given the weather." They stopped in a café on the way back. She had a glass of port. A little later, she felt dizzy. He took fright.

"That's dumb," she says, "he's always worried. There's nothing wrong with me. I'm ninety-one."

"And I'm eighty-four."

The sergeant laughs and congratulates them, then negotiates the taking of her blood pressure: 110 over 80.

"So you see!"

"Well," says the sergeant, "do you mind if I call a doctor anyway? Just to reassure everybody." After a few minutes of discussion, she finally agrees. The sergeant calls, makes polite farewells, then everyone heads back downstairs. The door to the ground-floor concierge's apartment is open; inside the occupant is sitting before a bottle of wine that he has nearly emptied. He rises and staggers. "Thanks a lot," he mumbles, "they're old folks."

The day continues with a fainting spell in a restaurant. A well-dressed young woman. Stretcher. Blood pressure. Hospital. "It's an act," diagnoses the sergeant. "Nobody faints with that blood pressure and that respiration." Next!

The next call is a heart attack in a building with a garden, a little more *chic* than the surrounding buildings. The man, very overweight, has already had problems. He's surprisingly calm, and therefore his wife and two children are suddenly calm, too. Over to the hospital once again, then we head for the mess hall to have an undisturbed meal, if possible.

At the mess hall, the sergeant apologizes for not providing me with a fire. I forgive him and together we pray that a fire will cooperate. "If only you'd been here last week," said another noncommissioned officer, concerned about his outfit's reputation. I try to convince him that I simply want to share the company's everyday lot. Since just three out of every 100 *décalages* concern a fire, that's the only quota I expect. My dining companions politely claim to believe me, but it's clear the firemen still think that the humble calls we've just answered are unworthy of a written account. Which doesn't mean that *sapeurs-pompiers* are ashamed of rendering the services requested by Parisians. But they only accede to this routine social work insofar as they remain firefighters; it is fire, with the myth surrounding it and the courage required to fight it, that confers glamour, authority, immunity, and charisma—in short, a state of grace that places them above the fray. And they also need to feel that the point of all those hours spent working out in the gym or conducting outdoor exercises is not simply to resolve spats between neighbors, ferry sprained ankles, and reassure ninety-one-year-olds.

Apart from the staff obliged by brigade regulations to live at the station, not many officers and NCOs reside in Paris or its suburbs. Of the six men at my table free to choose their place of residence, four have moved to the provinces. Two to Brittany, one to Dauphiné, another to Alsace. Since a normal shift is three consecutive days and nights, followed by a break of the same duration, and since high-speed TGV trains have put their homes within three hours of Paris (except for the Alsatian), they lead two separate lives, with which they seem delighted. Given that most of the lower ranks—composed of draftees performing their military service—come from the provinces or the distant suburbs, and that a good many of the brigade's career officers hail from the same places, it suddenly becomes apparent that Paris's firefighters aren't from Paris. Despite high unemployment, and despite the appeal of doing your military service in the BSPP rather than the army, Parisians rarely apply. "They're not interested in Paris," commented one staff officer, "they don't know how the city functions and they couldn't care less."

A noncommissioned officer has a harsher opinion. "They have no sense of responsibility." His tone is one of observation, devoid of moralism. "They're cocky, but it's a city of basket-cases: they call the fire brigade if they cut a finger while slicing fruit or sawing a plank. In the country, you'd call a taxi to take you to the emergency ward. In Paris, the red fire truck serves as taxi."

The scope of this Parisian attitude can be appreciated by chatting with firemen about calls provoked not by fires but by enemy number two (or one-and-a-half): water. Minor leaks are so frequent in the capital that the BSPP had to adopt a policy of refusing to intervene. (Responding solely to serious floods still accounts for 10,000 calls per year.) That's because a series of factors in Paris has contributed to maximum chaos when it comes to renovating old buildings. A rent control act of 1948, which enabled the poorer population to remain in its lodgings, discouraged landlords from undertaking any improvements other than the strict minimum required to maintain their property. That meant often ignoring pipes until they'd outlived their useful life. In cooperatively-owned buildings, meanwhile, stinginess or dissension between owners led to similar results.

The worst damage, however, has been done by real-estate agents and do-it-yourselfers. The former buy up buildings which they "renovate" by knocking down a few partition walls, repainting everything, and installing modern conveniences. (As late as 1965, two-thirds of Parisian apartments still lacked bathroom and toilet.) The latter group does the same thing, on an individual basis. And both groups set bathtubs on floors too fragile to bear the weight of a tub full of water, connect runoff pipes in the cheapest way possible, add numerous lateral pipes, confuse sewage pipes with drainpipes, connect into nearby plumbing not designed to accommodate additional flow, and display a blithe lack of concern for next-door buildings, downstairs neighbors, and the laws of physics.

The upshot is that Paris has some of the wettest highrise apartments anywhere. And if it's hard to find a plumber when you need one, that's because they're all busy repairing the damage caused by so many absurd renovations. The fire brigade has therefore decided to act only when there's a clear and present danger, when things are so bad that floorboards or staircases threaten to collapse. (Insurance companies, meanwhile, are increasingly refusing to cover flood damage.)

Firemen possess endless examples of Parisian selfishness, irresponsibility, and lack of sincerity, which they recount without acrimony. That's because, when you come down to it, they like this town. Obviously, they wouldn't be able to bear it if they didn't live someplace else or, for those living here, if they couldn't envisage the possibility of a future transfer to someplace like Lacq (in the Pyrenees), Biscarosse (on the coast south of Bordeaux), or even French Guiana (where Ariane rockets are launched). But they probably wouldn't relish a life elsewhere so much if they hadn't plunged so often into this strangely populated city, which they know better than almost anyone else. The men of the 7th Company, for example, not only deal with night-time muggings in Pigalle and with tourists stricken by food poisoning during a tour of "Paris by Night," they've also discovered artists' studios on Boulevard de Clichy; explored dark, weary bars; mounted the stairs of hotels whose walls would be wise to remain silent; and gathered up young, drug-battered bodies from sandboxes in public squares.

Those in the 10th Company, meanwhile, have fished absolutely everything from the Saint-Martin Canal, have put an end to battles between bums in the Gare du Nord and to brawls between drug-addicted prostitutes (triggered by baroque tales of unpaid debts or stolen clients). They've raced over to the Goutte-d'Or at the outbreak of a fire only to discover the great difficulty of forging a path through the multicolored crowd that poured into the streets to greet their arrival.

Over at the 5th Company, they still can't believe their eyes—which nevertheless saw, or at least took in—apartments on Avenue Foch more luxurious than anything seen on TV: gold and marble fittings, immaculate deep shag carpets, pools, Jacuzzis, saunas, hallways long enough to provide training for the brigade's marathon, kitchens as large as dormitories, and dining rooms the size of the fire station's courtyard. These apartments are "on file" as belonging to some emir, tycoon, or golddigging divorcée. "We wipe our boots real well before entering." Three weeks later, they climb a wretched service stairway in the very same building, reaching the grotty top floor where the maids' garrets are, and where timid occupants crowd. Since there's no central heating, an electric heater from prehistoric times triggered a small fire. From there the company's red van heads off to a playing field at Bagatelle, where a rugby match between two elite engineering colleges resulted in a dislocated shoulder. While being taken to Ambroise-Paré Hospital, the hefty rugby player dolefully asks whether he'll have to have a shot. The *pompiers* take him for a ride by announcing that his buttocks will soon resemble a pincushion. The student widens his eyes in alarm, only beginning to relax when his saviors begin discussing the likelihood of an amputation. An hour and a half later, when delivering a soccer player from Bagatelle whose ankle succumbed to a tackle, the firemen run into their rugby player again, now bandaged and waiting for his family to come and collect him—his thanks are accompanied by the news that he was spared the needle.

As call follows call over a year, firemen offer reassuring words, kind gestures, and rescuing actions some 200,000 times—succor none would enjoy without a professional scratch-and-catastrophe squad that works behind the scenes to forge this big city into a safe place to live.

(To the great relief of my hosts, I finally got my fire. Not a raging, ravaging fire. Just a mushroom omelet that got out of hand, forcing into the street two alarmed guys and a girl who were preparing a small meal in a two-room apartment furnished with Indian fabrics, cushions, and poufs. Once the fire was brought under control—with great speed, using a minimum of water to avoid producing more damage than the flames—the three diners displayed the heady attitude of those who've just experienced something that will make a great story to tell friends and acquaintances. A kind of inebriation follows gut-wrenching fear. Firemen witness it all the time.)

If postal workers and firemen are great unsung forgers of links between the capital's isolated individuals (whether isolated purposely or by default), then teachers knead diverse ingredients into a democratic, secular, universalist dough, trying to offer a homogeneous future to children originating from the four corners of the world. On the northern edge of the 11th arrondissement, bordering the 19th, is an elementary school of 271 pupils. Fifty of them are French (including sixteen from the French West Indies), six are Portuguese, two Spanish, two Irish, two Serbian, two Polish, one Albanian, and one Macedonian; that makes sixty-six Europeans. Then there are ten Turks (who have only one foot in Europe), fifty-one Chinese, seven Sri Lankans, three Indians, three Laotians, one Pakistani, one Cambodian, and one Vietnamese; that equals seventy-seven more-or-less eastern Asians. Plus twenty-eight Algerians, twenty-six Tunisians, twenty-one Malians, nineteen Moroccans, eleven Ivory Coasters, ten Senegalese, three Guineans, and two Gabonese, totalling 120 Africans. Finally come eight "American" representatives—six Haitians and two Colombians. Another school, in the 10th arrondissement, boasts 300 students from twenty-eight different countries. The director of a school in the 18th arrondissement reported that only five of his 295 pupils were "of Gaulish stock." (Most public school teachers use this term jokingly to avoid employing the phrase bandied by the racist National Front, namely "of French blood"). Here again, those of North African descent dominate, followed by Chinese, Sri Lankans, Indochinese, Malians, Zaireans, and even one Australian girl. In the 19th arrondissement, a teacher with thirty pupils decided to organize an imaginary banquet in which all the children contributed a recipe from their home country, supplied by their mothers; sixteen national cuisines were represented at this literary feast.

"Could you please put my son with fewer blacks?" wrote one parent to a school principal, while another wrote, "I've told my daughter to stop going to school, because of poor grades due to too many foreigners." The paradox faced by teachers in Paris's working-class *quartiers* is that they have to try to integrate children from abroad—whether French citizens or not—into a local population that is vanishing from their schools. When the proportion of aliens becomes too steep, many parents of "Gaulish stock" go to the local mayor to ask for permission to transfer their children to a school of "better repute." Rare—indeed, very rare—is the elected official who refuses to grant this favor. And when it is refused, parents simply send their children to private schools, if they can. Others, more heroic, agree to play the school-district cards as they're dealt—one devout, left-wing Catholic family in north Paris kept their three boys in a primary school that had fewer than 3 percent white French children. Two years later, they withdrew the boys. "We made the decision with a heavy heart, but we didn't think could sacrifice our children's education to our convictions. Their level was much too low, compared to their cousins attending 'normal' schools. Some people made fun of us, and others—in one of the associations we belong to—even suggested we'd become racist. But *their* kids had always gone to well-balanced classes, whereas the atmosphere in our boys' school was unbearable, given the kids who only attended from time to time, the ones who still couldn't read by fifth grade, the ones who spent all their energy trying to prevent the teacher from doing his job, and the ones who started fights in the playground."

Unbearable or not, most primary school teachers cope with it. That's because they belong to a group much more confident of its social usefulness—and much less subject to introspection—than their counterparts in secondary education. Anyone who teaches in a middle school or high school might legitimately question the point of discoursing on the Punic Wars, electrostatic screens, or the dative case in German to young people convinced that their future resides in unemployment lines. Whereas the skills taught at primary school, as one teacher says, "are needed even by the unemployed."

The very great majority of school principals and teachers therefore relativize the problems they encounter, which most of them discuss with good humor. "The children who create problems are those who get no support outside school. Those whose parents come from Black Africa or the West Indies, for example. The former live in infinitely varying families that place no particular importance on formal education, especially since many of the adults cherish the improbable dream of returning home some day. A vast proportion of the latter come from one-parent homes, which means they're raised by a single mother who already has enough trouble feeding and clothing her brood, much less finding the extra energy needed to monitor their school work. Turks also cause problems. In general, the children are keen to learn and integrate, but their parents create obstacles. They won't let their kids join extracurricular activities. They don't praise good grades, and refuse all contact with us. When we manage to speak to them, they explain that they don't want their children to stray too far from their traditions and that, in any case, they'll soon go back to Turkey. Sometimes, Turkish girls who do well suddenly stop coming to school from one day to the next. Letters are sent to the family, which don't get answered. A social worker is notified, who ultimately learns that the kid was sent to live with a grandmother or relative back home, 'for her health's sake.'"

Yet whether they be Turks, Africans, or West Indians, many mothers quietly make an appointment to see the school principal, especially if the principal is a woman. Who then becomes social worker, marriage counselor, and liberation strategist. Secret meetings take place in her office when the husbands are at work or busy elsewhere. Plots are hatched to keep the boy or girl in school as long as possible, get them into high school, enroll them in an extracurricular activity. They talk about how to deal with men, how to make cunning use of men's authoritarian habits. They get so bold as to call a meeting—supposedly educational—of mothers who want to shake off certain shackles, so that they can give each other mutual support. They point out everything that might help, step by step, to free these kids (and their mothers) from their milieu's inertia. School principals (male and female) tread carefully, and yet they often comment that a kind of collective memory of immigrant education has survived and been handed down to them. "These days, it's the Africans, but before them it was the Yugoslavs, Poles, Hungarians, Italians, Portuguese, Spaniards. They didn't create the same problems in the same way, of course, and their family structures and ways of thinking were closer to ours, but everything else being equal, they had to be helped to overcome the same fears, the same tensions, and even the same rejection. And most of the time, it was thanks to the women." Watch out, though, if husbands get wind of the plot. The problem is not so much that they make a scene, sometimes noisy, in the principal's office, but—much worse—they move away and enroll their kids in a different school. Or sometimes just take them out of school altogether, despite the problems that creates in receiving childcare benefits. Between the pupils who disappear for such reasons and those who simply leave because their parents' professional or financial situation has dictated a change in residence, no more than 5 percent of children in some disadvantaged districts (given priority attention and therefore known as ZEPs, or *zones d'éducation prioritaires*) stay in the same school all the way from kindergarten to fifth grade. These statistics don't seem to discourage teachers, for ZEPs in Paris boast the lowest percentage of job-transfer requests.

Maybe we have the Chinese to thank for that. Since the mid 1990s, the children have made up a steadily increasing proportion of the total primary school population. I'm referring here to Chinese from China, not descendants of Chinese who moved to Vietnam or Cambodia (whom Chinese from China regard with disdain) nor émigrés from former Indochina (esteemed even less), these two latter groups having basically settled in the 13th arrondissement of Paris, whereas the true Sons of Heaven put down stakes in the 3rd, 11th, and 19th arrondissements. In the 3rd and 11th, they've swelled an existing colony of compatriots (often from the same region) who began arriving in France early in this century, were employed as replacement laborers during the 1914-1918 war, and have consistently welcomed—Communism or not—a steady stream of fellow fortune-seekers. This stream having grown to the size of a little river, the Chinese community extended its realm to the southern 3rd, the northern 11th, and finally the southern 19th arrondissement. The discretion conventionally attributed to all Orientals is no mere myth. As proof, you only have to go over to the Arts-et-Métiers neighborhood, for example, on Chinese New Year's day. Hosts of Chinese of every age and sex pour forth from every floor of almost every building, generating a certain amazement on the part of fellow locals who had never suspected their existence. Ordinarily, apart from their presence in a few leather or garment shops, the Chinese are rarely in evidence—not only because a certain number of them only partially fulfill the requirements of legal alien, but also because it's part of their tradition to avoid attracting attention. A resident of a modern building in the 19th arrondissement, where fifty-four of the 102 apartments are now owned by Chinese (as compared to only two just five years ago), recounts: "In 1972 I bought an apartment in the neighborhood where Maurice Chevalier was born, and by the time I got used to the fact that it had become an Arab quarter, all my neighbors were Chinese."

Teachers, meanwhile, noticed the increasing Chinese presence long before anyone else, due to the number of children from the Middle Empire who were enrolling in their schools. And they soon realized they'd mainly have cause to celebrate.

It's not the discretion of Chinese pupils that teachers appreciate most (furthermore, they know the cost), it's the ardor for work combined with iron respect for the educational establishment. This ardor and respect are encouraged and maintained at home by a "family" that may not have blood ties to the child but which exercises an unflagging authority. Unflagging and, often enough, unchecked by any constraints on that authority. More than one teacher has ultimately discovered that Chinese pupils aged nine, ten, or eleven were working a good part of the night (after having done their homework) in clandestine sweatshops, in order to pay their bed and board (which in many cases was no more than a bunk bed in a dorm). That only increases the admiring affection felt toward kids who arrive without speaking of word of French and who, after two years of an "introductory" course designed to teach them the language and "bring them up to classroom standards," join a "normal" group only to find themselves at the head of the class within three months. And should, against all expectation, a young Chinese student display a lack of discipline or fail to perform any duty, there's no need for severe treatment—all that's required is a slight allusion to the deed on a correspondence form with the "parents," who promptly undertake to reeducate the guilty party. "So much so that we hesitate to notify them," admitted one school principal, "because we don't know how far they'll go. One time, a Chinese boy hadn't done his homework two days in a row. It bothered us because it might have been the up-shot of fatigue if his 'family' was making him work in a sweat-shop at night. So we didn't punish or shout at him. I just gave him a note for the 'uncle' who was housing him, to whom I wrote that we were worried to see that the boy wasn't doing his work. I composed it in such a way as to suggest—at least so I thought—that his 'nephew' was tired, which was sup-posed to make the uncle reflect. But the next day, 'Uncle' appears in my office with the child and, before I realized what was happening, forced him to get down on his knees and ask forgiveness. He shouted in the boy's ears, 'If you owe respect to me, think what you owe to a school principal!' Which just goes to show that the Chinese don't pose any discipline prob-lems. The worry they cause us is that they disappear as myste-riously as they arrive. The 'family' tells us they've been sent back home, or on to another 'uncle' in Canada or another part of Paris. We have neither the right nor the means to check these assertions, and what's more we don't think any-thing serious has befallen them. But we'd like to be sure that those pupils who showed the intellectual ability and desire to continue their education are given the chance to do so. I remember a little girl of six, enrolled by a 'guardian' who said she came from a province north of Beijing, who couldn't even say 'yes' or 'no.' A year and a half later, we had her skip a grade. Not only was she good at everything, but she won ev-erybody's heart, pupils and teachers alike, white, yellow, black, brown, red. The fall she was supposed to enter fourth grade, she didn't show up. The guardian said she'd been sent to live with another family member in the suburbs. I asked for her address, but he said he didn't have it on him. I never managed to get it."

Whether enrolling or withdrawing their wards, Chinese guardians plunge school principals into the heart of the mys-teries of the Orient. The guardians know that school author-ities have no right to refuse to enroll a child under twelve, and that this enrollment automatically entitles the child to a residence card. They quickly realized that, unlike the situation in totalitarian China, not all French bureaucracies are interlinked—or even in contact—and that teachers don't work hand in hand with the police. "They bring me a strapping lad who's at least sixteen, maybe eighteen, and tell me he's eleven and a half. Fortunately for them, they don't have whiskers, because otherwise I swear the kid would've had a sailor's beard. I know the Health and Social Services Department has a sophisticated method for determining real age through bone examination. Juvenile court judges use it when presented with little Gypsy thieves who inevitably claim to be thirteen. But where am I supposed to dig up a judge? So I enroll him but make it clear I'm not fooled. All my counterparts do likewise, and anyway who does it hurt? Obviously, sometimes I put up a fight—when I'm presented with a pair of twins and am told one is nine and the other eleven, whereas they both look eighteen. Or when an old, wrinkled Chinese man of seventy-two shows me a national health service card which includes the names of seventeen children under the age of twelve, eight of whom he wants to enroll. Frankly, it's unusual for them to be so unshrewd. I kicked the old geezer out and told him he was insulting me by taking me for such a fool."

Teachers in Paris constantly navigate between pupils from the Far East, North Africa, sub-Saharan Africa, Macedonia, and the French provinces, without letting any squalls blow them off-course (except for a few city schools notorious for unchecked alcoholism, depression, and couldn't-give-a-damnism). In the hallways and playgrounds of "well-run" ZEP schools, dozens of nationalities live together without antagonism. Which doesn't mean that calm reigns: "There's no racism between kids, but the atmosphere is tough, language is coarse, and fists and feet fly quickly. It's working-class violence of the type this *quartier* has always had. Calm periods interrupted by explosions. The only new thing in the school's

110

tradition—handed down from one generation of teachers to another and recorded on the books—is that theft between kids has now become commonplace. Otherwise, some things are amusingly permanent: our school was invited to the Christmas-tree lighting ceremony at the Elysée Palace twice, in 1974 and in 1993. When we were introduced to President Giscard and told him we came from the Belleville neighborhood, he took one look at us, let out an "Ah, Belleville," and continued on his way. Twenty years later, President Mitterand sighed "Belleville, that's nice," in the same paternal way, before going to shake hands elsewhere. Which perfectly symbolizes people's interest in this *quartier*—its name has a pœtic ring, but nobody wants to look at the reality. I wonder how many politicians realize there are ZEPs right in Paris itself. Ninety-six percent of the kids who eat in the school cafeteria benefit from subsidies. Their parents can't afford twenty francs ($3.50) for a meal that I'm convinced is the only balanced meal their kids get."

Sometimes, on leaving a primary school after a series of conversations with principals and teachers, I wonder whether they're related to Napoleon's embattled guards at Waterloo. All around them, institutions are crumbling or collapsing. Private schools are multiplying, cloistering children of the same religion or same ethnic origin. The Church of Scientology opens one school here, another there. Teachers, who have already watched middle-class kids vanish, stay behind with the ones who have only public schools to go to, and they keep the fires burning under the melting pot where differences are supposed to be forged into French-style universal values.

Teaching people to get on with one another is a task also performed by certain individuals in Paris, people who don't merely do their job but also try to bring a little urbanity to the city. Edouard de Corvisart is one such individual. He dœsn't live in the capital itself, but thirty miles outside it. In order to be at work by 5:30 A.M., he has to get up at 3:15. Edouard is not descended from Napoleon's doctor, Baron de Corvisart, but rather is station chief at the Corvisart Metro stop. A commuter once left him a little note that awarded him that noble name.

Edouard had launched an appeal to "his" regulars. Every morning since his appointment to this station on Metro line number 6, he wrote a little welcoming message on a marker board. "Good morning, today is the feast of Saint Arnaud—happy name-day to all Arnauds. The quote of the day is, 'Every revelation of a secret is the fault of the person who confided it.' (La Bruyère)." Obviously, Edouard noticed that users took the time to glance at his board, yet very few of them took the trouble to indicate their appreciation with a nod, gesture, or word. To get a clearer picture, he asked users, via the marker board, to participate by supplying quotations they deemed worthy of sharing. He signed it, "Edouard V., your station manager." As hits go, it was a big one. Unlike the ticketpuncher in Serge Gainsbourg's famous song, the Corvisart station manager knew he was no longer "the guy you never look at when you pass."

Edouard received a constant flow of suggestions, from La Fontaine's morals and Montaigne's aphorisms to Camus's epigraphs, Barthes's utterances, and maxims from various moralists. "Shackled heart, free spirit" (Friedrich Nietzsche), "Humanity is not a condition to undergo, it is a dignity to be won" (Vercors), "Poor in pleasures, they want to be rich in illusions" (Charles Fourier), "Loneliness is not a basket to fill, it is a plant to bring to flower" (André Sève), "There is no fair wind for those who know not whither they go" (Seneca). And even a saying that the sender claimed to have authored: "Love is like coffee, you'd better enjoy it before it cools" ("René").

Using all these quotations required great care. The only acceptable ones were those that wouldn't shock anybody, wouldn't be misunderstood, and didn't stray from a basic humanism underlying all beliefs and philosophies. There was no question of posting "If wives were a good thing, God would have one" (Sacha Guitry), or "Women have nothing to say but everything to tell" (André Gide). Nor even "Being left-wing has become a profession" (Régis Debray) or "Right-wingers sleep, left-wingers dream" (Gustave Thibon). Fine, on the other hand, was "Genius is childhood recovered at will" (Charles Baudelaire). Edouard de Corvisart soon learned the shoals to avoid, and, buoyed by his success, bought a visitor's book. Users filled it with forty-five pages of congratulatory comments. The book was placed somewhat behind the station manager's *loge*, or booth, so that the writer's anonymity would be preserved. Even when making positive comments, Parisians prefer an indirect, incognito approach.

After a long strike by Metro employees in the winter of 1995, Edouard de Corvisart returned to work a worried man. He hung up his quotation board again, contenting himself with good-natured humor: "In the old days, I hadn't been born, but I've been making up for lost time ever since" (Maurice Roche). The great majority of Metro users carried on as before. Others flashed signals of relief at the *loge*, as though both users and staff had jointly triumphed over some outside force. Parisians increasingly seem to interpret certain strikes as their own rebellion, conducted by intermediaries. Edouard was finally reassured some weeks later when, for a never-ascertained reason, a numskull in senior management decided to put an end to the program of posting short poems at the end of every Metro carriage. In the space of three days, a hundred protests were deposited at the Corvisart *loge*, demanding the reinstitution of "Pœtry in the Metro." Whereas, during the strike, barely twenty protests had been lodged.

Everyday Vignettes of Paris

Three infants were baptized last year, one more than the previous year. "That's an increase of 50 percent," says the parish priest with a smile. Two burials. Not a single child enrolled for catechism classes. No "marriage preparation" sessions. Nor any marriages, for that matter. Number of residents in the parish of Saint-Louis-d'Antin: about two hundred and fifty. Number of priests assigned to the parish: thirty-one. One curé for every eight residents?! Such a ratio was never attained, imagined, or so much as desired even during Catholicism's most fertile heyday, even in the most priest-ridden provinces. So why waste a whole bevy of curés on a handful of souls at time when the French have lost faith in religion, no longer go to church, and are challenging Rome with its attendant hierarchies?

Because Saint-Louis-d'Antin no longer really serves the parish located between the old Opera House and the Gare Saint-Lazare train station, where offices have replaced so many apartments that the aging population diminishes every year. On Sundays, one Gregorian Mass is sung at the church of Saint-Louis at 10:30 A.M., attended by a few elderly locals. During the week, however, eleven Masses are given—in French—every day between 7 A.M. and 8 P.M. (including three at lunchtime that follow one another faster than those in Alphonse Daudet's tale, *Trois Messes de Noël*). In a church that's three-quarters full. Full? With whom? With some of the 200,000 people who pass through the parish of Saint-Louis-d'Antin every working day, or who actually dwell here during office hours: western suburbanites that Gare Saint-Lazare spews forth, then swallows up, employees of the firms whose headquarters sit here cheek-by-jowl, staff and customers of nearby department stores both old (Le Printemps, Les Galeries Lafayette) and new (FNAC), and owners and clients of the countless little businesses (ranging from fast food to fast sex) that live off the hides of the behemoths.

The *quartier* teems by day. Traffic is always clogged (even on foot, so crowded are the sidewalks). By night, the area is a concrete arctic—cold and deserted—more or less bisected by a stream of cars heading toward Place Clichy, and vaguely coming to life when the audience exits the Mogador Theater at about 11 P.M. At dusk, prostitutes patrolling their patch of pavement are so few and far between that you'd swear they constitute some kind of emergency shift assigned to handle urgent cases. In the morning, on the other hand, even as day breaks, the whole squad lines up for duty. Apparently a certain clientele (said to be on the upswing) seeks a little relaxation before starting the day's work. Lunchtime is also busy for these ladies. They attract some of the same customers as Saint-Louis-d'Antin, just as the church of Saint-Eustache, in Les Halles, shares some of its regulars with the courtesans on nearby rue Saint-Denis. Nothing like a good confession while the sin is still warm.

With a mixture of irony, affection, admiration, and envy, the Parisian clergy has dubbed Saint-Louis-d'Antin a "self-service" church. The expression fits, for the establishment features all the "products" a church can offer. First of which is peace and quiet. A survey of the faithful by the parish team revealed that this was the biggest draw. A haven of peace in the midst of constant bustle is what is mainly sought by people who climb the steps of Saint-Louis one day or another.

They are often Catholic in name only, and sit in the pews for just a few minutes. Some never return, or only rarely. Others stay till the end of one of the almost nonstop Masses. No one asks anything of them, and the looks of the people all around needn't weigh on them since they'll never see those strangers again (unless they wish otherwise).

If visitors seek something more than a moment of peace and quiet or a "quickie" Mass, panels and leaflets in the church inform them of what Saint-Louis-d'Antin has to offer, in addition to Masses. First comes confession, an increasingly requested item. Depending on liturgical season and time of day, between four and fourteen priests are at the disposal of whœver wants to be heard in confession. Demand has grown so strongly that an upstairs room in the nearby presbytery had to be specially fitted out; it's constantly full in the weeks preceding Christmas and Easter.

The parish has transformed a building behind the church into a lecture and exhibition hall, called Espace Georges-Bernanos. It has an entrance on rue du Havre, or can be reached by going through the church itself, facing rue Caumartin. The hall exhibits, say, Alfred Manessier's designs for stained-glass windows for the church of Saint-Sépulcre in Abbeville, plus a set of documents on the rosary and its history since the Middle Ages. In the auditorium, meanwhile, a viola player is scheduled to perform Heinrich Biber's *Rosary Sonatas*. Or else there'll be an exhibition on the artistic traditions of the Chaldean Church, followed by the celebration of a Mass in the Chaldean rite and an encounter with its bishop. One lecture follows another. There were four in April on Saint Theresa of Lisieux; another one (repeated each week for a month) discussed the liturgical origins of Christmas. Some subjects are secular, or rather semisecular: "Matisse and the Dominican Chapel in Vence," "Ramses II and the Bible," "Veronese and the Marriage at Cana." Other topics delve into the twentieth century: "Helping to Find Your Place in the Company," "The

117

New Management: Christian Critiques and Suggestions," and "Human Rights versus Human Justice." Readings are also given—ninety-five hundred people filed in, day after day, to listen to a reading of Georges Bernanos's *Diary of a Country Priest*. "That's three times the capacity of the Zenith concert hall," points out the curé of Saint-Louis, who can afford to be modest about his success, accustomed as he is to the popularity of events he and his team organize for his roving parishioners.

Indeed, everything finds a taker here. Prayer groups meet once a week at 12:45 P.M. Public discussions (Thursdays, Fridays, and Saturdays) cover topics ranging from "Kings and Saints, from Legend to History" to "Georges Bernanos Today" or "The Fad for Books on Spirituality." Every Monday, some forty people follow a course on Biblical Hebrew; the Greek course draws a few less, the Latin course a few more. On Thursdays, another group meets for a course on the Old Testament. Wednesdays, the focus is on "Biblical Keywords." A contribution toward expenses is always requested, but never any form of allegiance. Saint-Louis-d'Antin is a parish designed for free agents. If they want to band together and become regulars, that's their business. At "self-service" counters, consumption can be adapted to appetite. In 1995, two hundred and fifty adults requested and received baptism here (since 1990, new catachumens have been increasing at a rate of 30 percent per year).

Most Parisian churches are full for Sunday Mass. Some are even packed, so anyone who doesn't arrive a quarter of an hour before the Introit won't find a seat. This "high audience rating," to use a showbiz marketing term, is partly a gimmick—the vast majority of parishes now conduct only one Mass on Sunday, whereas thirty years ago they offered three. Vanishing supply concentrates demand. No one, by the way, would dream of contesting the fact that religious attendance has plummeted in France. In Paris, it completely collapsed in the 1970s, only to pick up slightly in the 1980s, then more firmly since 1990. Saint-Louis-d'Antin's extreme adaptation to the restive individualism of the new faithful is a spectacular expression of the transformation of both the ecclesiastical institution and the people who go there in order to pick and choose whatever strikes their fancy.

Formerly, it was strong social pressure that filled churches. The opinion of neighbors, rank in local hierarchy, and clan traditions did more than belief in the apostles' creed to spur people into the 11:00 A.M. Mass (followed by a trip to the local patisserie to pick up a dessert for Sunday dinner). I recall a childhood friend who, though raised in the Catholic religion, believed not a whit of it, and yet accompanied her family to church every Sunday. Instead of a missal, she'd take a volume of Balzac from the handsome Pléiade edition, which she'd read meditatively throughout the service. Everyone in the family was completely *au courant.* Since this woman had a lot of character, I expressed my amazement at her conformism, not to say hypocrisy; she just pointed toward her house, and said, "I couldn't do that to them. It would cost my father too much." He was a lawyer and deputy mayor. She was right to think that a daughter who failed to attend church every Sunday would have cost him a good many clients and voters. Since she loved her family, as long as no one forced her to pretend to believe (that is to say, to take communion or recite the creed) she didn't mind being numbered among the practicing Catholics.

One could almost say that today the opposite is true in Paris, where social pressure is so weak—almost nonexistent—that it encourages an "à la carte" approach to religion. Every individual chooses according to the state of his soul, varying intensity, frequency, and form at will, without anyone coming along to say not to skip a stage or miss an event. The upshot is that however diverse their liturgical sensibilities and tendencies, churches now generate an atmosphere markedly different from the one that reigned there thirty years ago. As soon as the only people attending a service do so willingly (excepting preteenagers), the weight of social conventions and conformism fades away. The ceremonial ambiance becomes lighter, freed from the grayness of routine, and a ring of authenticity replaces the mumbled prayers that all of us born before 1955 still recall as "the rumble of the Mass." With all due respect, people go to church these days the way they go to the movies. They join a crowd without being smothered by it. You only have to observe the ritual of the sign of peace that the faithful have been invited to exchange in recent years—reduced to a handshake and the standard expression, "The peace of Christ be with you. Amen." You might think that, in a city where so few people know one another, a gesture of this kind would be embarrassed, embarrassing, furtive, and fairly silly. I've noticed the exact opposite. People turn toward their neighbor (a total stranger, who will remain one), smile wholeheartedly, and utter the phrase sincerely. The stranger does likewise, then everyone returns to their aloofness as though they'd simultaneously established a social bond and defined its acceptable limits.

Going from one church to another as luck—or rather, bike—would take me, it was a while before I noticed a second sign (after the "sign of peace") of the changed atmosphere and voluntary nature of presence at church. Just as Poe's *Purloined Letter* was hard to recover precisely because it was hidden so visibly, I noted the number of faithful right away but saw only statistical significance. Yet it wasn't the high attendance that was significant, but the fact that the vast majority of people attended right from the start of Mass. Anyone who lived through the period when being Catholic was a social obligation will know what I mean. They'll recall that, in those days, people who were somewhat lukewarm about religion arrived at church as late as possible; even catechism dropouts knew at least one point of canon law, namely that attendance at Mass counts as long as you arrive before the unveiling of the chalice, that is to say before the offertory (leaving just the last third of Mass, thereby escaping the readings from the Epistles, the Gospels, and—*mieux vaut tard que jamais!*—the sermon). The churches of my childhood filled slowly, steadily, in successive waves. Widows, pious ladies, and the curé's pets arrived early. Right on time, or nearly, came well-bred families in their Sunday best. Then, from the Confiteor onwards, a constant trickle brought, pell-mell, children called to duty at the last minute (right in the middle of a game of dodgeball), housewives who had lingered in front of market stalls, husbands torn away from the bar of a bistro, and couples wrenched from a soothing sleep-in, not to mention the absentminded, the lackadaisical, and the shamelessly awkward who made their entrance at the last second of the last minute. (The same people vanished as soon as the "I" of *Ite, missa est* was pronounced.) These days, the Paris churches I visited from one Sunday to the next were full before the first celebrant left the sacristy, and latecomers were not only few in number but appeared dismayed at having missed the beginning.

The restive individualism of today's faithful is accompanied by great mobility. People only go to Mass in their own parish if the spiritual and liturgical tendencies of the local curés and vicars are deemed suitable, and if manners please—in short, if they like the looks of them. If not, people seek a church more to their taste. The church of La Trinité, below Place Clichy, is known for its "charismatic" worshipers. Of the three aspects of God, they focus above all on the Holy Spirit rather than the fatherly God or brotherly Christ, and they pray that they may receive that spirit, recognize its presence and action. This church, favored by many young people, is packed to the gills. For someone who doesn't share their sensibility, services at La Trinité seem fairly gregarious though not very openminded, and tend to get carried away on great words around which worshipers whirl like dervishes, mainly seeking—it seems to me—to produce an effect of incantation or fascination rather than open a space for reflection or prayer. The word in question ("joy," "grace," "love," "truth") suddenly loses its meaning and acts only as a trigger for collective behavior. La Trinité is just a few hundred yards from Saint-Louis-d'Antin, so maximum Catholic collectivism dwells right next to maximum individualism. Other varieties also exist. At Saint-Gervais-Saint-Protais, a stone's throw from Hôtel de Ville, invokers of the Holy Spirit have stripped the church of most of its chairs, replacing them with stools or rugs. They accompany prayer with what fans of yoga and similar Eastern wisdom call "psychocorporal practices": special postures for a given prayer or part of the service, in an atmosphere that remains austere, minimalist, conceptual, zen.

Certain churches are favored for their sermons; others, located in *quartiers* that still retain a distinct personality, quite simply bring together all the practicing Catholics in the neighborhood—Saint-Jean-de-Montmartre, on Place des Abbesses, recruits within a radius of three hundred yards, while Sainte-Jeanne-de-Chantal, at Porte d'Auteuil, also appeals to the nearby faithful. Both churches are "all-purpose" institutions with personality profiles which, without being bland, feature peaks and valleys of modest height. The same seems to be true of other parishes on the edge of town, where my cycle led me. It's in the center of the capital that churches are most distinctive and assert their personality most vigorously. Saint-Merri, right near the Pompidou Center, attracts Christians committed to the Third World, whereas Saint-Nicolas-du-Chardonnet appeals to Catholics who still yearn for the old rites. They sing, "We want God! He must / Come first in this land / It was France's former trust / That made the nation grand", and they chant the *Pange Lingua* with a vigor that expresses all their despair at seeing the world pass by (or above) them, as well as their rage at not being able to stop it.

Notre-Dame-de-Lorette, at the foot of rue des Martyrs, stresses the international scope of the Church—its pastoral team includes third-world priests, such as Indians and Africans who have come to Paris to study, and who draw the faithful from those same regions by celebrating Mass in their native languages; Lorette's liturgy attempts to accommodate the diversity of nationalities living in Paris, and the church also organizes "anthropological vacations" to distant lands. At Notre-Dame-des-Victoires, meanwhile, people pray with a vengeance, so to speak, all the time. Marian worship is particularly important here, in an atmosphere more sober and monastic than the one found at La Trinité or Saint-Gervais. On the second Sunday of May, a special Mass is held in the afternoon for "everyone taking exams." Once again the church is full, communion is taken by many, and hymns are sung lustily. The priest's sermon apprises Catholics that "passing an exam does not guarantee a passing grade in life. Nor does failing one mean failing life." Then he adds this strange piece of information—"You won't pass because you've studied, but because God loves you," which threatens to lead all those who fail into blasphemy, making them wonder just how God feels about them. The walls of Notre-Dame-des-Victoires are entirely covered with ex-votos, most of which date from World War I, expressing gratitude to the Virgin for the safe return of a son, husband, brother, or fiancé. Since piety doesn't preclude a sense of humor, on the way out of church one student—passing between two walls dotted with marble plaques of gratitude—turns to his buddy and asks, "All those for exams?"

The mobility of practicing Catholics, whether regular or seasonal, and their determination to go where they feel most at home, are such that a survey at Saint-Eustache, in the heart of Paris, revealed that only 10 percent of the people attending Sunday Mass live in the neighborhood. Another 40 percent come regularly from the four corners of Paris, while 50 percent are just passing through (whether Parisians, suburbanites, or even provincials or foreigners). The aesthetic appeal of the church plays a major role in the decision to attend Mass there, as does its music—it boasts a large organ, magnificently restored and maintained by Jean Guillou, as well as a choir long famous for its director, Canon Martin, and kept to the same standards of excellence by his successor. In a nod to their heterogeneous congregation, priests from the Congregation of the Oratory (who have run Saint-Eustache since time immemorial), alternate a Latin Gloria or Credo from the *messe des anges* (the Mass most often sung before the Vatican reforms) with a Lord's Prayer or Sanctus sung in French, along with anthems handled by the semiprofessional choir. Faithful to the spirit of human variety at the former market at Les Halles nearby, Saint-Eustache's priests seek the greatest common denominator and point out that "catholic" means universal.

The universality of human distress, for that matter, is acknowledged at Saint-Eustache every day—and night—of the week, as though, despite the displacement of the market and the demolition of its cast-iron buildings, this patch of ground once known as "the belly of Paris" still serves as a point of convergence for all the wretched on earth who seek a little moral or material relief. As soon as cold weather sets in, a soup line begins forming in late afternoon. It snakes back for three or four loops, and includes men and women of every age and appearance. Bums in the style of Jean Gabin in the film *Archimède*, young people in rags, others in the generational uniform of jeans and bomber jacket, many fortyish and fiftyish men (some dressed in the remnants of their former social station, others in garments so big or so small that they clearly come from some charitable organization, still others dressed in sweat clothes baggy enough to accommodate a lining of newspaper).

In the decade from 1985 to 1995, one-third of all funerals at Saint-Eustache were for AIDS victims: drug addicts or homosexuals, aged twenty-five to forty, drawn to this church rather than another for countless reasons (leading to the founding of a parish association to help AIDS sufferers). They came to ask one of the various priests not only for what is commonly called "the succor of religion," but also to help arrange a reconciliation with family or friends who had rejected them on discovering their secret or their illness. "New treatments have made these funerals rarer," said the curé, "but we've established links with certain patients, and with some of their friends and family, that has made them opt for Saint-Eustache as their parish, wherever they live and whatever the basis of their new interest in the Church."

Like his counterpart at Saint-Louis-d'Antin, the curé of Saint-Eustache has noted a spectacular increase in requests for confession. Faithful to the parish's eclecticism, priests offer penitents a choice between the traditional approach (in the dark of the confessional) and the modern approach (face to face in the light of an office). In either case, confessors are struck by the very traditional way in which petitioners view the sacrament of penitence. All the old memories flood back—it is the forty-somethings and fifty-somethings who are returning to church—as the confessee runs down a "checklist" of sins: "I was greedy, I lied, I took the name of God in vain," etc. "An infantile way of examining one's conscience still prevails," explains the curé. "And sexuality is disproportionately important. When someone asks us to hear an urgent confession, ninety-five percent of the time it's a sexual affair that's tormenting him—adultery or a visit to a prostitute. We try to broaden their vision of sin and divine mercy a little bit, but it's not an easy task."

Churches are part of the scenery in Paris, they blend into the background. People look at them without seeing them. Familiarity has dulled interest and curiosity. They rarely think of entering a church unless they have some business there. And yet it's hard to notice one of the city's smallest—and, heaven forgive me, ugliest—churches without feeling an urge to look inside. Saint-Hippolyte is located on the edge of the edge, by which I mean Porte de Choisy on the southern rim of the 13th arrondissement. Crushed between the two high-rises flanking it, the church forms a kind of architectural joke with them. The strangeness of the survival of a building so unrelated to its environment creates a desire to know more. Perhaps it contains a treasure that somehow requires this humble abode? In fact, Saint-Hippolyte harbors nothing of the sort, nothing out of the ordinary, except for bulletin boards which announced, the day I looked inside, a special Mass that would be held in a few weeks' time to celebrate that rite of spring, Chinese New Year, the festival of Tet.

On the appointed day—9 February, that year—spring was still a distant wish. The church was packed half an hour before the scheduled entry of the twelve priests co-celebrating the service: six Chinese and six French, preceded by eight choir boys and girls dressed not in the usual albs and surplices, but in traditional dress from various provinces of China. Facing them was a congregation over half of whom were Chinese or Indochinese, roughly a third were white French, and perhaps a quarter were West Indian, the rest being African. The curé uttered a few warm words of welcome and described the Chinese New Year tradition. He was followed by an old Chinese priest whose wizened face was split in a grin both childlike and mocking, and who said a few words in his own language to the congregation, the Asian segment of which began to grin in turn. French and Chinese were used alternately for the Introit, the Kyrie Eleison (*San Zhou Chio Ni Chou Nien*), and the Gloria. The Book of Job (7:1) was read first in French, then in Chinese ("Job answered, 'Has not man a hard service upon earth?'"); Saint Paul's first letter to the Corinthians (9:16-23) in Chinese, then French ("Though I am free from all men, I have made myself a slave to all"); and the gospel of Saint Mark (1:29-31, where Jesus heals Simon's mother-in-law) in the same order in the two languages.

When it came to hymns, things were not so easy. Each worshiper was given a sheet of paper with the Chinese lyrics reproduced phonetically. The wizened old priest, whose smile was splitting ever wider across his face, invited the French—whose language he mastered perfectly, though with a labial accent straight out of a *Tintin* comic book—to join their Oriental brethren. It went relatively well at first, since the melodies were familiar to every church across the planet, enabling everyone to more or less deal with the words of the famous psalm: "Alleluia San Zhou De Pou Ren Ah!" But then the Chinese would go too fast for the rest of the congregation to follow or, to the contrary, would suddenly stop to modulate on a note or introduce a musical variation, at which point everyone else got ahead. So from collision to cacophony, everyone finally let the Chinese sing alone, while the old priest's smile split his face so deeply it looked like the top half might fall backward.

"You'll get your money's worth," announced the curé before his sermon. "Two sermons but only one collection." The church swallowed the two homilies—one in each language, of course, the second delivered by the old priest, who spread his good humor to his colleagues and the congregation (those who understood him, at least). Later, after the Credo (in French), a little Chinese girl and boy alternated in reading the list of people to be remembered in prayers, evoking many family separations and war victims. When the time came for the sign of peace, instead of the handshake described above, the congregation was asked to separate into two groups, one facing the other, which then greeted one another by nodding the head, Asian-style. Obviously, the French and West Indians overdid the bow by bending as deeply as possible, whereas the Chinese simply made a movement whose solemnity was indicated by slowness rather than depth. Since both groups contained people of every ethnic origin, the chaos was total and the entire church burst into laughter.

At the end of the Mass, after the usual announcements, the curé invited the congregation to perform a rite in honor of ancestors. Everyone was instructed to leave their place and go to the back of the church, where they would be given a lighted stick of incense, which was to be carried to the altar and planted in an earth-filled vase. Each person would then be given a red envelope (the color of happiness). As parishioners began lining up, two worshipers read a eulogy for ancestors. "At the start of this year of the ox, we, the Chinese of Paris, with friends from France and other countries, gather here to express with sincere heart our filial piety to our ancestors.... To God I owe my soul, to my ancestors my body.... Let us remember the gifts we have received."

Two lines have now formed in the back of the nave, ready to march forward side by side, incense in hand. At the front of the left line is a tiny Chinese lady in traditional dress, hair tied back, movements carefully controlled. At the front of the right line is a pro-basketball-player-sized West Indian of twenty or so, who fidgets and turns his head everywhere. He calms down once the starting signal is given, and moves toward the altar with the old Chinese lady. He holds his stick of incense rather nonchalantly in front of his chest; she carries it solemnly in both hands, at eye level, head lowered. As soon as the young man notices, he adopts the same pose; since his giant steps carry him ahead of her, he shortens his stride, falling back to her level, and a few moments later plants his stick of incense alongside hers.

As delightful and bracing as this allegorical scene may be— where black, yellow, and white march in the same direction to the same beat—it can't disguise the fact that in Paris, foreigners are more likely to be encountered in court than in church. Along with drug addicts, foreigners constitute the bulk of the "customers" at the eighth division of the Paris prosecutor's office, namely the one that handles perpetrators caught in the act. Without immigration papers, there's no chance of getting a job; if you don't have a job you have live to by your wits, and the chances are good you'll fall into the hands of the police sooner or later. The same scenario holds for people with a drug addiction but no money (indeed, sometimes the players are the same). From the local precinct, suspects are taken to the Palais de Justice (main city courthouse) where the eighth division operates.

There assistant district attorneys witness a constant parade of highly diverse nationalities, each with its own specialty (or specialties), some ingrained, others fleeting: for six months, several gangs of Hungarians rifled the city's parking meters; Romanians armed with large bags lined with aluminum (to foil detectors at the doors) helped themselves to clothes from department stores; Poles organized a network for stealing and fencing liquor (after all, clichés have to be based on something!). The ring was broken up when too many of its members consumed the fruits of their labor and, drunk as skunks, got into fights that attracted police attention. The theft and resale of cars, meanwhile, is one business generally conducted by émigrés of all the former Communist countries of Europe. Except for former Yugoslavs, who pack the Metro with teams of pickpockets, in competition—sometimes physical—with small gangs of Algerians. North Americans do a wholesale trade in dope; Latinos handle the retail end, while West Indians specialize in crack. Angolans and Zaireans are experts in forgeries: forged identity papers, forged bank transfers, forged leases, real checkbooks obtained with forged papers, and real apartments occupied with thoroughly phony leases—the prosecutors can only admire such ingenuity and imagination. Indians and Sri Lankans are also trying to get into the forgery game, but have not completely acquired the knack (yet?), and also tend to settle their disagreements with much more violence.

It has long been said that the only laws the Chinese violate are their own, and that they themselves take care of delinquents and the consequences of violation. But it's also been claimed that they serve rats in their restaurants under various guises, and that they freeze-dry their dead before sending them back to China (all the while recycling the identity papers). As far as rats and freeze-drying go, there are still people—including police officers—who were "practically" eyewitnesses and will swear to it by the gods. As far as criminality goes, it hasn't been covered by the code of silence for some time now. Police officers and judges are henceforth familiar with various types of racketeering, from the standard "protection" racket used by every mafia organization to home sequestration of fellow Chinese for whom a ransom is demanded of the family in China. There are also increasingly numerous cases of clandestine work and sweatshop exploitation of minors. As various ethnic groups integrate into French society, their specific forms of delinquency become general; one old DA remembers that early in his career Italians still dominated fraud while Spaniards were known for hold-ups. "None of that means anything anymore. It's only the Portuguese who are still brought in a lot for the same crime—marital violence."

In an office of the eighth division, an ordinary day follows the same litany. Two soldiers on leave, on a binge and broke, cornered a forty-year-old man in the hallway of a building and threatened him with an army belt. A former convict, paroled the day before, was caught stealing a car; he's a multiple offender and a drug addict (he'll go back to jail, but everyone knows he'll be back here again). A tipsy sixty-year-old beat his mother and sister; they refuse to press charges, and they don't want to be seen by a doctor. (Their son/brother will be held for a while, given a good dressing down, then released.) A discount-store salesman was selling records on the sly. A single mother stole a wallet—she needed the dough to

130

buy herself some dope. A Croatian tried to break into an apartment by forcing the door; the neighbor, a reserve general in the *gendarmerie*, heard him and collared him. A murder/suicide in the 9th arrondissement—a man killed his mother and then took his own life; investigators were sent to scene (most of the neighbors only learn of the affair in the next day's paper). Three poker players got into a dispute over 800 francs ($150); one of them went to get a riot gun he kept at home. On returning to his poker partner's place, a neighbor about to take his dog out for a walk saw the armed man in the elevator, and called the police. A retired legionnaire, aged sixty-five, killed his twenty-five-year-old lover by stabbing him in the heart (because the lover had been unfaithful, declared the legionnaire when turning himself into the police). "That's my third one this month," commented the assistant DA.

"Your third legionnaire?" I asked.

"No," she replied, "my third crime of passion between men. The first case, though, was more criminal than passionate—a prostitute who brutally killed his client, an American living in Paris. An absurd tale. The client had equipped his apartment with every possible lock and security device because he had a very fine collection of primitive art and ivory objects, and yet he let his killer in himself. Who, for that matter, took only the VCR. The second incident was a more classic case of jealousy: an aging café owner who slept with his waiter. The waiter, however, slept around, and so the owner strangled him and walled up the body in the basement. We'd probably be none the wiser if a waitress in the same café hadn't filed a complaint—she was in love with the victim. If I were to give statistics off the top of my head, I'd say that today one out of every three crimes of passion in Paris is committed between homosexuals. Of course it doesn't always go as far as murder."

Two kids aged fourteen and a half broke into an apartment, raped the sixty-year-old occupant, and left with her jewelry. "The kids'll turn out to be from a suburban ghetto," predicted an assistant DA. Two hours later, he was proven correct. Elsewhere, a case of breaking-and-entering—but when climbing back down the long gutter into the courtyard, the cat burglar fell and broke his leg. Every day in Paris, two hundred and forty others get away, even though the police claim they do everything possible to catch them. A student was found dead, knife in heart, in the Bois de Vincennes. A crime; no, a suicide—he left a note. Comes to the same thing, killing yourself that way.

Three Russian citizens on tourist visas were arrested by a patrol while trying to steal a car—one already stolen five months previously. They defend themselves by claiming they were drunk; they just wanted to see how a Western car was made. A quick decision has to be made on whether to arraign them immediately or give them a respite and release them— they're two acrobats and a clown in a circus whose show is due to start in a few hours. They're released and told to keep their noses clean.

Interspersed among all these cases, and at an obsessive pace, the police haul "illegal aliens" before one of the four assistant DAs on duty. Three times out of four the person is a black man. The hearing (which precedes and guides a decision on whether to send the suspect to court) almost always proceeds in the same way: with little hope but a great deal of conviction, the detainee tries to lie about his age (if he's still young enough and looks plausible), passing himself off as a minor in order to dodge courts and sentences applicable only to adults. But usually he's already on file in some precinct or other, or else a skeletal examination is carried out—in either case, the tactic fails. If there's no hope of the age dodge, the "individual without ID" can try to play on nationality. If his skin isn't too dark, he'll claim he was born in the French West Indies, and is therefore of French nationality. Computer files and the internationalization of police records make quick work of this allegation—before sunset, the prosecutors will learn that the man who said he was born in Bellefontaine, Martinique, on 22 August, 1974 was in fact born in N'gaoundéré, Cameroon, on 30 September, 1973, despite a driver's license confirming his assertions. The forged status of the license was visible to the naked eye, but it sufficed to convince a hotel with a reputable address to hire the Martinican from Cameroon to empty their garbage cans (and probably also guaranteed he wouldn't complain if paid less than the minimum wage).

A gendarme now brings another man, "Toto," before the DA. After a brawl of obscure origins in a closed bar, Toto is being brought into her office on charges of "violence committed in public assembly," for "damaging the property of another," and for "violation of laws concerning aliens." Since he has no immigration papers—"I lost them," he declares—he initially claimed to be a legally registered alien from Senegal. He repeats this story in front of the prosecutor, who now informs him that his fingerprints have identified him as T. M., a citizen of Gabon, aged thirty-eight, already convicted and legally forbidden to enter France. Toto then launches into a discourse that slowly develops into a chant. He becomes increasingly still, almost statue-like, tears welling in his eyes as rhetorical passages follow one after another, picturesque in their mixture of refined vocabulary and bureaucratic sentence structure with, from time to time, a shear in syntax (a little like wind shear).

"Oh Madame, I must confess that my life has been paved with difficulties, and I greatly fear that now my situation is bleaker still. Just think that I accompanied a friend to a bar run by an acquaintance of his, in order to have a glass of fruit juice. This establishment being closed, but my friend having knocked on the pane, the acquaintance opened up and offered us alcoholic beverages. After a friendly conversation we parted, but once in the street my friend noted upon his person that his bag had been left in the café. So he knocked on the pane again, which broke, which made my friend's acquaintance furious, who opened up only to insult us even though we offered to pay for the pane. The noise attracted his wife, who appeared in night attire and insulted us in turn."

Not without difficulty, the DA interrupted what was literally beginning to resemble a police report. "The woman claimed you struck her."

"How could I have struck that woman? You have to be somebody looking for trouble to strike a woman. As Christ is witness to my words I say, and I say with all my heart."

The DA suggests that we leave Christ to His cross, and stick to the facts. "You've been forbidden entry into France for ten years. You were convicted in 1993 of having struck a Metro employee who asked to see your ticket. You were sentenced to jail and forbidden to return to France."

"That is possible, Madame, I didn't hear it stated in court but I wouldn't call your word into doubt." The prosecutor is obliged to stifle giggles provoked by the detainee's consideration for her. He adopts a lecturing tone as he continues: "You see, I am one of those who think there are good people and bad people everywhere. And I believe it is important that magnanimous souls, like yourself, come to my aid, but I came to France at the age of twenty-three, and I was sacristan to a priest who, alas, is now dead and who"—the DA tries to interrupt Toto, who accelerates his spiel, so that only snatches remain comprehensible—"who found me a lawyer who, to my misfortune, has also died... which means that I find myself at the mercy of the authorities." By raising her voice, the prosecutor manages to get a word in, informing the detainee that he will be sent before a court that very afternoon, where his fate will be decided.

"Would you like a state-appointed lawyer?" she asks.

"I do respect lawyers, but no one is able to understand me or my situation." A lawyer is nevertheless appointed, and Toto marches off to his fate, the same that awaits all the visa-less immigrants who preceded him in this office: prison, and a deportation order which won't be executed if his country of origin dœsn't recognize him as a national (not uncommon), which will mean a clandestine life again, at least until the next brawl or dragnet.

Much of what occurs on the premises of the eighth division of the Paris prosecutor's office is a fool's game that fools no one. The judge knows that the person before him or her will probably be "back in circulation" sooner or later. The detainee realizes that he has just entered a period of increased misfortune, but that it will probably be of limited duration. The legal ritual to which both submit will become an abstraction once it has supplied the kind of statistics that political parties relish. Certain groups will use them to vaunt the severity they've encouraged in governments they've backed; their opponents will use the same empty figures to stigmatize the inhuman treatment meted out to illegal immigrants. But in reality, lack of clear, applicable rules means that it's enforcement officers and ranking police officials who lay down the law.

The hysteria over immigration, fueled by the National Front Party, has led to an everyday assumption of cheating, and to a ferment of identity checks and hassles that weigh on all foreigners living in Paris. Those who illustrate it best are the ones who have lived in Paris for a long time and belong to communities formerly spared the wœs, nastiness, and vexations of the registration-and-monitoring bureaucracy. "Mamma" and Issey, for example, have run a Japanese restaurant near the old Opera House for a quarter of a century now; their children, born in the 9th arrondissement, were entirely educated in the city's public schools. In the 1970s, rare were the Japanese who decided to emigrate, much less to France. "I had a scholarship to the Sorbonne, and my husband arrived at almost the same time, as personal chef to the president of a Japanese firm which had its European headquarters in Paris.

We met at some friends' place. The more we saw one another, the more we realized that, for both of us, the Japanese lifestyle, as seen from Paris, was too rigid, too heavy, too formal, and too hierarchical, and we didn't want to go back to that. I was twenty-two and was fascinated by the glamour of Paris, yet above all by the lack of stress and ease of contact. Issey has always had an independent nature. He dropped out of school, didn't get along with his father and, after having managed to establish some distance, wanted to maintain it. So he left his job. We both went to work in a big Japanese restaurant, then took over this one."

"This one" is of modest dimensions: a bar and a few tables on the ground floor, plus another room upstairs often occupied by a group of tourists. At the bar are Japanese customers who live in Paris, plus a sprinkling of French, many of whom once lived in Tokyo and speak Japanese. After 10:30 P.M., newcomers are discouraged from entering; the remaining customers are all regulars who have a bottle of whisky or sake with their name on it behind the counter. For a long time, life was good and the place was full. Mamma was known for her good humor, outspokenness, and patience when a drinker decided the time had come to confide. Issey is quieter, but a good cook. Lately, though, the downstairs room has often been empty. Fewer and fewer Japanese are moving to Paris. Those who would like to study here are having a terrible time obtaining visas. French consular services in Japan and elsewhere practice the old Soviet method: never say no, but find a good reason for always postponing a yes. Executive "salarymen" in Japanese firms, meanwhile, do their best to avoid being transferred to Paris since most of the time their families are denied authorization to join them. This brake on immigration has affected the prosperity of Mamma and Issey's little bar and restaurant. And since Japanese tourism fluctuates with the tide of terrorist attacks in Paris, and with the wave of bankruptcies of Japanese tour operators sunk by a price war,

Mamma and Issey have been reduced to living practically from hand to mouth. At which point the immigration authorities decide to make life difficult. Mamma and Issey have to renew their residence papers, an operation that usually lasts a morning. This time, it has lasted a month and a half. "They want new documents, which have to be examined by several departments. The other day, I said at the window that there shouldn't be any trouble with my card, given how long I'd been on their books. To which they replied, 'If you'd married a Frenchman, you would've had your papers faster.'"

Lately, Japanese restaurants have experienced a rash of inspections. Police, social security agents, health inspectors, tax officials. All quite legal, of course. But why so few in twenty years, and such a flood now? Everyone knew that a handful of Japanese students work as "undeclared" dishwashers or waiters. And that others work quietly for tour operators, or for service or emergency companies aimed at the Japanese community in Paris, or as babysitters, or as extras in commercials shot along the Seine to lend Parisian chic to products sold in Japan. The lifestyle of this tiny population of unofficial laborers was even the subject of a film directed by Kei Ota, *A la Carte Compagnie*. This minuscule fringe has been tolerated for a very long time. Yet now it's being treated as a threat to public order and an irreparable blight on the French economy.

A Japanese friend of one of Mamma and Issey's sons has just been deported. This son of a wealthy Osaka merchant was a student at the prestigious Ecole des Beaux-Arts. His father had bought him a three-room apartment in the 1st arrondissement at a cost of 900,000 francs ($160,000). He was hassled for weeks before being finally notified that his residence permit would be denied on the grounds that he couldn't supply them with grades for his courses at the Beaux-Arts—where grades haven't been given for over thirty years.

"Now I want to sell up and leave," says Mamma. "I'm looking into Latin America, especially Chile. But I'm over fifty, and the kids are completely Frenchified. I could never go back to Japan, at any rate. Because of my frankness." Frankness? "Yes. Here I've acquired the habit of saying what I think, of not hiding my reactions. That's what I liked about France. When the kids go to see their grandparents in Tokyo, every two years, they never stay more than two weeks. Its better for everyone that way."

I went to see the film by Kei Ota (every film shot in Paris can be found in the city's Videotheque). It's a rather agile work which deals humorously with the misfortunes of two young Japanese immigrants, a boy and a girl, who came to Paris on tourist visas and decided to remain within sight of the Eiffel Tower longer than authorized because they, too—a quarter of a century after Mamma and Issey—found their native country's social order too rigid. The dialog, however, is sometimes a little bombastic. It notably includes the following question: "Dœsn't everything look sad in the glow of Europe's twilight?"

Culture for Dummies

There's a certain kind of snake that can't stand the heat, and that won't head for shelter when it rains. This snake emerges every morning from early spring onwards, its long body continuing to stretch into the first days of September. Far from blending into the color of its surroundings, it is speckled with garish spots and bright hues. When it reaches full adult size, the snake curves in four or five loops as it crawls slowly but steadily forward. Its head disappears little by little below I. M. Pei's pyramid, under which it seeks its usual sustenance—masterpieces.

A masterpiece is a prey to be consumed in a group, if not a crowd. Barely have they scattered into smaller squibs in front of the Louvre's ticket windows, than visitors cluster together again—whether they've come alone, as a couple, *en famille*, or in a gang—and rush toward one of their favorite (indeed, sole) destinations. Which number four: Michelangelo's *Captives*, the *Venus de Milo*, the *Winged Victory of Samothrace*, and the *Mona Lisa*. It is the *Mona Lisa* that boasts the greatest number of signposts; there's practically no spot in the museum that fails to indicate the direction to head via an arrow below a black-and-white photo. On observing the haste with which visitors hurry along one of the paths leading to the Mona Lisa, and on noting their feverish, noisy disappointment if they go astray into Akhetep's mastaba or toward van Eyck's *Madonna of Chancellor Rolin,* you might think that Leonardo's painting was about to be sold, stolen, or even to self-destruct that very day, or that—like the Eiffel Tower in the Charles Trenet song—it had decided to run away to see if life is fairer elsewhere.

Running away would be completely understandable. Anyone who wants to know what "harassment" truly means should consider spending a few days in the room where the *Mona Lisa* hangs. There's a constant flow—nay, flood—of excited, edgy, squawking pilgrims. Their behavior is so repetitive that it appears to be the product of Pavlovian conditioning. Nine out of every ten visitors has the same twin goal: to photograph *Mona Lisa* and be photographed in front of her. Museum rules, indicated by multilingual signs and explicit pictograms, expressly forbid this. (Flashes damage paintings.) But it's impossible for guards to enforce this rule, unless they're equipped with a battery of machine guns or, at the very least, electric cattle prods. For that matter, when the high tourist season arrives, full-time guards manage to get themselves assigned to rooms that are less—much less—popular, abandoning their posts to part-time employees (mostly students) who will later recount their sentry duty with the *Mona Lisa* the way their great-grandfathers recounted the bombardments at Verdun.

Bursting into the room with their cameras already at chin level, blithely ignoring the other paintings hanging there (including Veronese's *Marriage at Cana,* which measures a colossal 9.90 x 6.66 meters), "monalisavores" crowd around the group that has already formed in front of the object of everyone's eagerness (a mere 0.77 x 0.53 meters). Up to five or six layers of bodies pile up in front of the feeble barrier designed to keep them at a distance. They're packed closer together than rush-hour commuters on the Tokyo subway.

This human magma moves like a jellyfish. Every segment tries to position its camera to get a picture of *just* the painting.

This exercise demands a superhuman alertness and sense of opportunity. Most monalisavores therefore give up and accept a vague approximation. Then comes the accomplishment of the second goal, which entails two phases. Phase one: photograph your traveling companion(s) in front of "the most famous painting in the world"; phase two: be photographed in the same place. Just as dozens of birds can amazingly wheel above a single tree without ever colliding, so this succession of operations—which everyone wants to carry out at the same time—surprisingly occurs without major clash, stinging remark, or incident of any sort, despite the general agitation. True enough, everyone seems to be keenly aware of the obligation to remain in front of the *Mona Lisa* only for the number of seconds necessary for the taking of a picture. Once this goal attained, they race to the *Venus*, or the *Winged Victory*, or the basement cafeteria. They haven't seen anything, but they've taken a picture. Pointlessly, as it turns out, since Leonardo's painting is protected by glass that reflects the glare of flashes—the pictures are never any good.

I once counted 121 people massed in front of the *Mona Lisa*, from an enormous American woman wielding video equipment topped by a spotlight to a kid armed only with a disposable camera. By fixing upon another hundred or so, I established that the average time elapsed between entering and leaving the room was three minutes and twenty seconds. Which shows just how contractile the jellyfish is.

This blob of camera freaks forms as soon as the Louvre opens (masterpiece-lovers are early birds), and only begins to lose some of its mass forty-five minutes before closing time. (Tourist buses don't wait, and there's still the museum shop to hit, in order to buy coasters of one of the paintings they didn't see.) This is the moment when remaining monalisavores are given some scope to refine their photo, elevating it from the status of souvenir to that of original artistic expression. In most cases, the originality consists of asking the per-

141

son to be immortalized to stand just beside Mona Lisa and imitate her pose and, if possible, her smile. Click. I also saw a young woman photocopy—sorry, photograph—her boyfriend in front the painting on bended knee, pretending to make a passionate declaration. Click. And a gentlemen imitating a teacher, arm extended, pointing to the Mona Lisa for universal admiration. Click. Or a couple, he to the left of the painting, she to the right, recorded on film in the pose of caryatids, thanks to an obliging third party. Click.

This is also the moment to ask the guards questions. Said guards are bushed. Ever since they came on duty they've been struggling to deal with the most grievous infractions: visitors who slide under the railing in order to be photographed closer, videocamera operators accompanied by lighting assistants bearing spotlamps of the lighthouse-at-the-end-the-world variety, prankish kids wanting to know if touching the painting will set off an alarm. Part-time guards, still trying to get over their discovery that the public doesn't behave in they way they had imagined, often believe and fear—in the early days of their temporary employment—that a visitor who approaches them with the obvious intention of asking a question will be disappointed by their lack of art historical expertise. Which is rarely the case. The inquisitiveness to which they are subjected has more to do with matter than with mind. At the top of the list comes a crucial question, expressed by representatives of both sexes and all ages from every continent, and posed in one of two ways: "How much is it worth?" or "It is true that it's the most expensive painting in the world?" When it comes to the first query, questioners generally accept the response that the guard doesn't know the answer. (As to the second, all guards soon decide to answer yes. Their patriotic spirit is thereby gratified, and the visitor enjoys the feeling of not having wasted valuable time.) And yet I saw one sixtyish and apparently wealthy visitor (English-style suit, goldplated wife) refuse to believe that no pricetag could be put on the *Mona*

Lisa. "You're afraid someone will pull out a checkbook and walk off with it, is that it?"

"No, sir, really, I..."

"Your superiors won't tell you how much it's worth, but they must know."

"No, really, I promise. It's not for sale. Anyway, museums in France aren't allowed to sell any of their artworks."

"That's just possible. But it doesn't prevent the paintings from having a price. Which goes to show you're lying."

"Huh?"

"Just what I said. Because in order to insure them, these paintings of yours, you have to declare their value."

There was no point in replying that the government is its own insurer (and if it weren't, where the deuce would it find the money to pay the premiums?). The man had already spun on his heels, making them resound on the museum floorboards the way only a man who has had the last word can make his heels resound. The part-time guard—a business-school student—remained dumbstruck. He was pulled from his stupor by a couple of Americans in their mid-thirties, apparently East Coast, chic, and casual. "Do you speak English?"

"Yes."

"Could you tell us something, please? What's so special about this Mona Lisa?"

The guard's openmouthed stupefaction skyrockets, then falls back to earth. "I don't know.... Just look at it. You have to make up your own mind." The couple is disappointed with this answer, which requires them to form their own opinion. They would probably have preferred to be informed that the *Mona Lisa* had been given top ranking by an international jury, or told where they could buy a book which, like Dale Carnegie's bestselling *How to Win Friends and Influence People*, would explain exactly how to form an opinion on a work of art.

143

A fortyish lady comes up, followed by a well-dressed teenager. Mother and daughter, obviously. Neither of them seem to be equipped with the least photographic device (God bless them). What's more, the question they want to ask concerns *The Marriage at Cana.* It looks as though the day might just end on a note echoing a love of art.

"Is it the biggest painting in the museum?"

It is. Most certainly. Mother and daughter exchange looks, sharing a feeling of great satisfaction, turn away, and take one last, brief glance at Veronese's canvas, which they seem to congratulate on its dimensions. Then they leave the room, content. The customer is always right.

Which is why the Louvre's honorable curators, if they would only lend an attentive ear to visitors' questions for a few days, as I have done, would soon realize the unsuitability of organizing the museum into special rooms devoted to Greek or Egyptian antiquities, to French, Flemish, or Italian painting, or to objets d'art from a given century or other. They'd abandon all their old habits, and would reclassify works according to famousness, value, size, and weight. There would be galleries of priceless paintings, galleries of extravagantly expensive paintings, galleries of unaffordable paintings, galleries of very costly paintings, galleries of pricey paintings, and galleries of undervalued paintings. Instead of labeling a painting with the name of the artist, date, and sometimes a word or two on its history, they could indicate its value (in French francs, dollars, yen, marks, and Swiss francs), its surface area, the amount of paint required to execute it, and the time it took to dry.

Even if museologists can't bring themselves to adopt this solution (dictated though it is by a desire to satisfy art lovers), they could—at the very least—allocate a single room to Michelangelo's *Captives* (currently on the ground floor of the Denon Wing), the *Winged Victory of Samothrace* (stuck at the top of the grand staircase over by the Sully Wing), the *Venus de Milo* (now photographable only after having put up with the *Piombino Apollo* and the *Panathenaea* frieze—or worse, depending on what side you arrive from), and the cursed *Mona Lisa*, which has to be sought in the Salle des Etats, which means wading past, in the best of circumstances, all the paintings in the Grande Galerie; lucky are the people who manage to avoid the Gallerie d'Apollon (a Paris department store used to have a slogan that ran, "At Printemps, I buy everything with my eyes closed"; the Louvre visitor's motto might be, "At the Louvre, I go everywhere with my eyes closed"). Maybe I'm being unfair to the Grande Galerie, though, which holds a distinct appeal for art lovers: I don't mean the works hanging on the wall, but rather the seats, set here and there, providing culture vultures with a place to rest after all their aesthetic thrills. The sitting position, however, is not to be overdone; art lovers prefer to sprawl, to slump, or—to use a colorful Quebecois verb, *effoirer*—"to slunk." The slunkers are legion. They suffer from serial fatigue: from getting up early, from having gulped down an insufficiently nourishing breakfast (or snack lunch), from having joined the snaking line extending from the pyramid, from having waited in front of the ticket windows, from having hunted for the four "must sees," and from learning *la loi de la jungle photographique*. "Culture cannot be inherited," wrote André Malraux, "it must be conquered."

Statistics and on-site observation concur: Parisians themselves rarely go to the Louvre. As children, they went with their primary school, and again in high school. As adults, they only return—and even then, not often—when they reach retirement age. Guides who lead groups of willing visitors throughout the year note that they include a constant and significant proportion of divorced women. Yet although Parisians don't go—or because they don't go—they'll swear to their relatives from the provinces (or their guests from abroad, or their colleagues at the office) that the Louvre not only represents the clearest sign of the cultural appetite of the capital's populace, but also the grandeur of what we have to offer the world, since admission tickets are sold in the millions and the sight of Pei's pyramid is now as familiar in foreign lands as the Eiffel Tower or the Basilica of Sacré-Cœur.

Or Beaubourg, that other great proof of the eminently cultural life we all lead in Paris. Yessiree! But just go to the entrance of the Pompidou Center (as Beaubourg is officially known) at opening time some morning, and follow the visitors. During the school year, two-thirds of them are college students who come to use the center's library, given the poverty of university libraries in town. The other third is composed of "cultural tourists"—foreigners and provincials. During the summer season, such tourists constitute the immense majority of people who cross Beaubourg's threshold. They take the multistory escalator, enthusiastically enjoying the wonderful view of Paris as they slowly rise above it; then they reach the uppermost terrace and delight in one of the finest vistas the capital has to offer. (If less charming to my eyes than the one from the terrace of the Samaritaine department store, which gives you the Seine and the Pont-Neuf as a bonus.) Having seen the sight—taking all the more pictures ever since cameras with panoramic lenses became widespread—"cultural tourists" occasionally have a drink at the cafeteria, then head back down the escalator and set off on the next stage of their worthy itinerary.

These scalers of lofty escalators are included in statistics showing that every year eight million people visit the Pompidou Center. Their number is added to that of the students in search of a decent university library. And the hordes formed by these two species have been analyzed as follows by an enthusiastic commentator (if somewhat under the influence of official circles): "These days, attendance figures at Beaubourg nearly match those of Disneyland Paris. On entering the Pompidou Center, millions of people have set foot in a museum of modern art (or, for many of them, a museum of any kind) for the first time in their lives. All the weightiness of conventional museums, all the psychological blocks about culture with a capital 'C,' have been swept aside. The Center has won the public's favor through the playful spin it puts on a rather serious image. The 'Pompidolium' now enjoys a predominant role, indispensable to culture within France and beyond our borders. That's one of the miracles of Beaubourg."

In addition to the reassuring chauvinism of this passage at a time when everyone deplores modern youth's disdain for the concept of patriotism, the author was quite right to employ the word "miracle" when hailing this accomplishment. Miracle it is, since none of these millions of visitors even noticed they had visited a museum of modern art. They went right past it on the escalator (twice: once up, once down), serenely unaware of fauvism and cubism, surrealism and abstract expressionism, or pop art and new realism, not to mention minimal art, conceptual art, or arte povera. Nary a soul visits the permanent galleries on the third and fourth floors of the building, except for high school groups. And the comments made by those students suggest that youth and modernity are not necessarily synonymous; their teachers, meanwhile, who stubbornly try to "explain" Mondrian, Delaunay, Tanguy, and Johns, remind me of old White Friars trying to transmit Christian morality to African natives blithely oblivious to purported sins of the flesh. Such visits almost always end in front of a sculpture by Tinguely, which reconciles everyone. When it comes to Jasper Johns, teachers at a loss for argument and unwilling to let the students slowly familiarize themselves with works that are almost totally new to them, often fall back on an argument guaranteed to win the flock's attention and esteem: "He's the most expensive living artist in the world today." A surefire winner.

School groups are matched by dense ranks of oldsters. At Beaubourg, just as at the Louvre, and at the Louvre just as everywhere else, senior citizens supply museums and historic buildings with a regular contingent of visitors all year round. They hope to broaden their minds during their retirement, making contact with a world of culture they feel they failed to appreciate or never got a chance to know. Their goodwill is total, their stamina surprising, and their desire to learn admirable.

Even as these pilgrims move in well-behaved squads through both floors of the museum of modern art, ceaseless currents are rising and sinking on the other side of the glass walls, carrying compact clusters of visitors from the Beaubourg plaza up to the terrace and back down again. Beaubourg has indeed worked the miracle of sweeping away "all the psychological blocks about culture with a capital 'C,'" since millions of people pass right by it—just a few feet from hundreds of major works of painting and sculpture—without caring in the least, without going to have a glance, without wondering whether it might be worth the effort, and also without realizing that the great wizard of statistics is crouching in the shadows, recording their ascent to the terrace (while they rise, carefree, with the escalator) as a cultural act and a tribute to modern art. But then again, Marcel Duchamp transformed everything into an artwork, so maybe the moving staircase is itself a mobile sculpture we haven't taken into account.

Back at the Louvre, once art lovers have completed their four stations, a good many of them will take advantage of their recent training by joining yet another line, this time in front of one of the restaurants in the underground mall, a den where cultural tourism meets gastronomic tourism. "Quick Burger," "Hector's Fried Chicken," "El Rancho Tex Mex," and "Tapas del Sol" line up alongside other "specialty" joints: spaghetti here, sauerkraut there, carrot cake further along, cheese-and-salad or spare ribs across the way. This is the place where people recover their strength and revise their battle plans: the Musée d'Orsay this afternoon (we can skip everything except the Impressionists); tomorrow, Monet's garden at Giverny; day after tomorrow, Auvers-sur-Oise, where Saint Vincent van Gogh lived. Grand finale: the Place du Tertre atop Montmartre, black with hack artists applying color to canvases whose main outlines were industrially printed in Hamburg.

One weekday morning in July, I found myself depressed by overly long observation not only of *Mona Lisa* picture-takers but also of all those people who pat the fannies of nude statues (which remain unmoved only because made of stone—Oh worthy, chaste Diana!). So I decided to go for a stroll in the Louvre's Cour Carrée, then lose myself in contemplation of the Seine from the nearby footbridge, Pont des Arts. Passing the toilets, I made a note—so that the book you're now holding would convey my concern for the tiniest of human affairs—of the unfairness of Nature, who obliges women answering her call to get into lines much longer than those formed by men in order to perform the same operation (which they execute much more expeditiously). I subsequently paused in front of the picture-takers taking themselves in front of Pei's pyramid in order to count them—out of reflex—when up came an Asian, slim and English-speaking (if somewhat difficult to understand), who wanted to know if it was reasonable to try to reach "d'Orsay" on foot.

I assured him it was, and questioned him in turn. Had he just come out of the Louvre? He had. What had he seen? The *Venus de Milo*, the *Winged Victory of Samothrace*, the *Mona Lisa*, Michelangelo's *Captives*, and Delacroix's *Liberty Leading the People*. I knew this latter work hung roughly halfway between the *Winged Victory* and *Venus*, yet I inquired of the reasons that led to a halt, rather than the indifferent passing which constitutes its ordinary fate. My interlocutor, a medical student from South Korea, explained that Delacroix's painting had attained the status of a holy icon in his country,

149

where student uprisings are common, and so he was delighted to be able to see the original.

He had arrived in Paris the previous evening, accompanied by two friends whom he had lost between *Mona Lisa* and Michelangelo, and whom he hoped to find in front of van Gogh. His first Parisian sight had been the Eiffel Tower—"beautiful scenery." That morning, he and his two friends had left their hotel (located out by Porte de Clichy) and headed for the Louvre. After the Musée d'Orsay this afternoon, they intended to climb to Sacré-Cœur in the evening. Tomorrow would be devoted to Versailles, leaving them just enough time to return to the hotel, pack their bags, and head for Roissy airport, where they were due to check in at 3:00 A.M. for a charter flight scheduled to leave at dawn.

Barely two days to visit Paris, I bemoaned out loud. True, but that was because the three buddies had purchased a "tour" which led them everywhere at a hellish pace. Having flown out of Seoul, they landed in Madrid. Their itinerary took them to Lisbon, Barcelona, Nice, Monaco, Rome, Venice, Munich, Prague, Brussels, Amsterdam, London, Edinburgh, and finally Paris. All in twenty days. What voraciousness! What stamina! Everywhere the program was the same: airport, hotel on the edge of town, "beautiful scenery," museum, museum, and museum. Wanting to make better acquaintance with a representative of this race of cultural Tarzans who could swing from museum to museum like apemen from tree to tree—so strange to my eyes—I invited the Korean student to have a drink at a public establishment in the enclosed garden of the Palais-Royal nearby.

The quiet harmony and beauty of the spot disturbed my companion. What was this place? I concocted a brief history—the palace of Richelieu, then Louis XIV, followed by the Regent, the revolutionary gatherings of Camille Desmoulins, the gambling dens, the ladies of easy virtue, and now the Ministry of Culture. Although he was more familiar with

French history than I am with Korean history, Wui Won—for that was his first name, which it took me a while to grasp, thinking I heard "we won" and wondering what win he was talking about—obviously couldn't follow all the details of my explanation, but he was able to conclude that the Palais-Royal with its garden was, in his words, "one of the important places of Paris." He asked me to confirm this assessment, which I did. Wui Won's face then clouded with puzzlement and annoyance. If we were in "an important place of Paris," why wasn't it mentioned in the guide that the tour operator in Seoul had given him? And if said document hushed up a sight as important as the one in which we now found ourselves, how many others did it omit, not only in Paris but in London, Rome, Prague, Amsterdam, Venice, and so on? I sensed that my companion was in the throes of retrospective angst: had he toured the right tour?

I tried to take his mind off this anxiety by attempting to get a clearer idea of how he toured the world. Had he had any time to wander aimlessly during the various legs of his journey? Had he and his two buddies made any interesting acquaintances? Did they like the various cuisines they'd been served? Was there a city or cities to which they'd like to return?

The schedule of museums and "beautiful scenery" hadn't allowed them to dawdle, especially since their flights from one city to another could only be done at set times, some of them programmed at inconvenient periods that "ruined" half a day. Furthermore, travel to and from the airports ate up time all the more precious in that they never stayed more than forty-eight hours in any given town. At that kind of pace it's hard to make any acquaintances; at the hotels and hostels where they stayed, they occasionally exchanged a few words with breakfast companions, but no more, except in Edinburgh where they ran into a small group of South Korean female students. Questioning Wui Won about what he saw in Edinburgh, which I know a little, I learned that he spent a total of thirty hours there (night included), which were devoted to the castle ramparts ("beautiful scenery") after a brisk walk up the Royal Mile—a street where every house provides a good reason to linger—then onto the Royal Scottish Museum, the Scottish National Gallery of Modern Art, and the National Gallery of Scotland (where a van Gogh hangs, overwhelming my companion with delight; but neither Raphael, Titian, Rembrandt, nor Velasquez was mentioned in his guide—we checked together—any more than Poussin's *Seven Sacraments*).

As to national or regional dishes, Wui Won had no opinion—for the excellent reason that neither he nor his friends had tried any. Back in Seoul they had already spent a good deal for their "round-trip," which included all travel and lodging. So they didn't have much money left for film, souvenirs, and nourishment. They therefore adopted the easiest and cheapest solution by always eating in fast-food joints, from Madrid to Prague and from Rome to Brussels. Fortunately, you can now find one in every city of any size, regardless of country.

But if he'd had the wherewithal, would he have tested the local cuisine? Probably. In fact, most willingly. He's curious by nature and not afraid to experiment. Is there any French dish he's heard of, that he'd like to try? Yes, there is—couscous.

Since our conversation had dragged on, I suggested that we have a bite to eat if Wui Won would agree to be my guest. The two dishes of the day at the establishment in question were fresh fish accompanied by julienne vegetables, or *boudin* (blood sausage) with applesauce. I explained what blood sausage was. Wui Won, to prove his earlier assertion of curiosity, decided to order it, and ate heartily, occasionally moistening his lips on a glass of wine whose effects he feared. He spoke of his family of affluent merchants, of an elder sister who already had an important job in industry; he mentioned the extensive corruption within the South Korean government and the student demonstrations he had taken part in; he described the way the medical profession was organized in his country, asked about the situation in France, and expressed his hope of winning a scholarship to study at Johns Hopkins in the United States. He asked me what the French thought about South Korea. I improvised a smoke screen of commonplaces. At any rate, it was time for Wui Won to try to find his friends at "d'Orsay." We exchanged addresses (though we'd do nothing with them), and as I stood up I realized that my invitation to dine had had a disastrous effect on my guest. Slumped in his chair, he seemed unable to get back into gear. It wasn't the food (nothing more digestible than blood sausage) or the wine (he'd barely drunk three sips). It was simply the effect of stopping: the first somewhat lengthy halt in nineteen days of a geocultural marathon, the first break in rhythm, first lapse in concentration. Wui Won was shattered. Climbing back into the saddle would be like hoisting cast iron. But it had to be done. Gathering up all his energy, like Napoleon's routed cavalry at Berezina giving their mounts a final spur to get them across the river, Wui Won sat up, stood, and struggled off in the direction of van Gogh, the next-to-last stop on his stations of the cross.

I returned to the Louvre. It was 2:00 P.M. by the clock, high noon by the sun. The snake slowly looped, dragging its feet. A few professional photographers offered to distract the waiting tourists by immortalizing them on a Polaroid. Not many takers. Beneath the pyramid, in the vast entrance hall, hostesses of unshakable friendliness and flabbergasting multilingualism (one of them is hexalingual, another pentaglot) answer the incessant queries of cultural tourists. "Where's the bathroom?" and "Where's the *Mona Lisa*?" are the two main questions. Sometimes a visitor comes up with an unexpected request. In front of me, a female U.S. citizen (who is massive, but I don't want people to think I'm anti-American just because I mention this detail every time I describe one of Jane Fonda's compatriots) wants to know where in Paris she can sit outside, in complete safety. The hostess, right on the ball, realizes she won't be believed if she replies that all public benches in the capital are generally safe. So she sends the American to the Luxembourg gardens, explaining that since the adjoining palace now houses the Senate, it is very well guarded. A convincing argument. The U.S. citizen is more than just reassured, she's positively reconciled to the very concept of big cities. And how can you get to this promised land? By bus, line 27 goes straight there. She only has to wait at the bus stop along the Seine.

"Is it safe to wait there?"

"It is, madame, definitely." The American therefore heads for the 27 bus stop. I remember unfolding the newspaper the next morning with the vague hope of learning that a U.S. citizen had been molested by a heat-crazed senator.

In addition to supplying information on the location of toilets and the *Mona Lisa*, hostesses are obliged to give the complaint book to any visitor who requests it.

So I insist that it be rendered unto me, forthwith! Not that I want to complain about anything. I'd just like to see what provokes the outrage of art lovers. Two subjects fill most pages. The first concerns money. People complain about having to pay full admission even though they'd presented a card, document, pass, or paper that absolutely entitled them to reduced rates: a certificate of inclusion in the illustrious Spanish Medical Association, proof of membership in the International Friends of Museums Association (Sydney, Australia branch), a card awarded to honorary teachers in Austrian schools, a document proving auditor status at an art school (therefore the equal of students, who get in free). Someone even complained of having been granted free admission but being asked to pay twenty-five francs to attend a guided tour.

Someone else was outraged at having to stand in line to buy a ticket, when he was just accompanying two grandchildren who, being under eighteen, were entitled to free entry—"why isn't there a special ticket window for people in my situation?"

When people don't complain about the money spent on getting into the museum, they complain about what they spent in one of the basement restaurants. "At So-and-So's, we were forced to buy something to eat when all we wanted was a drink." This protest, written in English, was signed by "a group of Irishmen." It was followed by recriminations and vituperations over the prices charged in various dining establishments and by unfavorable comments on the relationship between cost and value. Sometimes, the outrage has another cause: "*Everyone* who takes photographs should be *absolutely* thrown out. It's unbearable. If you need extra staff for that, let me know." Signed Emmanuel V., a Beaux-Arts student (followed by address and phone number).

Saving my own complaints as a scoop for my readers, I returned the book to the hostess, who was surprised at my abstention. Abandoning the idea of going see if the monalisavores were up to any new tricks, I decided to plonk myself on a bench in Gallery 31 of the Richelieu Wing, to see how cultural tourists deal with Rembrandt, to whom that room is entirely devoted. Between 2:30 P.M. and closing time, that is to say a little over three hours, Gallery 31 never contained more than five of us at a time. I even enjoyed a good quarter hour of salutary solitude, handsomely contemplating the vanity of things of this world. A while back I'd gone to Amsterdam to see the Rembrandt exhibition at the Rijksmuseum; obtaining an admission ticket required the patience of a saint and, once admitted, you were constantly bumping into people. Yet here, deprived of the media blitz accompanying a temporary international show, the popularity of Rembrandt's paintings was now in steep decline. (The same thing occurs at Beaubourg. While the museum of modern art remains totally deserted, retrospectives and temporary exhibitions on the top floor are overpopulated.)

Three mornings in row, I verified the loneliness of the artist who painted *Bathsheba, A Philosopher in Meditation,* and *The Supper at Emmaus.* It was matched only by the solitude of his not-so-distant neighbor in Gallery 38—Vermeer. The *Lacemaker* and The *Astronomer,* placed on either side of the doorway, had only rare takers. Three out of five people who crossed the room didn't even give them a glance. It's true that Vermeer's paintings are small, but since The *Marriage at Cana* ("the biggest painting in the museum") doesn't manage to draw any greater attention, I doubt that size explains such disdain. Furthermore, shortly after the Rembrandt exhibition in Amsterdam, infatuation over the one devoted to Vermeer was even greater. You'd think, if you didn't know we were living at a time of disinterested love of culture, that people's relationship to art has more to do with social—and sometimes high society—ritual than with a noble search for something that transcends our wretched lives.

A drunken Japanese tourist enters the gallery. I had noticed him earlier, in the Puget Courtyard, studiously consulting his guidebook. He sits on the central bench, facing Jacob van Ruisdael's famous landscape, called *Le Coup de Soleil* (The Ray of Sunlight). The Vermeers are to his left, but he doesn't turn his head. Motionless, leaning forward, he seems mesmerized by the Ruisdael. Intrigued, I wait several minutes, then begin to stroll around the room in order to see him from the front. He's asleep. He would continue to sleep—soundlessly, motionlessly—for half an hour, then, returning to life, would pull his guidebook from his pocket, stand up, and, passing the Vermeers with dazed indifference, head in another direction. Maybe the guidebook listed the most comfortable benches in the museum.

When I was a student at college, Dean Gabriel Le Bras was said to have specialized in the sociology of religion because, being obliged by his wife and his Breton background to go to church more often than he would have otherwise desired, he entertained himself by counting the faithful and classifying them by age, sex, and other distinguishing features. Having taken up the sociology of cultural tourism as a hobby, I confess that I, too, have known moments of lassitude, which I fought off by trying to guess the nationality of Louvre pilgrims based on their appearance alone. Verification was conducted by listening to them speak. Unfortunately, I have difficulty distinguishing the Korean language from Japanese, and Polish from Lithuanian. Nevertheless, my observations helped me to shed light on the unique role played by shoes as a tool of long-distance identification of the geographic provenance of a tourist.

On perceiving a pair of serious buskins designed for athletics or walking, with soles that are thick or tapered, one can safely bet on a North American (I'm referring to adults here, since all teenagers *à travers la planète* wear such shoes). But socks inside Spartan-type, open sandals, or shoes with leatherette laces, means you're probably dealing either with a Chinese visitor (assuming the skin is yellowish) or a citizen from one of the former Communist countries. It was while devising and refining the basic rules of this new science, calceology, that I made the eminently consoling acquaintance of Lyubomir.

I noticed him one morning among the few admirers of the Rubens cycle from the Medici Gallery (whose new Mussolinian-Calvinist presentation is highly debatable, the paint on the walls being a color that would kill any artwork). Accompanied by a slender, graceful blond, Lyubomir parted from her with a tender kiss in front of *Marie de' Medici Disembarking in the Port of Marseille,* emptying the contents of his trouser pockets into her hands. Said pockets seemed to have a storage capacity greater than the attic of the average family home. Finally he came up with the keys, which the

157

young woman took, returning the rest of the jumble to him, which he immediately dumped back into its containers. She was dressed entirely in denim; he was wearing shapeless gray trousers and a sweater of the same ilk. His shoes in brown imitation leather could only be the surplus production of some five-year plan. I wagered that he came from one or the other of the now-separated halves of Czechoslovakia.

That was the day I had decided to linger on the upper floors of the Richelieu Wing overlooking rue de Rivoli, which not long ago housed the Ministry of Finance. It's gently intoxicating to stroll from the famous portrait of John the Good to Poussin's *Four Seasons*, or from van Eyck to van Dyck via Memling. Little by little, you become completely cut off from the world. (I haven't ever heard, thank heavens, a cellular phone ring in a museum—yet. Maybe the bearers of this kind of equipment prefer to show off elsewhere. Or maybe the notorious "psychological blocks about culture with a capital 'C'" inhibit them from leaving their machines on when they enter the Louvre.) Soon enough, you no longer know exactly where you are. Not being pressed for time, knowing you can come back the next day, brings a peace of mind and relaxation highly conducive to establishing a relationship with the artworks. You can pause to study them, you can chose one or—more often—be chosen by one, get to know it, and scribble questions in your notebook so you can look up the answers at home. You become imbued with the feeling of doing something worthwhile, the way you get deep into reading a book or listening to a piece of music. As soon as the eyes become saturated—when they can still contemplate but not really see—you can refresh them by admiring the view overlooking the Palais Royal or by observing museumgœrs. That's how I "met up again" with Lyubomir over by Velvet Brueghel's way.

Most museumgœrs proceed from work to work and from gallery to gallery like those cybernetic toys which advance by careening off the walls. Reserves of nervous impulses keep them in constant movement, interrupted only when their progress drives them straight up against an artwork. There they skid for a few moments, then head off again as though ricocheting off the wall, in a direction which they maintain until a new collision sends them toward some unpredictable destination. Lyubomir's purposive tread and clear goal set him apart from other cultural tourists.

It was in Gallery 38, where the Vermeers hang, that our paths crossed again. Lyubomir was studying *The Lacemaker*. He spent a long moment before it, then shifted to *The Astronomer* on the other side of the doorway. The two canvases are small (the former measures 25 (20 cm, the latter 50 (45 cm). Then my purported Czech (or Slovak) began going back and forth, steadily peering at one, then the other, reassessing previous observations, carrying out God only knows what comparison, scrutinizing the works rather than just looking at them. I hadn't seen anyone behave in this manner since I began immersing myself in the Louvre. So after a generous half hour by the clock, when Lyubomir was about to leave Gallery 38, I accosted him, hoping to high heaven we had a language in common.

We did. (Unfortunately, it wasn't French.) Having introduced myself, and having learned that Lyubomir's name was Lyubomir and that his shoes and his good self were Bulgarian (as a science, calceology is still in its infancy), I ascertained that he was a twenty-four-year-old film student from Sofia. His mother, a theater director, had been invited by our embassy to spend several months in Paris studying the French theatrical scene. She had rented a room in Pigalle, which was free during the second two weeks of July while she was in Avignon attending the annual theater festival. Lyubomir and his friend Anna were taking advantage of the empty apartment, having hitched all the way to Paris together. Lyubomir found Pigalle, which he knew only from black-and-white movies, to be greatly disappointing in full-color flesh. By day, it seemed just like any other *quartier* in the 9th arrondissement, excluding of course its abundance of sex shops. By night, the hordes of lecherous Germans rolling from one sidewalk to another hardly reconciled him to Germania.

Lyubomir had specific goals at the Louvre and the Musée d'Orsay: Rembrandt, Vermeer, and Corot. Three painters of light. Comparison of *The Lacemaker* with *The Astronomer* alone made his trip worthwhile. *The Lacemaker*, shown almost in close-up and lit frontally from above, conveyed a feeling of intense concentration. *The Astronomer* was placed in a wider shot, and, surrounded by fabrics, objects, and furniture seen in semishadow, left a much more indeterminate impression, thereby stimulating the curiosity and triggering all kinds of hypotheses. I asked Lyubomir if he'd paid tribute to the *Mona Lisa*. He answered that the bustle and the crowd had prevented him from really appreciating the painting, but he was totally amazed to discover that a few yards away no fewer than four other works by Leonardo were on show, including *The Virgin and Child with Saint Anne* and *La Belle Feronnière*, before which no one halted. In any case, Lyubomir found the Louvre too big and couldn't understand what pleasure we took from such hugeness.

Our conversation then drifted to the absurdities of the French. Several French filmmakers and a few cinema critics had paraded through Lyubomir's film school. He described them bluntly as pretentious and artificial. He also found them too interested in philosophy and not enough in painting, too cerebral and insufficiently sensual. Then he asked me if I could help him find the Russian cemetery in Paris, which he hadn't managed to locate. Although labeled "in Paris," the cemetery is in fact located in a suburb, Saint-Geneviève-des-Bois. Why did he want to go? To meditate on the tomb of Andrei Tarkovsky, the director of *Andrei Rublev* and *Offret (The Sacrifice)*.

I like people who remember the dead. The only things I know about Bulgaria are the harsh image of Todor Zhivkov (the former Secretary General of its Communist Party), the much more appealing one of Sylvie Vartan (a French pop star of Bulgarian stock), the great reputation of its yogurt, and the longevity of its citizens. (Flaubert: "Someone of ninety is always robust; someone a hundred is always Bulgarian.") Plus the fact that the French expression *bon bougre* (nice guy) comes from *bulgare* (Bulgarian). Three more-than-sufficient reasons to invite Lyubomir and his girlfriend to lunch the next day. (I make a religion of dining.) After having inquired of their tastes and gastronomic desiderata, I arranged to meet them at a restaurant near Notre-Dame, where the *paté de tête*, *quenelles de brochet*, *andouillette*, and *tarte Tatin* remain above reproach despite the number of tourists to be found there during the high season. Lyubomir suggested that we take in Notre-Dame before lunch; I added the courtyard of the Hôtel-Dieu to the list.

I arrived very early, intending to complement my observations of visitors to the Louvre and Beaubourg with a few notes on those to Notre-Dame Cathedral. Outside, neither the left-hand portal (showing the Coronation of Mary plus bas-reliefs of the Labors of the Months), nor the central Last Judgment portal (with its weighing of souls), nor the right-hand Saint Anne portal (with scenes from the life of the Virgin and her relatives) were seen as anything other than a backdrop for a photo. Click. Then people dived into the south aisle of the nave, after have passed panels displaying the head of a dog, a smoking cigarette, and an ice-cream cone, all crossed out in order to indicate to lovers of religious art that Notre-Dame is neither a dog run, a smoking parlor, nor a gourmet restaurant. (I discovered that the first two instructions produced the desired effect, but that the third failed to do so, and that various ice-cream bars and popsicles accompanied sauntering visitors of all ages.) Below these pictograms is the sign: *Tenu décente*

(Decent Attire). Since the concept of correct dress is more social and conjunctural than natural—and therefore eminently evolutive—and since I would never wish to be numbered among of those who seek to reestablish "psychological blocks about culture with a capital 'C,'" I will merely lament the fact that the most naked of the countless scantily clad bodies in the cathedral are rarely those bodies one would wish to see.

Below the "Decent Attire" sign was a warning: "Beware of Pickpockets." Above it was a plea in seven languages: *Silence, s.v.p.; Stille bitte; Silencio por favor;* Silence, Please; *Silenzio per favore; Stilte a.u.b.*; plus some Japanese ideograms that must express the same prayer—issued, for that matter, in vain. If cultural tourists pay as little attention to pickpockets as they do to their attire and the volume of their voices, there must be no trade more lucrative in Paris than a picker of pockets at Notre-Dame. It must admitted that the density of the tide flowing toward the transept often means being separated from the people you came in with; whence the need to shout a name in order to rejoin them. Most of the other shouting back and forth is designed to check that so-and-so has remembered to take a photo of this or that, or to suggest posing in front of a given piece of precious metalwork in a side chapel or before a tomb in the ambulatory behind the choir.

Seized once again by the idea of using the simple methods of Dean Le Bras, I began timing visitors from the moment they entered the Saint Anne portal until they exited by the Coronation portal. The average time required to complete the tour that morning (including snapshots) came to seven minutes and thirty seconds. By way of comparison, the (free) guided tour offered every day at noon lasts between an hour and an hour and a half. Impressionism is more than a fashion, it's a way of fashioning one's life.

Deterred by the crowd, Anna and Lyubomir—when we finally met up—decided to postpone their visit of the cathedral until a more peaceful moment (the 7 A.M. Mass on Sunday?) and to climb the towers instead. The obligation to climb four hundred steps eliminates ninety percent of the visitors to Notre-Dame. All that remain are the most ardent photographers, those who must absolutely take the picture you can buy anywhere in Paris (notably on the square below), and which shows (in the left foreground) the head of a gargoyle with the cityscape stretching behind. True enough, anyone taking the picture himself can add the head of a traveling companion to that of the gargoyle. Almost no one passes up this opportunity—originality tends to become universal.

While Lyubomir had been sojourning at the Louvre, Anna—an apprentice costume and set designer—had roamed the small museums whose quiet and emptiness contrast so violently with all we'd observed prior to sitting down to lunch. She had found sustenance beyond her wildest hopes at places like the Musée des Arts et Traditions Populaires, the Musée de la Mode et du Costume (housed in Palais Galliera) and the Musée Nissim de Camondo (a former private mansion with lavish furnishings, overlooking Parc Monceau). I learned from Anna that the 15th arrondissement (one of the last in Paris, with no disrespect to its residents, where I would have expected to find a museum) housed one called Kwok On, endowed with a substantial collection of costumes, masks, and countless other items relating to the performing arts in Asia Minor and Southeast Asia. In exchange, I recommended that she visit the Musée de la Vie Romantique, tucked along a street in the 9th arrondissement, where she could see the authentic Romantic decor of a residential area fashionable in first half of the nineteenth century.

As one course of lunch followed another, I realized that my companions were both pleased and disappointed with their first trip to Paris. But mainly disappointed. They were first of all pleased to leave their everyday life behind, and to find not only the things they came to see, but even more. It was neither Rembrandt nor the Musée Camondo's furniture collection that left Lyubomir and Anna dissatisfied. It was Paris itself. They had stopped to appreciate all the beauty they noticed, had gone at least once a day to a quayside or bridge to experience as many of the Seine's miraculous facets as possible, and had happily wandered along Île Saint-Louis and through Nouvelles Athènes. And yet they never encountered anything that might link all these charming spots together: "*l'esprit de Paris*" Anna called it, rolling her Rs terribly. "You know what I mean?" I knew. Maybe not exactly what she meant, but I knew. A mixture of energy, of frivolity, of self-aware role-playing, of cosmopolitan mingling, of constant acceleration, and of not just being in the most beautiful city in the world but of enjoying the certainty of being in the one where people best appreciate what life has to offer, squeezing every last drop out of it. If that was *l'esprit de Paris*, I couldn't feel the spirit stirring, either.

To tell the truth, I started wondering if my home town wasn't insidiously beginning to resemble Venice, that extraordinary stage set which is less and less populated, where boredom sets in every evening at 6:00 P.M. Battalions of picture-snapping cultural tourists roaming everywhere give Venice a semblance of life in daytime. But it exists in a vegetative state, performing only the most basic functions. People who consider themselves shrewder travelers than everybody else—plus the few Venetians who still remain in Venice—say (and say to each other) that there are special routes for crossing town without meeting a single camera-bedecked belly, that tourists all cluster in Piazza San Marco and stay put. A consoling thought, maybe, but completely untrue. All of Venice is dedicated to its passing residents—and here "reside" means the opposite of "live"—just as the center of Paris, less and less populated, is reduced a little more each year to the function of international promenade featuring luxury goods and photo opportunities.

I kept my anxiety to myself and, since we all agreed that a lunch like the one we had just consumed called for a digestive stroll, Anna mentioned that they hadn't yet seen Saint-Martin Canal. After crossing a branch of the Seine to Quai de Gesvres, we took the number 75 bus safely to our destination. Less than a half hour later, while strolling on Quai de Jemmapes along the canal, Anna gave a little cry and gripped Lyubomir's arm. She pointed excitedly to the facade of the Hôtel du Nord with, just in front, the famous footbridge over the canal, where Arletty and Louis Jouvet had stood.

Although Lyubomir was aware that Marcel Carné's famous film, *Hôtel du Nord*, was shot on a studio set designed by Alexandre Trauner rather than on location at the hotel itself, he wanted to have a cup of coffee there. There were no empty tables on the terrace. Inside, the natural setting was no longer natural. Everything had been demolished except the facade, and an investor had turned the ground floor into a chic bistro, banking on the magic of the name to attract brisk business. As we sat in the back of the bistro, I explained all this to Lyubomir and Anna, then told them how, at the end of the 1960s, the Paris City Council had unanimously voted to cover the canal and transform it into a four-lane highway. I explained how, even these days, it took the unflagging vigilance of a local residents' association to prevent the square in the bend in the canal, on Quai de Valmy, from being transformed into an office building with a three-story parking garage. Suddenly, the bistro in the Hôtel du Nord got darker: a bus had just pulled up in front, blocking the window. A horde of cameras, dragging Japanese tourists behind them, poured from the bus. "More and more come by," the waiter told me. "The Hôtel du Nord now figures in most guided tours." I'm not an obsessive fan of allegories, but you have to admit that when buses pull up and unload cargœs of individuals who want to record the image of a site which is now nothing more than a facade, you have to be particularly careful to resist the temptation to turn it into a symbol.

165

Welcome to Our Preserves!

In the early 1980s, Paris rediscovered the Place des Victoires. (The city is accustomed to such renewals of affection.) Designed by Jules Hardouin-Mansart on behalf of Maréchal de La Feuillade in the late seventeenth century, Place des Victoires remained the preferred address of deep-pocketed courtiers and high-flying financiers for several decades. It was conceived, in the words of one historian, as a "stately setting," yet was constantly modified and jostled down through the years. The height of the buildings was raised, uniform dimensions went by the board, and the original plan was progressively abandoned until finally, in the last decade of the nineteenth century, a coup-de-grâce was given when the round *place* was gutted to make way for rue Etienne-Marcel. It therefore changed from a residential circle into a traffic hub, a simple intersection where no fewer than six streets henceforth converged. At the same time, the erection nearby of Baltard's pavilions for the redeployment of the wholesale produce market known as Les Halles made the new intersection one of the busiest and noisiest, especially at night and early morning.

In Haussmann's Paris, despite the charm that Place des Victoires miraculously managed to preserve, most of the residents abandoned their apartments, which were transformed into business premises of all kinds (which is still the case today). For over a century, this part of the 1st and 2nd arrondissements—a stone's throw from the Palais Royal and the *grands boulevards*, a hop-and-a-skip from both the teeming Halles and the grand Avenue de l'Opéra—remained a *quartier* rich in affordable housing and abundant, varied shops, many of them profiting from proximity to Les Halles, and all dynamized by the presence of numerous wholesalers (especially fabrics) sometimes in former residential mansions subdivided in countless ways (as also occurred in the Marais). It was common for employees to live within the quadrilateral formed by rue Réaumur, rue du Louvre, rue de Rivoli, and Avenue de l'Opéra, along with staff from the nearby Bourse and brokerage firms, the Banque de France, and the various small-time businesses that lived off these big-time firms.

At the end of the 1960s, all the produce trucks, refrigerated meat and fish vans, and carts of flowers or dairy products left to make their racket elsewhere when Les Halles market moved to the wasteland of Rungis south of Paris. For nearly ten years, the din was partially replaced by the racket of demolition vehicles and the swarm of machines of all weights and sizes on their way to contribute, first, to the destruction of Baltard's market pavilions, and then to the digging of the (temporarily notorious) hole in Les Halles, and finally to the building of the wretched shopping mall that dishonors, disfigures, and degrades Paris under the misleading name of Le Forum (about which, more later).

When these noises finally subsided, then stopped, interest turned to Place des Victoires. Les Halles and surrounding streets had become chic. The battle over their redevelopment had generated so much talk about the Right Bank (dismissed as "bourgeois" by Left Bank proponents of existentialism even though it harbored an integral part of working-class Paris, whereas their own Saint-Germain-des-Prés flirted with the ultrachic 7th arrondissement) that people who set the tone and launched fashions decided to establish their distinguished

168

abodes there, as did everyone who followed them in the ardent desire to appear original (on the condition of having plenty of good company).

After apartments with exposed beams, after Swedish (or, at the very least, English) cars; after steel or plastic furniture; after Afghan rugs, Turkish kilims, and Pakistani poufs; the quest for originality homed in on clothing, taking the twin paths of "casual/comfortable/sporty" (British style) and "destructured/austere" (Japanese approach). It should be recalled that this trend had been preceded by a period during which, from the sartorial standpoint, the doctrine had been "anything goes"—a manifesto that rejected appearances, showed disdain for dress codes, and opposed class divisions. Denim, velour, and carded wool (brown or ecru) long reigned unchallenged. Mao jackets and oriental scarves constituted accessories heavy with political and social meanings.

However, once the Khmer Rouge had finished demonstrating the truth of Maoism, once the benevolent Soviet protectorate had cut the Afghan rug route, once the wonderful path of communal life had been littered with broken loves sprawling in puddles of bitterness, and once all those who had chosen to live in castles in the air had wearied of paying rent to their psychoanalyst(s), the rumor went around that it was now completely OK to look out for yourself, for your own comfort, for your own beauty and well-being—which meant, along the way, spending a lot of dough on clothes. Even better, men—previously forbidden to indulge in coquettishness, at the risk of provoking persistent suspicions concerning their sexuality—were invited *coram populo* by their girlfriends' magazines (and even by more straitlaced weeklies) to recognize the feminine side of their ego and to indulge in the passion for appearances.

Those appearances, though, were not to be adopted on the basis of superficial criteria. They had to "convey values" or "mark a return to...." Thus goes Paris these days: being avant-garde means "returning to," echoing the approach advocated by Paris bus drivers who, a hundred times every day, shout at passengers jamming the aisle of their vehicle: "Advance to the rear, please, ladies and gentlemen." As to "conveying values," that's an exercise that Parisians have practiced since time immemorial, with neither pause nor rest, aware as they are of the example they must set for the provinces and the world.

This was the context in which Place des Victoires became a fashionable place—sorry, I mean "spot"—once it (and its immediate vicinity) became home to a host of retail rag traders. Kenzo set his bags down there and, since he's not short on talent, attracted lasting attention to his boutique. Other designers like Cacharel and Victoire, who wanted to mark their distinctiveness by setting up somewhere other than the traditional fashion districts, also opened shops facing the equestrian statue of Louis XIV in the middle of the circle. Customers drawn to one boutique discovered the others, and everyone's business got off to a bright start. In a matter of years, the entire *place* went over to clothes and shoes. The stationer sold his shop to an Italian clothier, while one of the two restaurants (justly famous for its excellent bistro cuisine) changed into a footwear outlet (the restaurant owner had backed the wrong horse once too often). The hairdresser couldn't refuse the offer of a ladies' garment maker. The fish merchant—whose lobsters and oysters had drawn Parisians from all over town—tiptoed away with his little critters; their tanks were replaced by gray polystyrene dummies wearing cocktail attire for astronauts, devised by an avant-garde designer. The real-estate value of business premises steadily climbed: the watchmaker, who had long rejected all propositions (at levels unimaginable just a few years earlier) finally accepted the offer of a manufacturer of "1950s American clothing" highly prized by teenagers and young adults. A few months later, dead bored and not knowing what to do with his jackpot, the watchmaker went down to the cellar of the building where he had moved with his German shepherd. With one barrel of a shotgun—bought the day before—he killed the dog and then, in the conventional language of police reports, "turned the gun on himself." When the 1950s-style clothier went bankrupt a few years later, the shop was bought by a vendor of "upscale" costume jewelry.

The fabric merchant whose warehouse occupied the entire space between two streets running into Place des Victoires was also the object of all kinds of attractive offers. He finally succumbed to an American chain of casual wear. Other shopkeepers in the neighborhood whispered—in tones ranging from envy to stupefaction—that he had demanded (and received) a monthly rent of 500,000 francs ($90,000) for his premises. Just opposite the circle, a German clothier leased two floors, but with a smaller total surface area—the rent was a mere 300,000 francs per month. (In both cases, conjectures ran wild over the amount of "key money" that was handed over.) The second restaurant on the circle sold out in turn; its windows had featured jeroboams and balthazars whose necks were covered in red wax and whose bellies bore the labels of strong, solid wines. They made way for wire figures sporting pale dresses designed for anorexic young ladies. Next door, a huge boutique volunteered to dress children under ten, offering them a taste of the vanity and conceits of appearances prior to the age of reason: 390 francs ($70) for a vest, 380 francs for overalls, 520 francs for a dress, 190 francs for a tee-shirt, 380 francs for a pair of shorts, and even 400 francs for a bathing suit. For an eight-year-old!

The same trend spread to neighboring streets. Those who hadn't managed to find premises on Place des Victoires itself fought over shops on the six radiating streets. A Spanish republican grocer and his wife (always dressed in widow's black) were paid 3,000,000 francs for their shop, more than it had earned them in forty years of trade. Since Franco had finally died, they returned as wealthy merchants to the land they had fled without a penny. The shop of the nearby glazier was snapped up by another avant-garde designer who specialized in clothes that displayed male anatomy to its best advantage; it sold navy-blue mesh tank tops of the "come here, young man" sort, which cost a fortune. The Tunisian fruit and vegetable store just down the street was transformed into a vast fashion stall beneath a logo that was becoming famous; the artichokes, eggplants, and potatoes were elbowed out by brightly colored duffel coats, sweaters, and pullovers in animal patterns, gleaming two-tone shoes, and smart accessories.

A few paces along, the corner patisserie was skippered by the baker's fiftyish wife. She was chubby, justly proud of her breads and cakes, and a stickler for details; if an apprentice baker arrived a little late, she would give him a dressing down by invoking the example of her model husband, who left his native Auvergne with nothing but a wife, and who now boasted an enviable reputation and honest prosperity by never failing to rise in the middle of every night to conscientiously knead his bread. If a sales assistant showed up with her lips too red, cheeks too powdered, or skirt too short, the baker's wife lectured her on the importance of respect for oneself and one's customers. She wound up selling her shop to a kind of genius of enticement, a Saint Laurent of frou-frou, a benefactress of striptease—that is to say, a lady who made delightful feminine underthings.

Step by step, within a radius of three or four hundred yards, the triad formed by garment, shoe, and accessory dealers (in order of importance) added to its trophy collection an electrician, a shoemaker, a stationer, a tripe butcher, three cafés, a sporting goods store, a knifemaker, and a restaurant (once famous for its wines from Saumur; its owner, since retired to his native province, sometimes returns to wander through the neighborhood, and is said to look up furtively and mumble when greeted by former clients). Also gone are a chocolate shop, a fish merchant, an Italian grocer who more or less catered meals from his back room, a gas station and garage, a stamp specialist, a florist, a plumbing and heating firm, a bookbinder, a record discounter, a lampshade maker, a retailer of religious items (statues of saints, edifying books, candles, rosaries, crucifixes, articles for Mass), an antique dealer who specialized in kitchen and dining objects, and even a funeral parlor (the shrinking number of people living around Place des Victoires apparently reduced potential deaths to a hopeless level).

A few names are probably missing from this memorial to shop owners who fell bravely on the field of battle against fashion (against "fancy goods," as they would have said in the nineteenth century). That's because, when compiling this list, it was difficult to find residents old enough—that is to say who have lived here for a mere twenty years—to have known the commercial geography of the neighborhood around Place des Victoires before the great upheaval. Even those who witnessed it with their own eyes have difficulty getting their recollections to agree.

"What was there before the American boot store, next to the tobacconist?"

"A bookstore, maybe?"

"That's right, a bookstore that specialized in military history."

"Oh yeah, right, and next to it, where the Japanese are now, wasn't it a philatelist?"

It's all a haze, they're amazed to find it so hard to remember, they who were born and raised here. They rack their brains like the elderly even though they've just turned forty-five.

"My parents worked at the Banque de France, and lived two hundred yards away, on rue du Bouloi. Whenever my mother comes back, she always says it's like a magician suddenly transformed all the stores."

The sale of a few warehouses and wholesale outlets to the triad has solidified the transformation and monotonization of the neighborhood. Meanwhile, the covered arcades nearby—Galerie Vivienne and Galerie Véro-Dodat—were renovated into luxury showcases for refined collectors and "designers" of every ilk, adding a further note of chic (underscored by the presence in one of these "historical-monument arcades" of the most outlandish of modern fashion designers, Jean-Paul Gaultier).

The Palais Royal, just two minutes southwest of Place des Victoires, performs the same function as the two covered arcades, namely that of preserving "collective memory," an ingredient without which Paris could not live in the present, like certain people gripped by a phobia rendering them incapable, though still sprightly, of walking without a helping arm to cling to. The stupid, criminal destruction of the cast-iron Baltard pavilions at Les Halles sparked new interest in the neighborhood, and the opening of the Pompidou Center in 1977 completed the Right Bank's rescue from limbo. So when Daniel Buren erected his bollixed columns of crummy marble in the Palais Royal courtyard, it sparked such a controversy (a shrug would have sufficed) that crowds flocked to this overlooked garden, bordered by arcades hosting a variety of timeless shops worthy of some spiritualist novel by Gaston Leroux.

The interiors of these stores were vigorously renovated—not to say totally *relooké*—in order to host still more "designer shops" (featuring perfume, household linen, tableware, knick-knacks) and up-to-date antique dealers whose more-than-expensive price stickers guaranteed neither the originality nor the quality of their merchandise. One of them specialized, with more intuition and shrewdness than taste, in haute-couture items from the 1930s to 1970s. Thus grandma's old dresses went from "thrift shop" to antique store, making a terrific qualitative leap, climbing from the status of souvenir (and sometimes disguise for costume balls) to that of work of art. At the same time, powerful reinforcement came from the nearby Marsan Pavilion of the Louvre, which was designated as the site of a new museum of fashion. (The old one, in the Palais Galliera, treated dress too much like a straightforward testament of its time—hardly more than a curiosity!—and not enough like crucially important proof of mankind's creative genius.) The window of one clothing store bore the following sign: "People who live in the past must bow before those who live in the future, otherwise the world would begin to turn backwards." Many leaders of the fashion crowd were showered with the honorary title of Chevalier des Arts et des Lettres, and a goodly few were even awarded the Legion d'Honneur. "Top models" began attracting more attention than most movie stars. They might lack speaking parts, but that only made them more international. And at any rate a model's fees, expressed in dollars, spoke extensively for her—or him.

Even as the fashion scene became highly—and especially widely—mediatized, industrial relocation was in full swing. Pants, blouses, polo shirts, tee-shirts, and sweaters were henceforth made in Korea or southern India, and sold in Paris for up to six times cost price. You can see how 600 percent profits might enable the lucky beneficiaries to bid millions of francs for boutiques in the newly fashionable fashion district. In only five years, most of the salable premises had sold out. The rest—those who stubbornly persisted in the idea of continuing to trade—ultimately succumbed later, with no known exception. One talented, bohemian antique dealer had turned her little shop into a highly symbolic bastion of resistance to the clothiers' hard cash. Just fifty paces from the sacred *place*, her store was the object of ever more attractive offers, which she refused (between two drags on her cigarette, assuming her attention wasn't completely absorbed by a radio broadcast on France-Musique) in a tone of commiseration. All around her, shops were caving in, one by one. The antique dealer held out. The offers, however, continued to swell; the craze for

175

moving into the area regularly resulted in astonishing deals (blessed by the banks, it goes without saying). A poor knife seller, sensing his approaching demise, complained that all the other merchants on his street and nearby roads were receiving attractive propositions whereas no one courted him. That was because his shop, which had formerly been patronized by the overflow of workers and visitors from Les Halles market, was minuscule: barely the size of a *chambre de bonne* (garret). Who, bemoaned the old cutler, would be interested in such a joint? The day eventually came, however, when he could joyfully post a sign announcing a "going-out-of-business" sale of his stock of knives, scissors, cutting implements, straight-edge razors, and shaving brushes. A seller of fancy berets had purchased his shop, paying hefty key money simply to get one foot—not enough room for two—in the holy of holies.

The antique dealer sold out not long after the cutler. The four hundred square feet of her store brought in enough money to entirely renovate her family home in the south of France, buy a shop one-and-a-half times the size in the Marais for herself and her daughter, and set up her grandson. She explained—and her voice had the ring of sincerity—that it wasn't the money that had forced her hand, but the change in population at the bistros where she usually had a coffee, a quick lunch, a decent glass of wine or honest shot of whisky, or just bought a pack of cigarettes. She had the impression that now she met only clones there: young men and women of the same age, similarly dressed, taking about the same things, drinking the same drinks and swapping the same gossip, all of them salespeople in the clothing stores. What money couldn't buy, monotony did.

A sales assistant in the new fashion neighborhood is a peculiar specimen. He (or she) initially gives the impression of being the precious scion of an illustrious family, temporarily forced by a series of unjust circumstances to earn a living by selling rags to unworthy souls. (Strictly speaking, for that matter, he dœsn't really *sell*—like the relatives of Molière's Monsieur Jourdain, he simply gives things away in exchange for money.) The discrepancy between what he merits in his own eyes and the state to which he has fallen spurs the assistant to dress in mourning—he dresses in black in all seasons. Sometimes, his grief is such that he shaves his head, retaining only the amount of hair formerly allowed to forced-labor convicts. He also wears shœs designed for forced marches (which, strangely, nail him to the spot). Nothing seems to amuse him, nothing can wipe from his youthful face the expression of weariness with which he seems to have been born.

His aloof bearing and preacher's dress suggest that the sales assistant's conversation might dwell on crucial metaphysical questions. Yet it more commonly dwells on his colleagues' love affairs and the latest tidbits gleaned in a nightclub, from a celebrity-gossip mag, or from television. These young men and women successfully give the impression not so much of being asexual as being beyond sex. That they've already been through it all. It's easy to see that a large proportion of the men are homosexual (indeed, they employ every possible code to underscore the fact), but you get the impression that instead of expressing a carnal preference it reflects a subjection to fashion, to chic Parisian lifestyle fashion. It almost seems as though homosexuality—in addition to black clothes, convict boots, shaved head, and bored expression—represents a clear sign of belonging to the ineffable world of "artists." "Michelangelo was one, Jean-Paul Gaultier is one, I'm one. And my lapel sports the red ribbon reminding everyone that AIDS is among us," in the same way other people wear the Légion d'Honneur, a Rotary badge, or Masonic square and compass—that is to say as a sign of recognition among people of distinction, even if distinguished by the threat of misfortune.

And yet, the virus turned these games of love and fashion to its advantage. In a single year, the curé at Saint-Eustache buried eleven of the ninety employees in one of the neighborhood's fashion houses. The priest was struck by the extreme solitude of their final months. No more family. Practically no more friends, either. As if all the people they formerly saw, who shared tastes (and risks), could only deal with AIDS as an abstract threat that added an element of immaterial, chimerical tragedy to existence. A virus that could be utilized socially, but not tolerated individually.

Whatever the case, illness and death prevented some of these young people from ever taking root in the neighborhood. And speculation spurred several clothiers who had just bought their shops to sell to other garment dealers, which meant that the staff moved on before they even had time to learn the names of the streets. Finally, the capriciousness of the sales-assistant crowd, plus the swiftness with which the least dispute became dramatic, increased the number of temporary stays and sudden departures. The upshot is that the *quartier*'s new population has never really peopled it. They're just extras, unable to give the neighborhood any real character. At the very most they've given it a look, and not a very exuberant one at that. By day, Place des Victoires and its surroundings are more full of agitation than life, since life supposes a soul. By night, it's dead as a doornail.

That's because its inhabitants have deserted it. Everything led them to do so. The transformation of everyday stores into the triad's boutiques meant that only a few grocers, butchers, and bakers remained—many of whom, finding themselves in a near-monopoly situation, raised prices even as they ignored quality. They thus gave certain residents a further reason to leave in addition to other rises in cost, the most important being real estate, which was soon taken to dizzying heights by competition between banks, insurance companies, and property developers. The value of some apartments increased fourfold in just a few years. The steady disappearance of restaurants reduced the attractiveness of Place des Victoires and environs—people from other arrondissements of Paris began coming less often. The poor reputation of the new Forum des Halles didn't make things any better. In just a few years, this part of central Paris became a "bedroom neighborhood," increasingly inhabited by what Americans call DINKs (Double Income, No Kids) and by "households" comprising a single person. Apartments were rented or bought by clothing companies who turned them into showrooms or offices camouflaged as company housing in order to get around zoning laws. Some buildings lost one-third of their residents in five years.

Along the southern strip of the 1st arrondissement between rue du Louvre and rue Royale, the extraordinary boom in international tourism has had the same effects—*mutatis mutandis*—as fashion had further north. The more touristy a *quartier* becomes, the more local business focuses solely on the passing population: fast-food joints, bars, clothes, souvenirs, gadgets, duty-free shops. Shops that target busloads of Japanese have proliferated south of Avenue de l'Opéra.

Never have so many people crowded between the Tuileries Garden and the Louvre colonnade, between Place Vendôme and Place des Victoires—but only on the sidewalks. The desertion of residents has led to the closing of schools or reduction in the number of classes (just like in rural Lozère). Some schools manage to remain open even though they don't meet minimum pupil requirements, but that's the fruit of discreet and ever-fragile connivance between city hall, local arrondissement counselors, the district education authority, teachers' unions, and the PTA (which sometimes includes members with political clout... who lose interest in the situation as soon as their offspring are no longer of school age).

Barely fifteen years after it began, this transformation is losing steam. Too much fashion killed fashion, and too much hype blunted hype. Economic crisis and a drop in consumption did the rest. In 1997, two stores on Place des Victoires vainly sought to sell or lease their premises (one of them tried for over a year). It's highly unlikely they'll be taken over again by a restaurant or fish merchant, by a baker or druggist. The former bakery turned lingerie store saw its underthings flee to the other bank of the Seine—the store now stands empty.

At the same time that the center of Paris is losing its inhabitants, it's losing its color. Or rather, it's becoming monochrome. Along with the fashion and cultural tourism neighborhoods, the Marais and now Saint-Germain-des-Prés illustrate this regression in their own way.

The main "gay" district of Paris is basically centered in the Marais, or more precisely in the rectangle bounded by rue de Rivoli to the south, rue de Turenne to the east, rue des Francs-Bourgeois (which becomes rue Rambuteau) to the north, and Boulevard de Sébastopol to the west. The people who live in or frequent this *quartier* have themselves dubbed it "the ghetto." One guidebook, cowed by political correctness into not calling a spade a spade, has found a charming circumlocution to designate the ghetto's highly visible population. "The Marais," it reads, "is henceforth inhabited and enlivened by a population of refined bachelors."

As silly as that expression is, it at least has the merit of pointing to the origins of the new settlement. In the early 1960s, many bright minds still called for—in the name of modernity, public health, light, and hygiene—the razing of that part of old Paris just to the north, east, and west of the Hôtel de Ville. This urban terrorism had very nearly been carried out on two previous occasions. Haussmann's plans notably recommended the cutting of an extension of rue Etienne-Marcel, mentioned above, as far as Boulevard Beaumarchais; later the "Voisin Plan" of 1925, backed by Le Corbusier in the name of functionality, would not have left a single stone standing on the central Right Bank, to be replaced by model cities of housing blocks built around gardens. This idea, periodically raised again, was partially and insidiously implemented through various real estate operations conducted before and after the war, with the benediction of city authorities. It was only halted by a clutch of historians, art historians, architects, and scholars. They formed a pressure group and, backed by the Commission du Vieux Paris (which included a few members of that group), they managed to have the Marais classified as a historic district in 1965, which meant it would be constantly monitored by the Historic Buildings Department.

(This is probably the moment, most unusual in a book, to ask readers to observe a minute of silence. During which, if you will, try to imagine what Paris would be today if certain erstwhile plans had been carried out: the Saint-Martin Canal covered over, transformed into a four-lane highway; the Marais razed and rebuilt as one vast housing project in the heart of town; Les Halles dotted with highrise buildings like the Montparnasse Tower; and the Gare d'Orsay, now converted into a museum, replaced by a building similar to the glass-and steel conference center at Porte Maillot, known as the Palais des Congrès. After such a vision, a second minute of silence may well be necessary to recover your breath and stop your head from spinning.)

In order to reveal the architectural and urban wonders beneath the worn, grimy, disfigured Marais, which had become one of the capital's most insalubrious neighborhoods—because the problems addressed by the Voisin Plan and others were very real, even if their solutions were abstruse—the neighborhood's saviors decided to organize a festival (which were not yet legion in those days) that featured outdoor events in the courtyards of various former mansions. It was a great hit. Even today, in fact, *Quartiers d'Eté*—the summer neighborhood festivals held all over Paris from 15 July to 15 August—demonstrate just how much the city lends itself to performances that valorize its varied indoor and outdoor settings, and how much charm it in turn gives to such events.

The festival drew favorable attention to the Marais. The rescue plan and various advantages encouraged a young and

181

relatively poor population to move in, attracted by the beauty of the buildings, the size of the apartments, and modest real estate prices (given the inevitable renovation work required). Such people were enchanted by the location, ambiance, and even quaintness of the area. They included artists and intellectuals who were unhappy with the changes that had occurred in neighborhoods where they and their kind had gathered comfortably, or who were driven out or dissuaded by the hike in real estate prices that normally followed the promotion of any part of the capital as an "artists' quarter." This new population was more bohemian than refined. Its average age favored nonconformism. It liked to mix with the original residents and delighted in discovering so many wonderful buildings, elegantly drawn streets, and vistas of unmatched grace. In Paris as in any other capital city, this energy, youthfulness, openmindedness, liveliness, diversity, and novelty were more than enough to attract some of those whose bachelorhood and lack of children translate into high disposable incomes, and whose fringe sexuality—statistically speaking—was drawn toward neighborhoods with a relaxed, welcoming, urbane atmosphere (that is to say, where you don't have to know or worry about the approval or disapproval of anyone whomsœver). According to one of these people, who moved into the Marais shortly after the festival began, "in the 1970s, you met more homosexuals here than elsewhere, but nobody thought of it as a 'gay neighborhood.' Or as an artists' neighborhood, for that matter. That's the kind of label often applied once the artists have left, used much more by real-estate agents than residents. Let's just say there were quite a few intellectuals and showbiz people, and since those professions are relatively unhierarchical and openminded at least in terms of mores, they were attractive to homosexuals, and so you noticed more of them around here than over by Vaugirard or Gobelins. It was friendly and nice. But our delight and pride in living in the Marais came from something else—the endless charm of this part of Paris, and the admiration we could see in the eyes of people discovering it for the first time."

Along with these enthusiastic individuals, real-estate developers were attracted to the Marais. They bought apartments redolent of history, then renovated and sold them to recent arrivals and parvenus who, like every freshly minted bourgeoisie, dreamed of acquiring a patina of gentility or, at the very least, old-world distinction. The transformation of the central Right Bank eminently coincided with the peak of the postwar economic boom. In an amusing paradox, this peak was also the great period for spiels on "modernism"—in art, architecture, and ideas concerning lifestyle—spiels whose militant virulence was all the stronger if delivered from a historic dwelling or location proud of its past. President Georges Pompidou, patron of modern artists and composers like Vasarely and Boulez, decreed that "Paris has to adapt itself to cars and should reject outmoded aesthetics," but he chose to live in one the of the best-preserved (and car-free) spots in the capital, Île Saint-Louis.

In repopulating the Marais, whose pre-1960 inhabitants were soon reduced to a mere a handful of specimens, nouveaux riches slowly began to outnumber the mavericks (of whatever ilk). The rich soon included a goodly number of foreigners—notably East-Coast North Americans—who loved the old buildings they lacked back home. Their interest in the Marais did nothing to lower the price of real estate. Finally, starting in the 1980s, high-flying corporate executives were joined by the latest incarnation of a moneyed bourgeoisie, namely the advertising, communications, and consulting types (image, strategy, decision-making *conseillers*). This PR crowd was followed by various species of applied, decorative, and performing "artists" (mercenaries who were better off than simple painters and sculptors), namely people who designed storyboards and layouts for advertising campaigns, fashion reviews, or lifestyle magazines, and representatives of what the French began calling *le showbiz*. At that time, money flowed thicker and faster in those circles than in any other, and those circles, more than any other, yearned for a "cultural status" that could be displayed as a visible sign of social success. Living in the historic center of Paris was an inescapable prerequisite of that status.

Like most of the original inhabitants, the mavericks from the early days of the rescue of the Marais abandoned their apartments. Often because they were unable to keep up with hikes in rent or real-estate values. And also because they had aged; their enthusiasm had waned, and they found their new neighbors only moderately appealing. The festival was going through painful death throes, and a certain Right Bank utopia died along with it.

The area was rich in ground-floor workshops and stores. The first to be sold were the ones that housed the business premises of Ashkenazi Jews who had made the Marais their home until the great Vélodrome roundup during World War II. Then the triple pressure of renovation, rising prices, and new regulations (designed to reduce noise, pollution, and traffic problems) forced out businesses linked to the neighborhood's traditional light industry. These were replaced—naturally—by clothing stores. Money attracted more money, and acquiring clothes went from being a time-honored necessity to a leisure activity. There was also a blossoming of art galleries, interior decoration stores, and antique dealers who often specialized in "antiques" from the 1950s and 1960s. Lifestyles had changed so fast that the preceding decades seemed to belong to another era, a period that had been "nice" if somewhat silly, oafish, "stick-in-the-mud," and certainly "pre-" something or other. So its objects were collected with paternalistic affection by the PR crowd and their henchmen, who were convinced they'd powerfully helped humanity to escape from that dark period. Whereas people once sought objects wrought from flint, bronze, or iron to place in their decorative glass cases, now they snapped up early Bakelite and plastic items from the dawn of the modern era, along with comic books, posters, pictures, or singles by stars of those bygone days, and even certain objects that up to then had passed for mere kitchen utensils.

Art galleries, numerous from the start, attempted take root in a *quartier* whose new population, it was thought, would be partial to works that were avant-garde or, at the very least, "up to date." This hypothesis turned out to be overly venturesome. Mainly because the zealots of modernism who moved into all those apartments in former private mansions with coffered ceilings were not about to risk good money on the purchase of paintings or objects unless the artist had already acquired fame and value. Advertising people's dealings with major brand names probably inhibited them from encouraging little-known artists (much less discovering any themselves). Those gallery owners able to stick solely with media-star artists and their disciples managed to hang on, especially if they were located near Beaubourg. The others moved out or metamorphosed into poster and print shops, since the flow of cultural tourists—swelled further by the opening of the Picasso Museum—guaranteed much more profitable sales than did original works by unknown progenitors.

In the early 1990s, the times donned a new suit of clothes and, like the devil in the medieval tale who, "when he was old, wore a hermit's garb," adopted an air of virtue, authenticity, and a return to values. Whereas flamboyant businessman Bernard Tapie had once been admired, now Sister Emmanuelle was venerated. Pop singer Jacques Higelin had been cheered, now crooner Charles Trenet was being applauded. Winners of all kind were formerly exalted, now people worshipped the Dalai Lama. A certain whiff of discredit—indeed of suspicion—began to cling to the dazzling professions that had prospered in the previous decade. This was highly dangerous, since the consultancy field is eminently based on trust: it survives on its reputation and accompanying set of beliefs. So the new PR bourgeoisie tried to climb on board and then overtake the critical bandwagon. What had been so praised was now burned, and in the middle of the bonfire they threw the Marais. They decreed that Paris was a hindrance to an authentic, balanced, pollution-free life. That the city prevented a return to traditional values—especially family values—whose skyrocketing popularity contrasted starkly with the "me-generation attitude" of the previous decade. The do-it-yourself guide to social success suddenly decreed that a spacious apartment in the historic center of Paris was "out." The Marais was replaced by the tony suburb of Neuilly with its nice buildings, discreet affluence, decent gaiety, and impeccable sense of social distances. The new bourgeoisie began feeling sufficiently sure of itself to mingle with the old and—who knows?—offer its daughters in marriage. For want of Neuilly, it was also acceptable to move to a small-house-with-patch-of-garden as still found in the 13th, 14th, 19th, or 20th arrondissements. Such properties were fought over. People also moved to Issy-les-Moulineaux—if possible, right alongside the Seine—nurturing the reasonable hope (promoted by Mayor Santini, an intelligent, shrewd media politician) that Issy would become the Neuilly of the early 21st century.

Once it lost its "in" status, the Marais underwent a new transformation, identical in nature and features to the one described above at Place des Victoires, if slower and less homogeneous. Stores carrying everyday items continued to disappear in favor of shops targeting cultural tourists. Due to a real-estate crash, some newly vacated apartments found no takers (as occurred in the rest of Paris). Finally, nearly one-fifth of the apartments were sold as *pieds-à-terre* to Frenchmen from the provinces whose relationship to the capital had been changed by airplanes and high-speed trains, or to foreigners whose local economies were booming. A part-time residence rate of 20 percent is still a long way from that of Venice, but the trend had begun.

So it was more and more a stage set—and less and less a *quartier*—in which the second Marais, "gay" Marais, grew. There was nothing new about a special neighborhood favored by Parisian homosexuals, nor the fact that it was located in the center of town. Depending on the period, it had shifted between the Left Bank and the Right (more often remaining on the latter). But "gentlemen's Paris" had always been a nocturnal affair; when it moved into the Marais from 1980 onward, it became a daytime affair for the first time, without ceasing to be welcoming and even lively all through the night.

Many homosexuals began refusing to live one life in daylight and another in darkness. They no longer wanted to be bilked by private, expensive, selective establishments. So they abandoned the clubs, bars, and restaurants located between Palais-Royal and Opéra, and became regulars at Marais bistros run by a few of their own kind who had decided to charge normal prices, where it didn't cost extra to be among friends.

In this new "pink nation," the concept of being "among friends" slowly separated into two attitudes, easygoing and activist. The easygoing crowd only wanted to be left in peace, to enjoy places where meeting other homosexuals was easy and possible all day long. They appreciated the tranquillity of a socially acceptable, even ordinary, homosexuality. Activists, however, wanted to make a violently distinctive sign of their sexual proclivity, waving it like a banner. For them, a gay neighborhood is a kind of fortress where they can rail against society's heterocracy. There's no question of a quiet life, because battle must be constantly waged against oppression. Since this oppression is more and more a *cosa mentale*—its nature having become increasingly vague in a society tending more toward anomie than rigid norms—the battle is conducted above all on the field of rhetoric and symbolism, and increasingly involves getting worked up within one's own camp rather than leading sorties outside. The several hundred shops and enterprises that target gay customers support the activists.

From one standpoint, then, "among friends" was just one moment in a life not meant to be reduced to or limited by sexual preference; from the other, it became an end in itself and meant constant subversiveness, notably characterized by crude sexual consumption as epitomized by "back rooms," and manifested in dress codes that swiftly become uniforms.

The melange of these two conceptions of the neighborhood—the latter being staged by "gay enterprises"—has led to "freely chosen segregation" in the words of one homosexual sociologist. Like all segregation, it draws together people who are alike and excludes those who are different. Whether you sympathize with the easygoing crowd or agree with the activists—or remain totally indifferent to both groups—what matters to Paris and Parisians in the nature and development of the gay Marais is that it has become a monochrome *quartier*, a preserve, a "ghetto" to use the local expression. It is now so marked that many homosexuals who place personal ads in the *Le Nouvel Observateur* explicitly describe themselves as "non-ghetto."

And a ghetto is the antithesis—not to say negation—of Paris, a city whose founding myth establishes it as a place where everything mixes. While that myth serves as a rallying, utopian ideal, it is no doubt also a lie or half-lie. Paris harbors a certain number of other ghettos, though not called by that name. Some parts of the 7th and 16th arrondissements are tight enclaves open only to the rich and powerful. But who would ever think of seeking *l'esprit de Paris* there, on Avenue Georges-Mandel or Place du Palais-Bourbon? And yet gay Marais is no more open to those "who aren't" than that avenue and square are to the working or even middle classes.

The monotony of the ghetto weighs on many homosexuals who moved there thinking it was a land of freedom, meaning free of labels. "I've been here for twenty years," confides a man who lives on rue du Bourg-Tibourg. "I've moved twice, but always stayed in the *quartier*. This time, I've canceled my lease and I'm going to set up in the 9th arrondissement. It's one thing to be homosexual and feel neither ashamed or embarrassed about it, and another to be constantly urged to bring that aspect of my life to the fore. Gay bars, gay restaurants, gay bookstores, gay clothiers, boutiques of gay sex aids, and before you know it gay grocers, gay florists, and why not turn Notre-Dame-des-Blancs-Manteaux into a gay parish or give the church on rue des Billettes to a gay Lutheran preacher? The high-profile approach that I already felt was a childish syndrome of sexual liberation has turned into exhibitionism. More and more stores display the *drapeau gay* (rainbow flag). Of course, I realize that a certain solidarity is necessary, not only because of AIDS but also because there are guys who are hassled at home or at work for the sole reason of being gay. And of course twenty-five years ago, when I was twenty myself, it would have seemed great to have a coffee at five in the afternoon in a bar where I could have chatted with other guys 'like me.' It certainly would have reassured me, made life easier and, who knows, provided some pleasant moments. But solidarity should be the fruit of personal choice, not social pressure, and anyway I don't see what this hysterical sense of identification has to do with solidarity. Whereas I know what the regional AIDS association is doing for people who have AIDS or are HIV-positive—I've been working for it for seven years, ever since my friend became HIV-positive. Confronted with the medical establishment's technical rhetoric, we were able to insist that the ill *person*, not just the illness, be taken into account. What do all these gay businesses have to do with all that, except to help bring in customers? It's the height of hypocrisy and deceit! The moneychangers in the temple are now preaching morality and saying Mass! You'd think you're at Lourdes! In fact, that's it: the Marais has become like Lourdes. Which doesn't suit me at all—my parents were teachers who defended secular values. Freedom is my ideal, not recruitment. Down with the sexual draft!"

Then there's Jean, who lives on rue des Mauvais Garçons: "I loved this address. What's more, when I arrived in Paris, I was offered two apartments. This one and another one, on rue des Vertus. I'd left Montélimar after a dispute with my family—my father got wind of things by reading my mail. You can't imagine what went down. But I was twenty-two and had a good science degree, so I hit the road, as the song goes. I lucked into a job in a pharmaceutical lab outside Paris, but I wanted to live in town and knew in or near the Marais would be best. Having a choice between rue des *Vertus* (virtues) and rue des *Mauvais Garçons* (bad boys) seemed a veiled message from fate."

Jean didn't regret his choice. In a bar just a stone's throw from his apartment he met Emmanuel, a student at l'Ecole des Langues Orientales who hopes to become an interpreter. The former is now twenty-nine, the latter twenty-six. Whereas the former has broken off with his parents, the latter has only his mother, who knows everything. After three years of "seeing each other"—says Jean, who likes to stress his southern provincial roots—they've decided to move in together. In the former's flat, or the latter's?

"No," says Jean. "We're using it as an excuse to get out of here. We're heading up to Belleville. I've been wanting to ditch my joint for a while." (Emmanuel lives with his mother in the suburbs.) "I was dazzled by the Marais at first because back home, freedom was just a dream. As to Avignon, where I did my chemistry degree, you've soon done the rounds. So, once in Paris, goodbye Mom, goodbye Dad! Everything seemed new and shiny and I had a ball! After two or three years, I calmed down. Too much of a good thing is like not getting enough of it—you eventually become pathetic. That's when the Marais began to get to me. Before, there were fags. Now there's nothing but fags. Even at the bakery, the guy stares at your crotch when you come in and your ass when you go out. So I began to think about moving. Straights, you see, think we always have sex on our minds. But I like to go into a 'normal' bar [he pronounces the quote marks] and talk with guys who aren't homo. It's terrifically relaxing. There's no ulterior motive, no hustling, no little voice in your head that says if he's not mad about you you're a loser. It's the same for girls who chat with fags—it's like a vacation, a truce, whatever. That's no longer possible in the Marais. A friend of mine says that as soon as you go out people look at you as if you were the Dow Jones—you can't help reading how much they think you're worth in their eyes! *Basta.* Anyway, I finally met Emmanuel. Since then I basically stopped going out alone, and thought less about moving. But now the occasion has come. We're out of here. Hooray for freedom. Because being in a straight neighborhood isn't going to stop me from giving my boyfriend a French kiss." The boyfriend seems to be counting on that, and asks for proof, just in case. Jean complies, exaggerating things, thereby defending the reputation of Latin lovers. Emmanuel finally pulls himself away, delighted at this highly demonstrative sign of affection; pretending to suffocate, he gasps, "Air! Gimme air!"

"We'll get plenty of air, Manu," quips Jean. "That's why we're moving out."

Whereas by day the Marais, straddling the 3rd and 4th arrondissements, may seem like a preserve, at night the ghetto subdivides into countless enclaves, each of which hosts its own special crowd. Some establishments recruit on the basis of a given preference within the homosexual preference. Most of them appeal to fans of leather and what was long called *amour vache* (nasty sex) but is now given the more technical

191

term of S&M. (Some people also say *sado-maso*, but that sounds a little provincial.) Other divisions are based on age. Once past forty, if you haven't devoted sufficient time and money to ward off the effects of age, you'd be advised to have a drink in some places rather than others. It's not that you'd be turned away, but certain ways of dropping the gaze equal dismissal. Social milieu leads to further distinctions. One bar features designer jeans, cashmere sweaters, and pricey deck shœs. Another draws a crowd with a master's degree or better. A third, in contrast, is where sales assistants and hairdressers gather. The fourth is described as a rendezvous for twerps— which means you'll mostly meet middle-class forty-some-things who like to have a drink after leaving the office, still in suit and tie. Yet another, located over in the Opéra *quartier*, is mentioned with sad irony as the place where old people gather—meaning fifty-somethings (and even worse) who've forgotten they ever had abdominals.

Accompanied by three young men from the Marais, all with fine bodies and younger than me by a generation—who enjoyed serving as my guides by convincing themselves they would have some fun at my expense, and who dubbed them-selves my "bodyguards"—I spent a certain number of nights roaming a distinct number of establishments in and around the holy rectangle of the ghetto. Given the mismatch in our ages, we were never completely at home anywhere. At one place people were amazed—silently but perceptibly—by these three dolphins escorting a killer whale. At another, we were made to feel it was hardly seemly for a man who is "stale" (which the dictionary defines as "having lost freshness while still being fit for consumption") to draw in his wake not one but three choirboys who didn't even seem to be gigolos (who, for that matter, would have been as unwelcome as my trio of sherpas).

Nothing aggressive, though. In these establishments every-thing—or almost—is expressed with the eyes. A simple shutting down, a silent message to make you realize you could never become one of the regulars, whose habits you happen to be disturbing. There was even a bar where the entrance of our foursome brought conversation to a halt and turned more than one head. That was because, while following my mateys, I'd been filling one of the pipes I always keep at hand, which I stuck between my teeth as we arrived; the use of this pleasure device was apparently perceived as a declaration of nonconformity to the mores of the occupants of the place. This impression was confirmed a few nights later when, still guided by the same team, I showed up at the door of an establishment famous for its "foaming parties." (For astronauts, spelunkers, submariners, laborers on offshore oil rigs, and all other people who have long been absent from civilization and its benefits, a "foaming party" means that at about 2:00 A.M. the dance floor is covered with a nontoxic foam. Once the foam, which doesn't hinder breathing, rises over the dancers' heads—and even before—they can take advantage of this cloak to explore other dancers and manually invite them to attain mutual bliss.) We therefore stayed at a marginally quieter bar—where a few statuesque go-go dancers writhed more mechanically than convincingly—until after midnight, and only then headed over to the Tuesday night "foaming party" (the one for men). I let my tugboats join the line with all the other excited, young, fluorescent men, and as much by reflex as to give myself an air of composure, I drew my wretched pipe from my pocket, packed it, and lit it. Just then it was our turn to undergo the scrutiny of the bouncer-cum-appraiser before buying our tickets. He looked at my companions, pointed his finger at me and said to them, "We only take homos!" Obviously, we all swore that we'd come straight from one another's embrace, and I even added that I'd already been to the club before. The appraiser granted us the benefit of the doubt but, after this night-time tour of a Marais dense in ghettos-within-the-ghetto, these two balls-up over the pipe seemed to indi-

193

cate amazingly rigid codes and a naive, almost fetishistic, belief in appearances. Yet this rigidness and this belief struck me as belonging to a mental universe diametrically opposed to the one originally targeted by the gay movement, the one of stereotypes and classifications.

Such as it has always been described in literature, the homosexual universe is a melting pot where encounters occur between individuals whose social backgrounds should have kept them apart. Such as it is developing in the gay Marais, this world of "freely chosen segregation" is a world which not only mimics, but even exaggerates, exclusion based on age, social background, and erotic tendencies, not to mention everything that's done to discourage people not attracted to men from spending a moment there, even if they'd like to enjoy these charming city streets. The establishment of the Marais as an open zone in the late 1970s and early 1980s, a zone free of prejudices, was experienced by many homosexuals as a wonderful advance in the social acceptability of their mores. So doesn't the transformation of that zone into a series of ghettœs-within-a-ghetto constitute a restriction, indeed a rejection, of that freedom?

To this question, my three mateys answered yes, more or less, but that "it's more complicated than that, and anyway the segregation within segregation is not as strict as it might seem to a passing, outside observer, and what's more, there's a general trend in fin-de-siècle Paris for people to seek out the closest of their own kind." Perhaps. And yet, in the course of the exploration they organized for me, every time we halted in one of their regular bars or restaurants, we made ourselves at home and took our time, whereas whenever we visited an establishment that didn't correspond to their profile, they hurried things up and soon suggested we head someplace else.

As to the inevitability of the trend to flock together with birds of increasingly identical feathers, an amusing and friendly chance encounter several months later enabled me to question its veracity (and at the same time introduce my guides to a male meeting place they didn't know). One day, while dawdling in the 10th arrondissement where the Saint-Martin Canal flows, I met Hervé, a teacher in a tough intermediate school outside town and one of the leaders of the valiant and efficient battalion of neighborhood residents fighting to save Square Villemin, located on a bend in the canal at the junction of Quai de Valmey and rue des Récollets. What I immediately liked about my first conversation with Hervé was the way he described the brawl with developers and city hall not in the preachy tone of an activist, but in the same voice normally used to recount a rugby match, carnival, student hazing, or particularly entertaining ruckus. Thirtyish, with lively, pleasant eyes, immediately friendly without being overwhelming, he seemed to represent a rare breed, namely a small guy who isn't afraid of the big guys and who doesn't need authorization from any clique or dogma to say and do what he thinks is right. He even had about him an air of a latter-day Gavroche—or Paris scamp—that I despaired of ever finding again.

After our first lunch, eaten in a local workmen's restaurant, Hervé offered to show me the area around the canal, introducing me to a bookseller who was more of a mother hen than a businesswoman, and to the owner of a restaurant (set price menu for FF 42, or $7.50, including a small carafe of wine) who knew her *quartier* better than anyone and loved it like her own home. Along the way, Hervé and I continued to make acquaintance and, while crossing Arletty's bridge, he explained that he was not only a defender of Square Villemin and editor of an excellent rag devoted to the 10th arrondissement's past and present, but also the head of a *gai-musette* association. Gay dance hall? *Kézaco*, I queried in old Paris slang: "Come again?"

"I'm attracted to guys," he answered, "and to meet them I'd go to nightclubs every now and then, like a lot of people. I didn't much like the music they played there, and even less the dance floors where everyone shudders and shakes all alone, mostly dancing with their own reflections in the mirror. I was looking for a place where you can take a guy in your arms, and everything that goes with it. I didn't manage to find one, but every time I went out I noticed there were lots of other guys who seemed equally frustrated and were looking for the same thing. So I had the idea of organizing a dance based on music ranging from the charleston to rock, from the tango to the twist, from slows to waltzes.

"The first dance was such a hit that I repeated it, all the more enthusiastically for having met the guy who I've been living with for two years now. Then we founded a nonprofit association and organized one dance every three months. Word of mouth brought in more and more people, so we rented a large hall and the dance became bimonthly. Now there's one on the first Friday of every month, and all kinds of people come, even straight couples. We've even been asked to organize dancing lessons."

I repeated this news to my Marais guides, who admitted they had vaguely heard of it. They agreed to accompany me there on the next "first Friday of the month." We decided to dine first, but at the early hour of 8:00 P.M., because Hervé advised me not to arrive too late if I wanted to get into the dance hall (located at the very northern tip of the Marais, over by Arts-et-Métiers, and normally frequented by a standard clientele). When we showed up, one of my companions, who constantly predicted that hardly anyone would be there, pointed out that it was only 9:30 P.M. and that we were going to be bored to tears. But there were already at least 200 people inside the hall which, an hour later, had to turn new arrivals away because of safety regulations. On the dance floor twirled couples of every age, every gender, and every color, from forty-year-olds in suits and ties to kids in jeans and tee-shirts, a few eccentrics of various ages, and a goodly number of gentlemen who might have been grandfathers (including a couple of delighted seventy-year-olds who amazed the other hoofers by the grace and skill with which they went from one dance to another). Hervé played the role of disk-jockey, asked people what they wanted, announced the beat, and, from time to time, asked a sidekick to demonstrate the steps to people who lacked a clear idea of them. The general good humor finally infected my companions, who had briefly resisted it, as though an ambiance so good-natured, straightforward, and amazingly natural first confused and perhaps even disappointed them (since it deprived them of the dark, complicated, hidden side of homosexuality). Or as though this melange created an atmosphere so rich that they found it hard to breathe. After having gone over to greet Hervé (tickled pink at proving the success of his operation), I heard a voice call out to me, "So, Monsieur Meyer, doing research or walking on the wild side?" I turned around. It was a recent former student of mine at Sciences Politiques, where he had been not only brilliant and conscientious, but thoroughly conventional. He introduced his friend, and asked me to dance the next rock tune. To this very day I feel ashamed at having turned him down.

On leaving the dance hall, we were given a leaflet. It stated that, "Gay Paris has become uniform in recent years. The same rules apply everywhere—earsplitting decibels, glossy mag fantasies, fleeting encounters, and, in the end, a type of exclusion and sectarianism: girls on one side, guys on another; straights forbidden; over-thirty-fives not admitted unless weightlifters; techno fundamentalism, etc. Meanwhile, AIDS is decimating our ranks, defying us. We have decided to resist by promoting the spirit of *gai-musette*. This spirit is growing from dance to dance. Our parties bring together people of every kind. Young dance with old. Straight friends come along. Some people invite colleagues from work, others bring along their neighbors from across the landing. A particularly warm atmosphere occurs every time we dance a farandole, the Madison, the French cancan, or a carpet dance. What's more, dancing with a partner makes it easier to meet people. All these happy moments seem like precious gifts, and convince us that *gai-musette* is on the right track!"

It is probably this reference to possible happy moments that differs so sharply with what I'd felt in the ghetto. Not that Hervé and his friends are simpletons who claim to have found blissful homosexuality. (*Kézaco?* Is there blissful heterosexuality? Where do you find it, who's found the recipe?) But they do their best to give happiness a chance; it's up to everyone to seize that chance. I liked their unforced energy, their openmindedness, their urbaneness, their straightforwardness, their refusal to play the role of the damned of the earth (or of radical subversives). The ghetto is not only stifling and hypocritical, with its activist facade screening all the business and money, it can also be silly, when you see people strutting with such assurance of their almighty worth that you'd think you were at a parade of turkeys. Yet it's the ghetto that remains high-profile, because it's located in the center of town and is thought to be typical of the gay lifestyle. (*Kézaco?* Is there a heterosexual lifestyle? Can you take lessons in it?) And it's a center of town whose vitality is dulled by a ghetto where life became grim and banal even as its buildings were being resurrected.

The banal insipidness of the center of Paris first became apparent on the Right Bank, when Les Halles market was moved and its Baltard pavilions demolished. Then the streets of the 1st and 4th arrondissements were transformed into fashion showcases and tourist obstacle paths, followed by the ghettoization of a Marais whose renovation has been a technical success and a human failure. This Venice-like dulling took a little longer to reach the intellectual quarters of the Left Bank, but most of those bastions will have toppled by the end this century.

Shortly after May '68, Boulevard Saint-Michel was the first Left Bank site to fall. French youth, after having been the object of much worry for a number of weeks, basically emerged as a new market, a veritable Far West. The generation grew to believe—and was convinced by others—that just being twenty wasn't good enough. You had to advertise it. Youth was sold the young look, immediately adopted by anybody who didn't want to seem old. The "Boul' Mich" thus sprouted stores—from Place Edmond-Rostand to Quai des Grands-Augustins—selling external signs of youthfulness, especially the most distinctive of such signs: clothing. At the same time, the Latin Quarter acquired new tourist value—it was the place where a revolution nearly succeeded, where youth almost toppled the established order. Few social or public events have enjoyed such rapid commercial fallout. "It was wild," reported one of the few residents of rue Serpente, "people would stop us on the sidewalk and ask if we knew exactly where 'it' had happened, and if we'd been there. A lot of them were looking for something to photograph. But the few trees that had been ripped up were quickly replaced, even as the boulevard was being paved rather than recobbled, just in case the college students got it into their heads to erect barricades again. And that was what gave two brothers (or two cousins, I forget which, who each had souvenir shops on lower Boul' Mich selling 'May uprising' posters that passed for authentic but were just facsimiles), that's what gave them the idea of selling souvenir cobblestones, cobblestone paperweights, authentic cobblestones. We later found out that many of them were supplied by our son, who roamed the city at night on his scooter, looking for streets under repair, filling his backpack with stones. It provided him with spending money for four or five years."

The Saint-Séverin sector—bounded by the river, Boulevard Saint-Germain, Boul' Mich, and rue Saint-Jacques—was first the victim of a half-repressive, half-electioneering decision to turn it into a pedestrian district. This created a kind of pocket that collected guitar pluckers, panhandling singers, fire-eaters, preachers, and nutcases of all kinds. Visitors found it all very picturesque, residents unbearable. The noise, filth, dope, and constant brawls wound up convincing natives to flee and merchants to sell out as quickly as possible. The process of touristification completed this transformation, so that rue de la Huchette, rue Saint-Séverin, and rue de la Harpe became the heart of a nasty clutter of unscrupulous bars and snack-food joints all drenched in the constant odor of fried and refried oil. Once the suburban RER train network arrived, the drop-outs who hung out at Saint-Michel were replaced by suburban ghetto kids (at least until the newly completed Forum des Halles absorbed them). And with that, the stores on Boul' Mich changed hands and began offering—notably in terms of clothing—merchandise that was increasingly cheap and increasingly uniform.

That was when a reform of the University of Paris led to a decline in the student population—the Sorbonne was henceforth just Paris IV, one of twelve numbered colleges in town, alongside a growing number of universities founded in the provinces, making it less necessary and less common to "head up to the capital" for college. In 1968 and subsequent years, the college in nearby Nanterre became famous and assumed a leading role. In the 1970s, the Sorbonne lost further prestige to the Ecole des Hautes Etudes en Sciences Sociales, located on the other side of the Luxembourg Gardens, on the former site of Cherche-Midi prison. Replacing the final exam system with regular grading and acquisition of course credits (copied from American colleges, with greater or lesser success) led to a profound change in university lifestyle, which began increasingly to resemble a high-school lifestyle, indeed a cramming lifestyle. This change, reinforced by an increased number of hours of mandatory classroom presence, delivered the coup-de-grâce to what had previously characterized a French university student's life—freedom and, fairly often, a carefree attitude. The rise of unemployment did the rest by developing the cult of higher education to an absurd level. People wound up no longer speaking of "a bachelor's degree in literature" or "a master's in law," but "*bac* plus three" or "*bac* plus four," the *baccalaureat* being the high-school certificate and the three or four (or more) being the number of years of university education completed thereafter. College students became higher high school students, increasingly focusing their existence on classroom attendance, becoming mere extras in the life of the neighborhood. The Latin Quarter's day was over.

That left Saint-Germain-des-Prés, a part of the capital that had long combined the charms of history and the glamour of literature and fine arts with a favorable reputation for nonconformism and an aura of youth. Saint-Germain held out longest against the banal uniformization of central Paris because beyond the existentialist scene and the lore that grew around it over the years, this part of the 6th (and tip of the 7th) arrondissement—enclosed like the Great Wall of China by rue du Bac, rue Dauphine, and rue Saint-Sulpice (beyond which lay another world)—long preserved its social and professional specificity. Just as Faubourg Saint-Antoine had been the furniture-makers' *quartier* (traces of which still remain today), Les Halles the courtesans' *quartier* (same comment), Le Mail the center of newspapers and printers, and Les Gobelins that of tanners and dyers, so Saint-Germain-des-Prés is the neighborhood of publishers, books, and ideas. In fact, it covers all or part of four of the city's eighty administrative *quartiers*: the 24th (called Saint-Germain), the 21st (La Monnaie), the southern part of the 22nd (Odéon), and the eastern tip of the 25th (Saint-Thomas-d'Aquin). Some people claim that the area's vocation dates back to the founding of the scholarly Benedictine abbey of Saint-Germain in the mid-sixth century, while others feel it is more reasonable to trace it to the eighteenth century, when the term *éditeur* (publisher) first emerged.

Whatever the case—and whatever one's interest in origins—the neighborhood acquired a solid, substantial personality even though its main business was carried out at home (and therefore barely visible, being concretized only by an unusual density of bookstores). It had nothing to do with the Latin Quarter in the 5th arrondissement, which was the realm of professors, that is to say members of an institution that defined beauty, decreed the truth, indicated what had to be learned, and announced what was officially acceptable. Instead, here was a republic of those who discuss, dispute, and speak in their own name alone. Over there was a corporate body, here a jumble of atoms. There, everyone was supposed to contribute to the success and glory of the alma mater; here, it was everyone "out on his own," happy loners pursuing their own dreams. This contrast is exaggerated, of course, but that's how people perceived and desired it. It was possible, obviously, to go from one realm to another; professors published things other than scholarly works, and writers could earn a living by accepting a university chair. But travel in one direction or the other was usually accompanied by a pseudonym, underscoring the separation between the official and the personal.

Simul et singulis, "Together and Alone," the motto of the troupe of actors comprising the Comédie-Française, might also apply to Saint-Germain-des-Prés. This well-bred individualism—that is to say one which tries to preserve the city's charm by respecting a code of urbanity—marked the neighborhood and above all the population, which included not only publishers and retailers but all the trades involved in making books: printers, graphic designers, binders, stitchers, remainderers, illustrators, drawers, engravers, translators, copy-editors, layout artists, salespeople, agents, go-betweens of every ilk, autograph sellers, used-book sellers, book stall owners, etc. Around this polymorphous tribe clustered other "intellectual workers," including, obviously, professors, filmmakers, photographers, and actors. I'm not claiming that this crowd—whether intellectuals, publishers, or artists—is in any way God's gift to humanity. In fact, when writers gang up they are definitely to be avoided. Luckily, they are fish who prefer to swim alone or in small groups rather than in schools. They therefore leave only light, barely perceptible traces in Paris. Furthermore, like everyone targeting a highly personal goal, they display an egotism—sometimes even egocentrism, indeed egomania—perfectly suited to Paris, whose motto is "everyone for himself." People who are convinced of their own self-importance, who are self-sufficient, and who prefer the company of texts to that of fellow citizens don't bother others much. Except when a writer feels that fellow citizens are not doing him justice, are balking at buying his output, and are stingy in their tributes (when tributes there are). In this case, the writer (or artist) changes into a madman, although he saves the spectacle of his excessive outrageousness for his publisher and friends: the former he insults, the latter he hits—then switches; he drinks himself into a complete stupor; he telephones at all hours of the day on a new whim; he threatens instant infidelity; he struggles to reconstruct the thread of the plot which is preventing his rise, the jealousy which is belittling his work; he begs for prizes and, if he receives one, grovels to attain higher status by being invited to join a jury. He maligns, slanders, lies, stabs in the back, courts, copies, and steals. He fears newspapers, and avidly gleans fabricated information on the sex lives of his colleagues, passing these details on with an added bit of dirt. He constantly weighs up the influence of various people, and has no horizon other than his own navel. "Let's not talk about me! What'd you think of my book?" This thumbnail sketch has been attributed to so many writers that it must depict them all (except the author of these lines, miraculously vaccinated at birth against all of the flaws reviewed above).

All these shameful turpitudes remain unobtrusive, however, since they only affect the tiny professional scene. Because of or despite them, writers and artists still are the people via whom ideas and styles are developed and transmitted; modes of expression and talents are conjoined, challenged, or fertilized; and commonplaces are revitalized. There's no disputing that it would be better if all writers and artists died (myself excepted), leaving neither widow nor family, so that we would have to deal only with their works, with their best side. Unfortunately, every period is obliged to put up with a certain quotient of living writers; in order to survive frequent encounters with such vile beings, there's nothing like constantly maintaining the distinction between talent and character, work and person. Social life has a tendency to confuse them, but since it always—or almost always—does so by attributing the character of the talent to the artist, and the quality of the work to the person, it comes down to the same thing. That, moreover, is what sustains the fine and noble utopia subtending life in the Saint-Germain-des-Prés *quartier*.

It should also be acknowledged that intellectuals, essayists, novelists, and—to a more limited extent—journalists display a real curiosity about what's happening in their world. This could be attributed to the fact that Saint-Germain long hosted a profusion of cabarets (which nurtured so many marvels), galleries (where so many risks were taken), and hundreds of other spots where ideas and plans were hatched, where lasting friendships and solid appreciations were formed. It is important to avoid judging a *quartier* by the biggest premises on the biggest street. The general public is familiar with the names of four or five publishers currently (or recently) based in Saint-Germain-des-Prés. Yet as many as 420 publishers have been listed in the 6th arrondissement, with another 208 in the 7th. I lived for a while above one of them, whose rather narrow display window presented just a few of the publisher's books—those with the most "general" appeal: *The Motif of the Tree in Paul Valéry's Poetry; Short Sentences in Montaigne's Oeuvre; The Life and Work of Raymond Poisson, Actor and Poet;*

Time and Narrative in the Work of Sébastien Brossard; The Rhythm and Melody of Literary Phrasing in the Work of Monsignor Félix-Antoine Savard, etc., etc.

That particular publisher, like so many others huge or tiny, is no longer to be found in Saint-Germain-des-Prés, yet it is he who embodied everything concerning the literary neighborhood, more than Gallimard, Fayard, or Flammarion. Or rather, it is he who embodied everything about Gallimard, Fayard, and Flammarion. It is he who best expressed the small publisher's role of gold-prospector, and the lack of consideration to be expected from society. People whose only image of the publishing world comes from writers who make it onto TV cannot understand what Saint-Germain-des-Prés was like, any more—perhaps even less—than people who watch the Five Nations Rugby Tournament or *temporada* bullfights on TV can imagine what rugby or the *afición* mean to little villages where they're an everyday affair, where fame begins when you become known in the neighboring town.

Just as, when it comes to periodicals, the major dailies and weeklies are like isolated trees that hide the forest of prosperous specialized and trade publications, so in book publishing, major literary publishers mask their colleagues who come under one of the 106 publishing categories that run from Art to Zoology via Esoteric, Regional, and Spiritual. Saint-Germain-des-Prés was *their* turf.

"When I was transferred to the 6th arrondissement," recounts a former police inspector, "I was only moderately pleased. I'd already 'done' many arrondissements known to be lively, not necessarily from a criminal standpoint, but in terms of personality—the 18th, the 11th, the 16th, the 10th, the 20th, and the 9th. I didn't have much of an idea of what the 6th would be like except for Brasserie Lipp, Les Deux Magots, Café Flore, Le Drugstore, and streetwalkers (who were becoming scarce by that time). But in the end it was the arrondissement I was sorriest to leave. First of all, I was struck by the residents' welcoming attitude, and by their sense of identity. They made a point, as you got to know them, of letting you know that they were Germanopratins and that the world was divided into Germanopratins and everybody else. Don't be mistaken, they weren't being arrogant or contemptuous. They just felt luckier than everybody else. Not because they enjoyed particular wealth or an especially pretty section of Paris—after all, there are much prettier ones—but because they enjoyed a special lifestyle. As the months and years went by, I realized they were right and I began to feel it myself.

"Saint-Germain functioned at a different rhythm, a different pace. Maybe because a lot of people did jobs that weren't characterized by urgent deadlines. In publishing, some books are talked about for so long that you're amazed when they finally appear. And then there were lots of upmarket craftsmen—framers, binders, people who have more than just business relationships with their customers—whose lives were enhanced by the work they did.

"The local police station was therefore the focus of collective initiatives relating to everyday problems, like changing parking regulations, modifying the direction of a one-way street, or requesting the closure of a street one evening in order to hold a neighborhood festival. Many store owners would get together to organize special days featuring this or that, and it was all pretty lively and enthusiastic. I'm not saying there weren't local feuds, too, but I'd say they were Italian-style feuds, more theatrical and loudmouthed than lastingly hostile.

"You know, there's an anecdote I always tell when I talk about the 6th. In every arrondissement I was stationed, there were always problems over noise. Whenever someone had a gathering or housewarming party, other residents in the building would begin calling us at 10:00 P.M. Everyone thought it was the hour when making a racket became illegal, although in fact it's at any time. We'd politely answer that we had more serious work to do—which was often true—and advised the callers to go ask for quiet themselves. They did no such thing, of course, but they'd call back half an hour later to claim it had done no good, asking us to intervene again. So we'd usually give in and send a car over. Every time, we asked the troublemakers to simply have the kindness, the next time they held a bash, to warn the rest of the building. In the best of cases, this led to a handwritten sign in the entrance hall or elevator. But in Saint-Germain, I was soon struck by how few calls we got for incidents of this type. I carried out a little investigation and learned that when people planned a party, not only would they go in person to tell their neighbors, but often they invited them—and a lot accepted. I wouldn't say the majority, but a lot of them. In Paris! Hey! For me, it was a neighborhood of courteous, relaxed individuals unconcerned about their reputation, status, or social conventions."

A good many of these "courteous individuals" have moved on. For one simple reason: money. Here, too—why should it be otherwise?—property speculation by banks and insurance companies did its work, only to backfire on them later. Saint-Germain was a highly attractive neighborhood. By the 1970s, business executives in the service sector wanted to give themselves a cultural veneer. Publishing and related professions were probably pleasant jobs, but the level of wages, even at the top, couldn't compare with what you could get in high-tech service fields, where salaries were easily three or four times higher. The demand was sufficiently strong and deep-pocketed to prompt people to sell out, one after another. Property fever swelled this stream into a river, then into a torrent. More than one publisher, for that matter, played along: some couldn't resist the desire to make money on their buildings, while others had to sell to amortize heavy losses incurred by investments in television. Still others greatly expanded by swallowing up competitors who had poorly anticipated developments in the book market; once they were big, these companies began spitting terms like "corporate logic," "synergy," and "rationalization." They wanted to have everyone right under hand, and moved out to the 13th, 15th, or 8th arrondissements. It was as though "publishing" no longer referred to the same trade, and they wanted to underscore this change by leaving the old neighborhood. Old, and therefore clearly old-fashioned.

Then things ran their course as they had on the Right Bank, around Place des Victoires and the Marais district. It was just that the pace was slower. After the real-estate crash, many apartments remained empty, others became *pieds-à-terre*. Schools closed, sometimes after a lot of skirmishing. The confounded rag trade gained more ground, swallowing up shops. Then came a series of thunderbolts: one after another, it was announced that Le Drugstore and its movie theater were to be replaced by an Italian clothier, that the record store would yield to a very chic jeweler from rue de la Paix, that the bookstore on the corner of rue Bonaparte and rue de l'Abbaye would be replaced by another clothier (French, this time), and that half a shop specializing in medals, jewels, trophies, and cups would be taken over by a luxury luggage maker who up till then had stuck to Avenue Montaigne and Avenue Marceau.

The near-simultaneity of these transformations created a shock. People realized that it wasn't the beginning, but rather the end, of a process, a process whose first sign had been the arrival of none other than Le Drugstore, mourned today even though it represented the first veritable violation of the spirit of the place, the first alien incursion into this *quartier* of frivolous students and never-gonna-grow-up adults, the arrival of Scrooge in the land of Peter Pan. Through an ironic twist of fate, at the very moment these lamentable things occurred, the Bibliothèque Historique de la Ville de Paris held an exhibition tracing the life and wholehearted fame of the city's cabarets. The show pointed out that the last cabaret disappeared from the Left Bank (rue de Seine) in the mid 1970s. It also revealed that these establishments—so gloriously entertaining and rich in budding stars—had not folded for want of new talent, but through the combined effects of systematic administrative persecution in the name of safety regulations and increasingly voracious national health taxes. Starting with that hemorrhage, night life in Saint-Germain-des-Prés was slowly but surely bled dry. People became worried, took action, and founded no fewer than six preservation associations whose main activity involved criticizing and disparaging each other, even as they bragged about collecting more famous signatures than the other organizations. Sometimes, however, they managed to grouse in unison. But very late in the day.

The first clear sign that the *quartier* was turning had already occurred several years earlier. It concerned the new Saint-Germain market, a covered market hall built on the site of the fair founded by Louis XI and housed in a rather graceful early-nineteenth-century edifice. First slated for demolition, it was saved by a coalition of residents who obtained its renovation. The work lasted so long that most of the saviors had moved away by the time the new market was inaugurated; they were thus spared the bitterness of seeing an expression of the city's natural vitality become petrified and silly. So silly that it should figure in Paris guidebooks, sociology textbooks, and architecture manuals as a crowning illustration of how late twentieth-century vanity ravaged trade in the capital. Ordinary stores were not entitled to set up under the new market. A few food stalls were admitted, but in as little space as possible and as chic as can be—a wine cellar and a caterer, but no butcher or tripe seller. Most of the new "galleries" were allotted to boutiques, twenty-one in number: ready-to-wear clothes, lingerie, shœs, accessories, leather goods, jewelry, gifts, perfume, a hairdresser, a beauty parlor. Nothing but good, classy trade. Nothing but image-conscious stores. The floor was paved with bathroom tiles. Display windows rose to the ceiling, all identical, all aligned, and all featuring designer objects arranged by professional decorators. All had lacquered ceilings with recessed halogen lighting. Music played throughout the building from nearly invisible speakers—the same airport-type muzak that dribbles into travelers' ears from one travel hub to another across the globe. Even the fruit-and-vegetable man was contaminated by this super-promotion of trade into a high-tech profession: his fruit was aligned straighter than the Garde Républicaine and more groomed than their horses. And when it came to his vegetables, everything was done to make you forget the fact they were extracted from the earth (not to say mire) or plucked from branches exposed to every wind. The eggplants seemed polished with a chamois cloth, the tomatœs looked varnished, the leeks must have been scrubbed with a tooth brush and the potatœs were so well turned out that they were handled with a surgeon's gloves in order to avoid dirtying them. There's no chatting—much less calling out from one stand to another—in this new, sterilized market. Whispering, confiding, murmuring, and twittering are more suited to what still bears the ordinary label of market but which will probably be soon dubbed a "commercial transaction mall" named after some famous figure who preferably had nothing whatsœver to do with merchandizing. Since the neighborhood now has more pretensions to culture than places where culture develops and thrives, I wholeheartedly suggest dubbing it the "Henri Michaux Commercial Transaction Mall." (Or maybe René Char. But above all, "Transaction" must be left in the singular. It's classier.)

When it comes to markets, for that matter, the 6th arrondissement can pride itself (or shame itself) on hosting the two most extreme examples of fin-de-siècle modernity: the pretentious funerarium described above and the "organic" market on Boulevard Raspail, where city-dwellers cluster in a dense crowd to pay weekly and costly tribute to nature. The cider sold there is 3.2 times more expensive than it is where it was produced; household soap is retailed in the form of chips scented with honeysuckle or enriched with wheat germ; spicy sauerkraut is advertised as "old-style" and sold by a mustachioed man whose whiskers have prospered thanks to some pigeon's organic turds; the macaroni is whole-wheat and lives next to a salad of spelt and lentils in sesame oil, soy sauce, groats, and black beans (looking a little shabby, as though it might not make it through the winter). There you can buy sheepskin slippers, vests of the same ilk, unprofaned honey, Indian candles (to be stuck in the ear, which they clean as they burn, by creating a vacuum effect), slimming cream, jars of pumpkin-and-chestnut soup, eau de Cologne made the way it was on the banks of the Rhine when the French captured the city in 1794, potatoes and carrots dark with earth (as though proving they belong to the natural order), and even fish which apparently—given their presence in this sacred place—swam only in organic waters. Also sold at the market are intellectual tomes like *Cosmic Imagination, A Wealth of Squash, Spasmophilia Explained and Cured by Etiokinesiology, Lunar Ecology, Biological Rhythms, Nature and Progress,* etc.

Whereas the retailers cultivate a "green" look, their many customers often project a casual preppy image: corduroys, English shoes, Irish sweater, jacket in twill or leather, plaid cashmere scarf, plus cap or hat "made in Connemara." Parked on the sidewalk are their minivans, mini-Jeeps or powerfully engined playthings in original—but manufactured—colors. The outfit lacks nothing. The image is "playful yet responsible." Saint-Germain's population of "modest intellectuals" (like "modest farmers" of yesteryear) has been replaced by this crowd which marches to external signs the way people used to march to the sound of guns.

That is what fully hit home when the chic jeweler, famous fashion designer, and classy luggage dealer moved into the heart of Saint-Germain-des-Prés: all the *quartier* has left to offer is a sign, an appearance, an "air," a trompe-l'œil effect. It hardly matters how superficial that sign is, since it is aimed mainly at passing customers who barely scratch the surface of things (if only for lack of time). "It's culture that brings added value to an area these days," I was told by the manager of one of these new showcases in Saint-Germain, who added, "it's an international fact." He should have said, "a *whiff* or *recollection* of culture." Destined to become the Faubourg Saint-Honoré of the Left Bank and fated, like that fashionable avenue, to lose its population as standardization sets in, the Saint-Germain neighborhood will surely retain a few specimens of its former activity and its former population, as is the case at Place des Victoires, Les Halles, and the Marais over on the Right Bank. After all, Paris won't be unbuilt in a day.

If necessary, the new "upscale" outlets will find a way to subsidize or support a few examples of the *quartier's* former way of life. Unless they simply buy them up—what's the annual revenue of a publisher, even a major one, compared to that of an international firm selling haute couture, perfume, and jewelry? It will be important to maintain the area's "added value." The center of Paris hardly needs inhabitants. Just a few will do, but with strong purchasing power. The clientele actually targeted by the trade in luxury items or "fancy goods" is a passing one. Sixty million visitors came to France last year, fourteen million of whom passed through Paris. It is with them in mind that Mercury, the god of commerce who has always made and unmade cities, has remodeled the center of the capital. In selling tourists a movie set, and in offering what remains of its residents a stage on which to parade, the heart of Paris has been turned to stone.

Parisian Daze

It was inevitable. And now it's irreversible. Those are the two main arguments used by the city's policy planners and decisionmakers when confronted with the petrification of the heart of Paris. "France," they explain, "may have mastered all the latest inventions and techniques, but the rest of the world still sees us as the land of luxury, courtship, elegance, festivities, and art—with Paris as its showcase. This is true not only for the majority of people who have only recently been authorized to leave their countries and take vacations abroad, it's even truer of people who see us from afar and know us only in terms of broad outlines and general stereotypes, the same way we know them. That's the case with Asians, who are destined to become an increasingly large part of the army of tourists. People are looking for an image. So it's stupid, pointless, and even dangerous to try to sell them a different one. Paris is a straightforward product. You'd be surprised to see how market studies all over the world show that people describe it in the same way, almost in the same words. You have to know how to exploit that strength.

"As to changes in the composition of Paris's socioprofessional population, notably in the center of town, that's a worldwide phenomenon. Even as city-dwellers' incomes have risen, their lifestyles have become increasingly individualistic. Now that economic upheaval has wrecked so many social traditions, they're more concerned and more demanding about the quality of housing and facilities in which they've holed up. When it comes to urban values, they favor individualism, which for that matter is a basic part of French—and especially Parisian—mentality. When it comes to bringing some life to the city, you might say that tourists have taken over from the residents."

If I had to down a bottle of wine every time I heard these slick sociological generalizations, doctors would be lobbying me to leave my liver to science. But simply repeating rubbish and lies, even with a great deal of conviction, doesn't make them true. It's not true that the centers of major cities are changing like Paris—just go to London. Or New York. Just try to find a city, comparable to Paris, where so many apartments remain unoccupied. Just name another capital city where the municipal authority itself owns such a high proportion of real estate, such a high proportion of housing. Just cite a city where municipal government buys up so many buildings.

As to Paris's reputation for elegance, dissipation, arts, and night life, it may still sell in Tokyo, Seoul, Beijing, or Taipei, but maybe not for long, to judge by its rating in Europe and North America. What new artists have surfaced in Paris, which is no longer even a major art market for works of any period? How many great fashion designers have recently sprouted on the banks of the Seine, compared to Milan and London? What is Paris night life next to a night spent in the British capital? Even in Barcelona, people have more fun in a wider variety of ways. It's one of Paris's peculiar features to have deported its working class to increasingly distant suburbs without managing to encourage the truly wealthy to stay or move in! These days the city offers neither working-class dance halls nor exclusive bashes.

There is, nevertheless, still a handful of professionals who organize grand festivities. Some of them have been working

214

in the capital for decades, and they all provide the same "market analysis." Says one: "Marie-Hélène de Rothschild, who died in 1995, was the last Parisian to keep alive the tradition of throwing parties for fun. These days some grand society receptions are still organized for the wedding of a financier's daughter or the coming-out party of an industrial heiress, but the vast majority of parties with panache are merely PR operations by major firms, who foot the bill. « Useful" guests are invited. Some payoff is expected—it's all coordinated with advertising policy. People want to create a "coherent image," they don't even think of having fun, much less a blast. They *communicate*. And they're bored stiff. Only the lower classes and aristocrats know how to spend a bundle. Only the likes of Pierre Fresnay and Jean Gabin in *The Grand Illusion* know how to let themselves go. The working classes now live beyond the beltway, while aristocrats and their modern counterparts all live in Geneva or London or God knows where. Paris is a Mecca for the middling bourgeoisie, a species that counts its money and spends only when it can be put on the expense account.

"In his memoirs, Jean-Louis de Faucigny-Lucinge recalled that when his mother was planning a ball, her secretary drew up a list of guests on which she discovered the name of a glamorous jeweler on Place Vendôme. The princess crossed the jeweler off the list and said to her secretary, so that he would remember the lesson: 'Never any tradesmen!' These days, it's just the opposite. The Jockey-Club set seeks invitations from 'tradespeople' and enthusiastically agrees to play walk-on roles in PR operations."

The clientele of grand hotels in Paris displays the same tendency. Much of the hotels' income comes from oil sheiks (rather than from some Baron de Gondremarck out of an Offenbach operetta). Yet that clientele is known for living within a closed circuit. "This year," reports the head of one grand hotel, "we had fourteen suites and sixty-three rooms occupied by a Qatari princess and her entourage for six weeks. A week before her arrival, ten trucks delivered twenty-two tons of luggage. For seventy-two hours, we moved furniture and installed clothes racks and chests of drawers in certain bedrooms that were to be used only as dressing rooms. One of the salons was requisitioned to store the luggage, all in crocodile skin. The princess arrived at night, veiled, with her cortege of friends and retainers. I took her up to her floor and never saw her again. Hotel staff gave everything to one or another of her servants, and was forbidden to enter the bedrooms. In the kitchen, we always had to keep a chef on duty to respond to any request at any time: cold apple juice at 5 A.M., a sherbet at 2 A.M., or soft-boiled eggs. The princess never left her rooms. She had a magnificent video unit set up, and brought hundreds of cassettes. Her husband came to spend one day with her. Nor did her attendants go out. When the princess wanted to make some purchases, the fashion designer or jeweler was summoned, and then had to deal with a kind of all-powerful matron, who was also veiled. Everyone left one night, and the trucks came to pick the tons of luggage, which had multiplied."

"From April to October," said the manager of another hotel of similar reputation, "we had a whole floor reserved by a Saudi princess and some of her children. Their servants got down to work a week early, with piles of luggage. The princess had 150 pairs of shoes for herself alone. Or rather 300, since there was a spare set of everything, absolutely everything. Half had to be placed in the closets, while the other half remained in the chests in order to be ready for an instant departure. The servants set up everything—when the princess and children arrived, clothes were in the wardrobes and commodes, pajamas and nightshirts were on the beds, and playthings were on the edge of the bathtub. A ground-floor salon was set aside to store the things bought in Paris—and there was a lot of it!

216

"The princess and her people led the same lifestyle for six months. In the evening, rather late, they'd go dine at a Lebanese restaurant. Then they went to some nightclub or other with the older children and a lot of bodyguards. When they danced, the bodyguards stationed themselves around the dance floor, but in a sufficiently discreet way so that no one was bothered. Then they returned to the hotel. More than once, one of the princess's attendants let us know that she wished to buy something from a jeweler's or dressmaker's despite the very late hour. We knew how to contact the store manager and, at 2:00 A.M., advised him that he'd better get cracking and open up the store. He didn't balk, given the bills he subsequently sent us to pass on. I can't reveal any details, but just to give you a rough idea, their food bill ran to 200,000 francs ($35,000) for a single day.

"They practically never deviated from this circuit. The princess would get up about 5:00 P.M. Once, the kids went to Disneyland. Two Rolls-Royces and two Mercedes with bodyguards. Since they had tutors, one of my assistants asked a tutor if he wanted any information regarding concert halls, museums, or movie theaters. The tutor kindly declined the offer. When they left us, in the early fall, they were heading for a grand hotel on the Riviera."

The change in clientele at the grand hotels is hardly a social tragedy, any more than the death of high-society parties. Yet it's another sign and another element in the devitalizing banalization of Paris, which people now treat like a Club Med vacation village. Unlike the cosmopolitan millionaires who preceded them, the new regulars at swanky hotels entertain no relationship to Paris, except to increase the flow of money pouring through it. The city offers them only a change of scenery and a chance to spend money. Nor can it expect anything from them in return. Here again, Paris has been reduced to the status of stage set or symbol.

A symbol all the more tenuous and distant for the eleven million visitors to EuroDisney, rechristened Disneyland

Paris. Although years of financial difficulty have made the management of this amusement park parsimonious with information, it's well known that a growing majority of Mickey's customers don't spend the night in the capital. Nor do they even pass through, since the park now has its own high-speed train station and airport links. For that matter, fewer and fewer tour operators who "sell" Disneyland now include Paris. They prefer to offer either other European cities, or other destinations in France that can be "done" within a day's bus ride from the Disney hotels (Loire chateaus head the list). The international press concurs, alluding to Paris as a museum of urban life (*Newsweek*), a city without a soul (*The Independent on Sunday*), or even "a city in its last gasps" (*Gazeta Wyborcza*) where "nothingness reigns in the streets" (*Süddeutsche Zeitung*).

This dulling of Paris was in no way inevitable, but rather the outcome of a series of urban development decisions and policies. In no other industrialized capital has development and change been so dependent on national and municipal governments (and their bureaucracies). The transformation now affecting us began with a master plan drawn up by the government in the mid 1960s and increasingly pursued into the mid 1990s. The decisions that led to the departure of Paris's working-class population were public decisions. Meanwhile, the unbridled speculation in the late 1980s, which delivered the final blow to the city's vitality by fundamentally affecting the population, was mainly a ballet of fools and thieves in bank and insurance firms, led by state-controlled corporations monitored by the Ministry of Finance. Real-estate tax laws contributed to—and continue to contribute to—the transfer of an ever-growing number of buildings and apartments from private ownership to the "institutional" sector. Meaning to the city administration itself, which now owns 13 percent of the housing stock and 50 percent of the land. It is also landlord to 300,000 tenants. None of this municipal wealth goes to the least fortunate Parisians who, on the contrary, were asked to make way for the middling bourgeoisie that emerged from the postwar economic boom. The city subcontracts management of 3,600 stores and rents 14,200 business premises. And the national government claims its share along the way—it owns over 2,800 of the 55,000 "solely owned" buildings in the capital; back in 1935, it owned a mere 362. By buying heavily in the historic center to upgrade its administrative offices, the government has strongly contributed to the city's petrification. Even private transactions are subject to political pressure. "In 1996," recounts a real-estate agent, "I had an unusual deal—a private mansion with garden right in the center of town. Something that comes up only once in a career, if you're lucky. I immediately received bids, including two pressing offers from an Italian financier and an English industrialist. In the time it took me to set one bid against the other, I received a visit from somebody at the foreign office who told me that a royal prince from the Middle East wished to acquire "my" mansion, and I was strongly urged to sell to him. Which I did, without losing any money, for that matter. It was clear that if I wanted to avoid having tax inspectors on my doorstep...."

Ever since the 1977 reform that endowed Paris with an elected mayor, city management has been constantly burdened by that mayor's nationwide political ambitions, reducing the capital to a launching pad that doubled as a cash cow. The scandals that erupted in the 1990s (and probably many others which haven't surfaced) showed just how the renovation of various arrondissements served as a magnificent source of "phynance."

Less thoroughly investigated (and even less indicted) is the issue of how one political party's grip on Paris has actually altered its population. And yet it just so happens that over 80 percent of the buildings—both old and new—in the city's "portfolio" are located in former working-class arrondissements. Pork-barrel construction and renovation contracts spurred "contributions" to the ruling RPR party. Allocation of the housing itself, meanwhile, was based on two criteria—personal patronage and the goal of turning Paris into a bastion of the "managerial bourgeoisie" which political theorists identified—correctly, as the past twenty years have proven—as a reservoir of conservative, mainly RPR party, voters. Paris has not only been "cleansed" of plebeians, it has been the object of a veritable repopulation scheme conducted by former mayor Jacques Chirac and his crowd, much the way gardeners or forest wardens might decide to thin a little bit here, replant there, and add new plants and varieties where desirable. Thus a certain species—formerly one among many—has emerged and thrived: the neo-Parisian. The scientific sociology of this species has yet to be written, but its broad lines appear from its basic ethnology. Which, at any rate, makes it possible to hazard a portrait of *Homo neo-parisiensis.*

Wherever observed, encountered, or overheard, a neo-Parisian whines (in the same way a hoopœ hoots, a camel roars, a stag bells, and a jay warbles). His speech is one long, multifaceted, unending lament. First of all, he regrets the disappearance of—Parisians. Or more exactly, of the street urchins known as *Parigots.* He complains, mourns, and sometimes even rages that working-class scamps (not always on the up-and-up) are no more to be seen loitering in streets or squares, or heard talking in the drawling, rolling, mocking accent so often exemplified in black-and-white flicks by actors like Raymond Bussière and Julien Carette. Ever since he's arrived in the capital, the neo-Parisian has vainly sought these characters with their caps cocked over one ear, cigarette butt dangling from the mouth, bottle of cheap red wine and a sausage in their bags. Nor has the neo-Parisian seen any brash females (personified on-screen by Arletty and Suzy Delair) with their ready wisecracks, upfront feelings, unashamed flirtatiousness, and refusal to be fooled by their men or by mankind; the neo-Parisian expected to hear their quips fly from the doorways and shops of his *quartier*. He longs for those Piafs, Fréhels, and Sauvages who sang of the splendor and nastiness of Paree, backed by an accordionist who fortified himself with a "glass of red." I've heard it said a hundred times if I've heard it once: "It's unbelievable how there are no Parisians left!" And in vain I've tried to point out to my interlocutors that this absence can be explained by their very own presence. That even if they weren't living in one of the new buildings that replaced the dumps housing all those missing *Parigots*, then they lived in a "renovated" or "refurbished" apartment carved out of what had been two or even three little flats, each formerly occupied by a whole family that has since left for the working-class towns outside Paris. No rational explanation, however, can assuage a neo-Parisian's regret (least of all that particular explanation).

Also heading the list of his disappointments comes the disappearance of bistros. "It's unbelievable how there are no bistros left!" True enough, they've become rarer and rarer, apart from those in the business and tourist districts. When neo-Parisians raise this subject, they open wide the sluice-gates of rhetoric, explaining that the corner bistro is the soul of Paris. That no other city in the world produced such an inspired invention. That it's a place where everyone is equal, where you can meet everyone who brings life to the community. That foreigners envy Parisians their bistros. That some have even tried to copy them but that the copies are just pale, soulless imitations. That many people come to Paris just for its bistros. For the sound of a hardboiled egg cracking on the metal counter of the bar... for the *café au lait*... for the basket of croissants on the counter... for French bread-and-butter... because nothing can replace the savor of things served at the bar. Not to mention the terrace, where you can steal away from work for a moment or two, where you can watch the girls stroll by, where amorous rendezvous are made....

A neo-Parisian is the equal of Demosthenes when it comes to the vanishing bistro. Even Brigitte Bardot, on the subject of baby seals, can do no better; nor can a representative of the Ministry of Culture when defending the greatness of local heritage before a regional commission. So you just have to let the neo-Parisian rattle on. Once he's finished (because even the finest orations must come to a conclusion, which in this case is usually "it's unbelievable!"), encourage him to change the subject. Then, when he's ensconced in another topic of conversation, take him back to the bistro unawares: "You often go to one in your neighborhood?"

"Me?" comes the reply, "never. There's a caf' near work where I go have coffee with people at the office, but around here, no, never."

Suggesting that there might be a potential relationship between a lack of customers and the extinction of bistros would not only be pointless, but in poor taste. You'll meet with a better response if you muse out loud that maybe his *quartier* should be endowed with subsidized bistros populated by salaried *Parigots* (even if they have to take the suburban train home to the end of the line every evening).

Neo-Parisians don't go to bistros because they stay at home. In arrondissements that have run the city's redevelopment gauntlet, bank managers at local branches—regardless of bank—can confirm this conclusion. Because when neo-Parisians can afford it—and most of the time, the still-youthful managerial bourgeoisie is flush, especially when it benefits from certain advantageous rents set by the city in its role as landlord—they invest their savings in one of three ways: renovating and furnishing their apartment, buying or fixing up a country home, and saving for retirement. In order to attain these three objectives (to which should be added the kids' extracurricular activities), they restrict their budget for restaurants, concerts, movies, theater, and outings of all kinds. Installed in their apartments (never has the etymology

222

of "apart" been so clear), neo-Parisian households willingly borrow money to improve the bathroom (Jacuzzi tubs heading the wish list) or upgrade the video system. "Home theater" is booming among this crowd, which means buying a giant television with a screen "just like in the movies" and a set of speakers reproducing sound effects each more deafening than the last. (Obviously, neo-Parisians top the list of cable subscribers, satellite subscribers, and Canal Plus subscribers.) From what we know of these new Parisians, it's safe to assert that between their voluntary confinement at home and their enthusiasm for spending weekends in their country houses, they deprive Paris of their actual presence most of the time.

Nevertheless, neo-Parisians do go out from time to time. In order to pursue a quest and dream—the quest and dream of finding Vieux Paris. But since "Old Paree" can no longer be found in Paris (or anywhere else), they collect its vestiges. Anything "retro" is on the uptake. City Hall obliges real-estate developers to keep up appearances, that is to say to retain old facades, even if, behind those facades, they carry out shameless depredations and egregious architectural aberrations. We've lost our soul, so let's save face. Let's not admit that after having failed to respect Paris and the diversity of its population, we're unable to join the list of generations who built this town by expressing a period—our own—through architecture. Or maybe it's just that we don't have anything to say.

This window-dressed urban development, this cardboard Paris, is embodied and echœd by neo-Parisians who flock *en masse* to public places that have escaped refurbishment. Not far from the grim Place de la République there exists a restaurant—long famous and still very expensive—whose walls haven't been repainted since before the war, where smoke and steam have accumulated in successive layers, where a brown cast-iron stove still reigns (I wouldn't swear that brown was its original color), where mirrors have been stricken with a kind of metallic impetigo that has triggered a proliferation of blackish rot, where the imitation-leather benches are on their last legs, where lamps provide intimate lighting despite themselves. This restaurant was long—and to a large extent still is, despite the death of its legendary owner—the place whose address would be murmured among east-coast Americans as a precious secret, a key to becoming one of the "happy few." Such was their image of "authentic Paris"—filthy, uncomfortable, gastronomical, and so very picturesque. And such is today, with only minor differences, the image that neo-Parisians cherish of their city.

Over at La Bastille, or by La Butte-aux-Cailles, near Folie-Méricourt, around Les Quinze-Vingts, at Les Epinettes, Ménilmontant, and Belleville (I'm exhuming all the old neighborhood names, in order not to be outdone when it comes to going retro), the most heavily patronized places are former *bougnats*, coal depots that doubled as cafés, now decked out with their engraved facades, heavy wooden tables, stools of similar ilk, and tiling once covered in sawdust "so that spitters can spit properly." And don't forget that final touch of Parisian authenticity, namely curtains and table-cloths of checked gingham. It's precisely in these vestiges of the past that it's hardest to find a table on weekends (especially in the fashionable nightlife district that has succeeded Les Halles and now runs from La Bastille to Saint-Germain de Charonne via rue Oberkampf and rue de Ménilmontant). That's where neo-Parisians await the ghosts that will restore some life to their city. Or sometimes their search will take them to the dance halls down by the Bastille, where they wind up encountering more of their own kind (everyone having temporarily abandoned worsted fabrics for denim).

A shrewd restaurateur, if unable to lay his hands on such a miraculously preserved setting, will turn to a café-restaurant from the 1950s (although a 1960s version will do). He must then add furnishings, perfecting the atmosphere by scouring flea markets or antique dealers for potbellied juke boxes, table soccer games with real wooden handles, lampshades in molded plastic, etc. The main thing is to add some new to the old. Nothing beats, say, a video store in a former butcher's shop with all its fittings—front grate, high cash desk where the butcher's wife sat, tiles on the walls, and, of course, facade decorated with marble plaques advertising the excellence of the meat once sold there. Such a melange combines the retro element with a touch of ridicule that neo-Parisians confuse with humor, because they don't realize it's an avowal of impotence, something as grotesque as garden gnomes in the countryside.

Nostalgia is an insatiable beast, however, and so neo-Parisians also want Vieux Paris at home. They enthuse over the black-and-white photos—and enchanting they are—by Robert Doisneau, Willy Ronis, Brassaï, and Cartier-Bresson, which they buy in the form of postcards, posters, albums. They can't get enough of images of life in Paris, although it would never occur to them to spend a cent on a color picture taken after 1965. You can sell them pictures of Les Halles market (demolished), the Vaugirard abattoirs (leveled), the Rose palace on Avenue Foch (razed), Montparnasse Station (vanished) the day a steam locomotive plowed onto the sidewalk, or the miniature Bardo palace (evaporated). But there's no question of offering them Beaubourg or the Institut du Monde Arabe, nor even the Louvre pyramid. And above all not the new Bibliothèque Nationale de France or the Bastille Opera House.

This has given birth to a memory industry, a factory of phony recollections. After postcards and posters, books of nostalgia have arrived *en masse*. There is so much demand for such items that one publishing house specializes not just in *Vieux Paris* but in the much narrower niche of Paris in the 1930s and the immediate postwar period. With shrewdness, determination, and talent, writers now specialize in interviewing survivors and prospecting for photographs. The upshot is a series of books, under the "I Remember..."imprint, which attempts to interest Paris in its immediate past, arrondissement by arrondissement. "I Remember the 14th Arrondissement" when it was nicknamed "Little Brittany" and featured Breton festivals, when it still had little huts with farmyards, when you could see writers sitting on the terrace at Le Dôme, painters at La Coupole, filmmakers at Le Sélect, card games being played in courtyards and brass bands performing at the town hall. "I Remember the 15th" when it had a horse market on rue Brancion, the Vél d'Hiv' cycle stadium with its famous six-day race, the elevated Metro with its arcades where all kinds of itinerant peddlers peddled dreams, when there were fruit and vegetable markets along rue du Commerce, a Negro Dance Hall on rue Blomet, and an "industrial cathedral" of a car factory in Javel, where André Citroën preached progress. "I Remember the 12th" when there was a train station at Place de la Bastille, wine merchants at Bercy, swimmers in the Seine, strolling knife-grinders and bread hawkers on Faubourg Saint-Antoine, and cigarmakers on rue de Charenton. "I Remember the 10th" when the canal was full of barges and people put on their Sunday best to go to a show at the Alhambra. "I Remember the Marais" when it featured Turkish baths on rue des Rosiers, a market at Enfants-Rouges, the Pacra music hall, and chair attendants at Place des Vosges.

But doesn't this gluttony for memories cause indigestion, especially when it's other people's memories you have to swallow? Isn't it poisonous to defrost imported, prettified, dolled-up memories—a postwar Paris without its tuberculosis, or its slums, or the stench of some of its industrial neighborhoods?

Apparently, neo-Parisians scoff at such risks, blithely sweeping aside these objections. Scarcely have they had their fill of an "arrondissement-by-arrondissement" past than they clamor for a citywide past, for a thematic past, for even a passé past. They're well and heartily served: *Chroniques de La Rue Parisienne* offers a glimpse of picturesque tramps far more Parisian than today's dropouts and "homeless," of cape-clad police officers so much kinder than contemporary cops, of fishermen blessed with a lot more luck than their modern counterparts, of painters on Montmartre much more gifted than the current variety, and even of young girls so much more virginal than nowadays. And if that weren't enough, here comes *Les Métiers Oubliés*, about the city's forgotten trades: bootblacks, doughnut sellers, water carriers, old-clothes dealers, streetlamp lighters, vinegar merchants. Then there's *Les Magiciens des Boulevards*: automatons, fortune tellers, animal tamers, barkers, itinerant photographers. Neo-Parisians who value nothing more than law and order even buy retrospective thrills in the form of *Apaches, Voyous et Gonzes Poilus*, a book on "hoods, thugs and tough guys," that is to say on the Paris mob from the early twentieth-century to the 1960s, featuring, in order of appearance, Riton le Tatoué, Pierrot le Fou, Tronde de Gail, Nonœil, René la Canne, Jo Attia, Jacques Mesrine, and the late lamented Antoine Mondoloni (1931-1969). This latter was the only professional killer who never declined a contract, and we wouldn't want to forget the memory of a man endowed with such a modern, professional *at-ti-tude*. Clearly, Paris should think about changing the motto on its crest from *Fluctuat nec Murgitur* (Float, Don't Flounder) to "Advance to the Rear."

As if cherishing an idealized phantom weren't enough, neo-Parisians nurture constant rancor and complaints against the modern city. They scarcely seem aware of internal contradictions—in the same breath they complain of the lack of liveliness and the excessive noise. If it's the noise of a honking horn (whose use is illegal but which the police tolerate); or a store alarm that screams every time a bus goes by, or with a passing crack of thunder; or even strange noises whose cause turns out to be as mysterious as it is unrelated to an attempted break-in, then the complaint is obviously justified. But neo-Parisians get upset by "noise pollution" much less violent and far more human. They telephone the police station because the comings and goings of customers at a nearby restaurant creates a hubbub that bothers them; because a café closes too late (or, in spring, has a bustling terrace where people talk too loudly); because teenagers—in *quartiers* that still have any—hang out in gangs whose commotion sometimes leads to a ruckus, shouting, disputes; because kids are playing soccer in the courtyard or on the sidewalk, thereby disturbing a peaceful session in front of the TV; or because they're going around and around on scooters or, worse, motorcycles; or because Arabs—"I'm no racist, but..." —are holding noisy (and incomprehensible) conversations in the street. But if sound were added to all those black-and-white images of the Paris they so love, neo-Parisians would be stunned—and probably incredulous—to discover the din in the streets in those days, including the racket, yelling, and rows made by the scamps and brats whose portraits they find so touching. Just as country-dwellers welcome the high-speed train as long as its tracks don't come near them, so neo-Parisians want liveliness, friendliness, and gathering places in Paris, but only at a good distance from their own dwelling—otherwise, they're on the phone to the cops. Anonymously, nine times out of ten. And occasionally pretending to be one of their neighbors.

Whereas Captain Cap, a character created by nineteenth-century humorist Alphonse Allais, suggested moving cities to the countryside, neo-Parisians would like to move the provinces into the capital. As towns grow and swell throughout middle France, they strive to match Paris in symbolic grandeur—every mayor of a mid-sized city secretly dreams of having a large theater, a museum of contemporary art, a megamultimedia center, maybe an opera house—whereas in the minds of neo-Parisians there lurks the fantasy of a capital brimming with little public parks (where you can take your dog to urinate), with micro sport centers (where you can keep in shape), with residential zones (where you'll be right at home enforcing draconian rules on quiet, sanitation, and children's games), and with a level of air pollution no higher than in the forests of the Vosges Mountains, the hills of Aubrac, or the plains of Berry. Make no mistake about it, we're talking about the very same neo-Parisians who, when they are owners of a country house, harass local municipal authorities because the church bells ring angelus too early, or go to court because their neighbor's chickens and roosters make such a racket that it's hard to sleep late. These same neo-Parisians take charter flights to New York, where they're dazzled by so much vitality, and to major Third World capitals, whose wonderful liveliness they describe so enthusiastically on their return. One word has traditionally typified Paris and its population, especially since the advent of the industrial era, a word celebrated throughout the entire œuvre not only of Balzac but also of Aragon—"energetic." Whereas typifying the urban ideal of neo-Parisians requires a hard choice between two adjectives—"languid" or "inert."

Not long after the emergence of this synthetic population—the upshot of Chirac's electoral genetic engineering and the deification of the middle classes—Paris saw a new socioprofessional category appear in its midst, known in bureaucratic language as the "cultural service sector." This expression casts an extendable cloak over the standard artistic professions (theater, cabaret, revues, music, movies, visual arts, photography, literature) and adjunct trades (interior decoration, costume design, set design, lighting, sound and technical direction), along with the audiovisual sector and booming businesses such as fashion design, advertising, journalism, public relations, consultancies, "event agencies," and so on. The members of this guild have grown exponentially in the last quarter of the century, and are now estimated to number three or four hundred thousand in France, a significant portion of whom who live in Paris.

The upper crust of these professions—comprising people with steady work and substantial salaries—has not chosen to move to one special neighborhood, as did Hollywood. At the very most it favors a few restaurants, nightclubs, and bars—a given bar in a hotel on Avenue George-V, a Chinese or Italian restaurant in the 8th arrondissement, and so on. The most flamboyant of them, joined by those fluttering around them, have their gathering zones—rue Boissy-d'Anglas, rue Saint-Honoré (for another few months), Les Halles (a while ago). The ambiance of such zones recalls the "fashionable" beaches at Saint-Tropez—locals describe them nicely as "the ball-flexers' rendezvous." But the vast majority of the "cultural service sector" is comprised of seasonal labor (like farming in the old days), that is to say temps and short-term contract hires of every size and stripe who survive by juggling sundry sources of income with unemployment benefits. They are the proletariat of culture, if you take the word "culture" in its widest sense and acknowledge that this proletariat dœsn't actually live in wretched poverty. Below this population of day laborers is a protean group of people who have not yet truly joined the active ranks of these professions and who, while waiting and hoping that their turn will come, are part of the "cultural service sector" on a purely ad-hoc basis. They are culture's subproletariat, living off minimum welfare grants and other subsidies they manage to get, topped up by revenue from "little jobs" usually done off the books.

In theory, the Paris contingent of the "cultural service sector" should turn the capital into a hive of creativity admired and envied throughout the world, starting with Paris itself. And yet the capital's artistic scene actually gives an impression of abundance rather than dynamism, of imitation rather than inventiveness, of stiffness rather than backbone.

In an average week, remaining within the city limits (and therefore within reach of public transportation) you could attend—assuming you were born with the gift of ubiquity—nearly two hundred concerts of all kinds of music, roughly one hundred plays, seventy-five music-hall or café-theater shows, thirty-five cabaret shows, and over one hundred exhibitions (a fifth of which are devoted to photography). Yet the individual productions of these various "cultural sites" are simply juxtaposed; they don't seem to add up, complement, challenge, or echo one another. One theater director who has occasionally shaken up the capital and stirred the Avignon festival quipped, "Paris has become Avignonized." The proliferation of shows has occurred at the expense of the consolidation of a few strong—and usually rivalrous—figures whose productions, confrontations, and disputes used to punctuate the city's artistic scene. The dominant rhetoric of "everything is one hundred percent cultural" has created an artificial ideological equality between various productions, implying that any ranking would lead to disgrace.

There isn't—any longer—any major artistic debate in Paris. Such debate has been replaced by discussion of the well—(or ill—) founded cultural policy being pursued by the government. There's no dispute over trends, tendencies, schools, avant-gardes, and what they all advocate, because there are no longer any trends, tendencies, schools, or avant-gardes. People struggle to reignite a bland debate over public as opposed to private funding, which hinges on subsidies, percentages of the culture ministry's budget, and the awarding of grants. Debate is stifled all the more since, if a voice is raised to ask a question worthy of Hans Christian Andersen's *Emperor's New Clothes*—"Did the public, whose money is being spent, attend? And did it enjoy itself?"—then defenders of official art immediately issue cries of fascism or "revisionism." Paris in the late twentieth century has developed a watchdog mentality that's beginning to resemble McCarthyism. If anyone

231

should express surprise that such a thing as a government-sponsored avant-garde could exist, he or she is denounced as clinging to the past, therefore an enemy of culture, and therefore an "objective" (and retrospective) accomplice of the Nazis. And this is occurring in a city that long passed for witty, frivolous, openminded, and above all curious. Here too, politics has deadened life yet again. No more question of new discoveries, tradition, inventiveness, repertoire; there's only one subject of concern—power, and how to get it. Or get close to it. Follow in its wake. Benefit from its largesse. Paris today has far more courtiers and stipend-holders than Versailles did in the days of Louis XIV. (But how many Molières, Racines, La Fontaines, Mansarts, Le Nains, Mignards, Lebruns, Lullys, Charpentiers, or Campras are there?) Today's artistic scene in Paris reeks of stale school dorms.

Given this collapse of cultural debate—this atomization of production, where all shows are declared free and equal hits (an equality which not all spectators seem to buy), every artist or aspiring artist has to advance blindly. The "Avignonized" Paris scene throws into the street a goodly number of orphans who navigate by dead reckoning, unable to find points of reference with which—or against which—to orient themselves. Meanwhile, the rest (and the bulk) of the troops, who perceive culture above all as a fashionable Eldorado, form patronage cliques that follow their gang leader and flash their switchblades at anyone who threatens their turf. Finally, television has completely razed the landscape, lowering mentalities and providing the arts scene with nothing but demagogic emotiveness, servile zealotry, and a perversely ideological (yet lucrative) buddy-system. Since anything shown on the small screen can supposedly be turned into gold, the less privileged sectors of the cultural proletariat produce dozens of beginners struggling to become clones of "seen-on-TV" celebrities, clambering onto every stage where they hope to be noticed by some foreman in the audiovisual industry. I even witnessed, in an 11th-arrondissement theater, a comic doing a take-off of a mimic—one who'd been featured on TV.

When it comes to arts and entertainment—if you'll excuse me for using those two words in the same breath—Paris is duller than dull. Let's not mention the feather boas in those grand revues where people now only go in organized groups (a company celebrating the millionth garbage-grinder to roll off its production line, or a senior citizens' club on an all-inclusive outing). Let's forget Pigalle (you'll soon be able to find more humanity, spontaneity, and fantasy at Disneyland) with its busloads of Germans who seem to ape actor Francis Blanche aping Germans, or busloads of Japanese who seem to be participating in a *Japanese in Pigalle* episode for one of those multiskit films from the 1960s.

Instead, let's seek out those small theaters and concert halls alleged to nurture budding talent whose mature glory we'll admire in the future. It would be misleading to say such theaters are sold out, or even reasonably full. I realize that any comparison, insofar as it intimates a potential value judgment, represents a violation of the rights of the artist (and probably even constitutes the first step on the path to fascism), but after consulting people who witnessed the success of cabarets in the thirty years following the Liberation, one is led to wonder what it is about today's society, which is more populous, wealthier, and more educated—and infinitely more concerned about flaunting its culture—that spurs so few Parisians to go out in the evening. And why it is that most people in the audience haven't even paid for their tickets—may as well let the cat out of the bag—but have been given freebies? Why so much incest? Ah, that establishment in the 4th arrondissement where two singers disguised as Pierrots, accompanied by an accordionist in overalls, tried to put some rock into old Bourvil's repertoire! (There were at least a dozen of us in the audience, although I suspect the plump lady who applauded so vigorously was not a complete stranger to the accordionist, any more than the five guys with her were to the two Pierrots.) Ah, that Piaf show in the deepest 9th arrondissement had everything of the great Edith: little black dress, cross around the neck, simple spotlight, and very same voice (almost)—except that no one was inside the voice. (What? Piaf? Bourvil?? All that was yesterday, or even the day before yesterday! That's right: the same period as those black-and-white photos by Doisneau and Brassaï, the same warmed over *Vieux Paris*.) Ah, that singer who made a videotape of himself, then sang duets (and even trios) on stage with his own image! Ah, that imitator who formerly starred on television, from which he was banished for I know not what disgrace, who now does skit after skit in which he tattles on the shabby lives and mores of other stars of the little screen, half to take revenge and half to convince himself he's still part of their world!

And concerts? Nary a week goes by in Paris without massacres being committed on Vivaldi (*The Four Seasons, Stabat Mater*), Bach (*Brandenburg Concertos*), Fauré (*Requiem*), Pachelbel and Albinoni (*the Canon* and *the Adagio*), Purcell (a medley of airs from *King Arthur, The Fairy Queen,* and *Dido and Aeneas*), not to mention the inevitable Slavic chorales with their pathetic mysteriousness.

Of course, sometimes you come across, in a café-theater in the 2nd arrondissement, a witty trio of English female musicians who mock the greatest hits with a great deal of spirit, or a quartet of actor-musicians whose completely original and impeccably executed gags make you laugh till you fall from the cheap bench. Yes, you can, of an evening, in a church, hear a male choir—all Brits who live in Paris—give a clutch of curious souls the opportunity to discover Josquin des Prez, Palestrina, and Tallis. Yes, you can, in a wormeaten hall in the 13th arrondissement, hear a highly sensitive interpretation of Debussy's *Sonata for Piano and Cello* by a Germano-

234

Turkish duo who wound up here by circuitous paths. But if you want to know what these hundreds of second-tier shows and concerts—below the top-billing performances (which could hardly be said to dazzle with brilliance)—really feel like, one image comes to mind: a church-pageant. There's no fundamental difference between the scene in Etienne Chatillez's film, *La Vie est un Long Fleuve Tranquille*, where a vicar in foppish ecstasy sings "Come back, Jesus, come back," and most shows playing in the small halls that supposedly constitute the underlying fabric of the Parisian artistic scene.

This provincialization of Paris's artistic scene resembles church-pageants insofar as the term designates a type of theatrical performance, recital, concert, or comedy skit in which what really counts is neither talent, work, nor intentions, but goodwill. Most cultural events produced in Paris, rather than facing artistic judgment (and therefore debate), benefit from a kind of humanitarian asylum and immunity (when they're not already part of official networks and aesthetics). The only critical commentary—and here I'm using critical in the sense of appreciation, both positive and negative—tolerated by such events is limited to a phrase empty of precise meaning, namely the vaguely flattering comment long employed by all putative art lovers unable to form their own opinion: "How interesting...." The modern variant has become, "How fabulously interesting...."

The apotheosis of this pitiful situation came, for me, during one or another of the increasingly frequent "open studio" events in Paris, in which "artists" exhibit their year's output at home or in some more-or-less abandoned public site. Originally, these events were conceived by painters, sculptors, and photographers who lacked the means or fame required to attract galleries, or who wished to exhibit in places less intimidating or less removed from the public they sought. Quickly overwhelmed by a flood of daubers and tinkerers convinced of their talent, the founders of the "open studio" idea now try, with more or less success, to shelter together and hoist distinctive signs in order to avoid being smothered by their own invention. It has to be admitted that, in comparison to the bulk of the "works" on show, all those dried-pasta necklaces, fired-clay ashtrays, and yogurt-jar vases that kids make (or made) as ghastly Mother's Day gifts suddenly seem worthy of the Louvre.

In her two-room apartment on the eighth floor, halfway up the hill in Belleville, a woman is holding a weekend exhibit of drops of resin that have been heated, colored, then trapped between two plates of glass. On the shelves of a bookcase in the corner are volumes by airport-novelist Paul-Louis Sulitzer, alongside titles by Michael of Greece, Paulo Cœlho, Pascal Sevran and a dozen of Goncourt-prize-winning novels. She holds forth on heated resin and unpredictable shapes more loquaciously than Proust's Madame Verdurin on Vinteuil's sonata. She's asking between 800 and 1,200 francs per work ($150-225) depending on size. For the duration of the "open studios" event, she has put a cloth over her television set.

In a garage, a man has written in red letters some four inches high on a wooden panel daubed in gray, ART IS A DIRTY JOB BUT SOMEONE HAS TO DO IT. (I wouldn't swear to that.) He has reproduced this sentence (this philosophy?) on a tee-shirt, and is standing next to his panel, with a somber (or profound?) expression.

In a spacious, light apartment whose rooms are arranged in an unusual, amusing fashion almost devoid of furniture, a couple await their customers. On the walls of each room are hung panels of particle board to which old clothes and used shœs have been nailed, depicting a figure of a man or woman. In the upper part, the head is sketched with thick lines of color. You could take a whole one home for 12,000 francs ($2,250), or a torso only for 4,000 francs ($750). I dropped by on a Sunday, around 2:00 P.M., and then again five hours later. All the works were still on the wall.

Not that people didn't come. To the contrary, there were lots of them, going from one "site" to another, respecting a sex-shop silence every time they entered. Visitors pace up and down seriously between the works, taking great care that their expression betray neither perplexity, nor boredom, nor disapproval, but merely a thoughtful, benevolent appreciation (probably similar to the one they give their children when the latter bring home scribbles or modelling-clay sculptures). It is moreover this conventional attitude that is the most painful thing—it reminds me of Mass in the Versailles of my youth: the same obligation, same conformism, same hieratic poses that serve to mask a lack of sincerity and personal interest, and the same involuntary capitulation to social demands.

Sunday daubers and tinkerers are not a recent development, of course. You only have to do the rounds of flea markets, secondhand shops, and even the Drouot auction house to realize that bland or pretentious canvases and permanently stillborn objets d'art weren't invented yesterday. Their inventors, for that matter, don't harm anyone, and this pastime would be inconsequential if the cultural demagogy of the last quarter of a century hadn't elevated such pieces to the status of artwork all the while shielding them from critical scrutiny. The less debate there is on art, the more it is replaced by "churchly goodwill" or cultural McCarthyism, making it easier for people who commission and profit from official art to do business in the thick fog of a world devoid of criteria, of discussion, of freedom.

Nor is it new—in art or any other field—to find a clique of cads marching sometimes in front, sometimes behind, the power-obsessed crowd, trying to confer the status of dogma on their own self-justifications. But what is new, in Paris more than elsewhere, is that—unlike Molière's Trissotin—these people now hold the high ground without having to suffer the darts of satire or the blows of polemics, without running the constant risk of seeing their masks yanked off.

237

When it comes to intellectual life, as with social life, Paris is a town in a mindless daze.

To my eyes, there's a physical manifestation of this daze, this vacantness, this collapse—namely, the void left by the redevelopment of Les Halles. What the Voisin plan proposed for the Marais (a housing-project suburb within the city walls), the Pompidou plan actually carried out for the "belly of Paris." (Maybe it would be fairer to add to the former French president's name a list of all those "senior civil-service vandals" who pitched in or acquiesced to his plan.) Of course, it was obvious that the fruit and vegetable market could no longer remain in the center of town. Urban historians even argue, with solid evidence, that Second Empire planners already erred in not moving it from Les Halles, which had been the site of the market since the days of King Philippe-Auguste (1165-1223).

But transferring the market to Rungis, outside Paris, in no way required that the Baltard market pavilions be demolished, nor that the wretched hole known as Le Forum be "erected"(?!). These two abominations represented the culmination of a process of debasement and depersonalization of Paris, triggered not by financial circles (merely the accelerators and beneficiaries) but by the technostructure crowd with its pride, its unreasonable thirst for power, and its extravagant pretensions to shape the city and inflect lifestyles as much as possible. The founding act of this process was probably the 1956 statute repealing the height restriction which limited all Parisian buildings to thirty-one meters (100 feet). This decision, in addition to the satisfaction it gave real-estate developers, betrayed a total absence of understanding of Paris, a city of melange and exchange, a city of *quartiers* with their own strong identities (which allowed photographers to show their talent, just as typical city characters did), and therefore a city with a diffuse lifestyle lived horizontally, at street level. This repeal led to successive massacres along the Seine riverfront, the southern Ternes neighborhood, Porte Maillot, much of the 13th arrondissement, Place des Fêtes, and Belleville. It gave birth to monsters that came increasingly close to the center of town, such as the Montparnasse tower and the Zamansky tower in the former wine market on the Left Bank. It provided a way to measure, during all these real-estate operations, the determination of elected officials to save Paris—and to observe that the required determination was nonexistent and unlikely ever to exist.

Government ministers, prefects, and the Dr. Strangeloves of urban development were henceforth guaranteed impunity and became intoxicated by their armchair creation of a greater Paris region with new suburban towns and a new capital; and they were still driven by the age-old hate and sense of threat that French governments have always felt for their capital city and its population. They then produced their masterpiece in the very heart of Paris, accomplishing the great technocratic dream: raze the past and write the present as though History began with themselves.

No thought was ever given to what might befall the city and its inhabitants following the transfer (again, technically justified) of a commercial activity that had marked it and them for five hundred years. No consideration was given to the extraordinary role played by Les Halles as a spontaneous social regulator, a *quartier* where poverty and everything that comes under today's term of "social exclusion" might find asylum, subsistence, company. This didn't make poverty enviable, but simply endurable. There existed, in the center of Paris, a free zone that had both a real and symbolic existence, now forever denied to the numerous "new poor" and the homeless (known in France by the bureaucratic acronyms RMists and SDFs). This zone is now also denied to all those beings who have made any kind of break with society, to whom the city—and mainly the Halles *quartier*—provided a

239

safety net for centuries Official sociologists paid no heed to the disappearance of this shelter (today they'd say "zone of liberty"). In their eyes, no free zone could function as regulator and integrator unless they decided on it, designed it, and dictated its regulations, implantation, boundaries. They and the decisionmakers felt that the *quartier* of Les Halles was the last thieves' den to escape economic, political, and social rationalism. So they dismantled it down to the last stone.

The utopian dimension of their plan and the premeditation of the murder of the center of Paris can be appreciated if you realize that in addition to the Baltard pavilions and the market square, ten streets were razed and one hundred thirty buildings in perfect condition were demolished. No other city—except maybe Bucharest under Ceaucescu—suffered such government vandalism. No political party was able to efficiently channel the constant, popular demonstrations—bringing together Parisians of all stations and ages—which attempted to prevent these terrible exactions; they were repressed with a brutality that amazed and often outraged even those newspapers closest to the government.

Competitions for plans to replace the market were organized by community defense associations. Despite the quality and interest of a great number of entries, none of the proposals were examined by the national or municipal government. It was out of the question to let the sociability of Les Halles survive, or even to save the buildings that had sheltered it; a rich, Paris-loving American offered to dismantle the pavilions at his own expense and rebuild these masterpieces of cast-iron architecture wherever desired (still at his own expense). The director of the city's technical services department replied that the operation was technically impossible—even though just a few months later it was performed on a pavilion at Nogent-sur-Marne at the request of the local mayor (a member of the Gaullist party in power). The very act of demolition was savage, as can be confirmed today simply by going to the Videotheque de Paris and viewing the documentaries and news clips of the day. Having just arrived in Paris myself, I witnessed the silent gatherings of distressed, serious faces marked with profound sadness, eyes moist with tears as steel balls hanging from wires attached to cranes shattered the pavilions' pillars, one after another, forcing those graceful umbrellas (under which an entire city once sheltered) to topple. I saw figures burdened by grief and shame come furtively to contemplate the mortal remains of that architecture and the last vestiges of that life before the trucks carted them off to the scrap heap. I write this so that no one will think that Parisians gave up without a fight, or that they didn't instinctively know the cost of such vandalism. Some of them have left moving accounts—penned, photographed, or filmed—of their awareness of this terrible loss. Others pieced together "memorials"; in a chapel along the north aisle of Saint-Eustache a naïve, colorful bas-relief depicts the closing of the last market day at Les Halles on 28 February, 1969. It provides a glimpse of what the defenders of the Baltard pavilions and the magnificent brick-and-iron cellars were mourning—they were mourning Paris itself.

One Sunday afternoon in 1996, when I was strolling along lower rue Montmartre, I heard sounds of a Mass being sung at Saint-Eustache, at that unusual hour. I went in. It was the annual Mass that *charcutiers* hold in honor of their patron saint, attended by a thousand or so of those sausage-and-cold-cuts butchers prior to enjoying one of the most opulent buffets that I have ever admired. There they discussed the fortunes and misfortunes of their ever-so-useful profession. They were far from all the television lights, cameras, and reporters, on a Sunday afternoon in the former church of Les Halles, at a time when even tourists didn't visit religious buildings. The charcutiers weren't there to mourn the spot where they once came to buy wholesale supplies; they're now quite used to Rungis which, for that matter, has its own—if rather standoffish—charm. They were there to keep alive the memory of a way of living and residing. No one asked Paris to remain stuck in that way of living and residing; only that, in its inevitable evolution, the city would remain faithful to the spirit, strive to reinvent it.

Instead, we got the Forum des Halles.

Does anyone remember that this underground wart was initially supposed to be an upscale mall? That the mixed private/public firm charged with designing and building it had vaunted it as the future showcase for French luxury goods? (Ah, those mixed private/public corporations, what a wonderful recipe for wheeling-and-dealing, incompetence, and irresponsibility!) Do people recall that, based on this buoyant outlook, in the early 1980s Yves Saint Laurent and Cardin opened boutiques in the gimcrack galleries on the highest underground floor, Level 1? They were joined by Ungaro and Tarlazzi and shoe stores of the same ilk, which had been assured that the Forum would become another Faubourg Saint-Honoré, further supercharged by the site's modernity. Below these aristocrats came Levels 2 and 3 for "mid-range" stores. You have to admire the simplicity of this concept: the less dazzling were located closer to the bowels of the earth, the more distinguished were closer to the heavens. As simple as it may have been, the regular customers of Faubourg Saint-Honoré apparently weren't buying it, for they stayed put. Or else they were put off by the architecture—panned by *The New York Times*—and the atmosphere. Nor did "mid-range" customers make the move. After the first year of trading, stores that let themselves get involved in this business had a cumulative turnover of just 26 percent of initial forecasts.

The chic crowd may not have sent any delegates to the Forum des Halles, but the punks, guitar pluckers, and panhandlers sure did. They'd been evicted from the esplanade in front of the nearby Pompidou Center soon after the center's opening, and were all the happier to move into the Forum since its "streets" were covered. Their ranks soon swelled with bums drawn by the same conveniences, along with prostitutes of all sexes, and with drug dealers who quickly saw the attraction of all those escalators, emergency exits, access corridors, storage alleys, and rear bays. Since all the hallways serving the three underground shopping levels enjoyed the status of city streets (only recently revoked), it was impossible to close the Forum at night. More and more black-market businesses sprang up there. The technocratic eggheads in the mixed public/private corporation hadn't thought of that.

So they installed fifty surveillance cameras wired to three command posts and organized regular guard patrols, accompanied by dogs at night. In addition, the municipal police force provided one police station, four uniformed officers on patrol, two plainclothes agents, and a ten-man rapid intervention brigade held in reserve—on the surface, in open air— for any sudden disasters. The private guards were given instructions to "discourage" punks, guitar pluckers, bums, and panhandlers. Store owners got into the habit of calling the command post every time they spied a "bleach head" or other specimen of what they called "the mob." The police took care of tracking dealers and prostitutes (both sexes). Modernity seemed to be losing its zest.

It was decided—by top management of the mixed public/ private corporation—to give the Forum a new look and to "reposition" it. The president of the firm declared that all three levels would become nothing less than "a laboratory of innovation in terms of public relations, business, and creativity in the sphere of leisure and cultural activities." He also announced that a rich, upmarket clientele was no longer welcome (the unwelcome parties seemed oblivious to the affront) and that two social categories identified by market-research gurus would henceforth be entitled to the label of Forum customers: "assimilated innovators" and "consistent pioneers." These labels—worthy of Giraudoux's *Madwoman of Chaillot*—wrapped a semantic fog around the population of nouveaux riches that emerged after (and often in the wake of) the events of May 68. In order to entice them, "free expression" and social conscience were offered as bait. One wall over by the Bourse exit was allotted to graffiti, aphorisms, and proclamations of all kinds, in such a way that—audacity of audacities—consumer society could be trashed (read: "challenged") on the very walls of its own temple. But it turned out that no one came to use the wall designated for free expression, except for a few male passers-by strongly driven by social circumstances to respond to an urgent call of nature. The mixed public/private corporation therefore called upon a professional and mercenary protester, hoping that he would scrawl striking phrases that would prime the pump and encourage rivals. No such luck; the Forum's official graffiti artist, Mézèque (for that was his tag and pseudonym), remained practically the sole user of the wall. He wrote dangerously subversive aphorisms like, "If only we could turn the sympathy of the fattest into bread-and-butter for the skinniest!" (I rarely go to the Forum des Halles, but I can't pass by Mézèque's former wall without thinking of that pathetic clown and everything he symbolized.)

In addition to this modest contribution to the birth of direct democracy, the mixed public/private corporation affirmed its social conscience by installing—on Level 4 (a Metro and suburban RER train station)—a large cube of glass that it allocated to associations such as Consumer's Choice, School for Parents, and The Handicapped Consortium. On the window of the cube, dubbed an "Activity Center," the mixed public/private corporation effectively wrote: here, you don't consume. There they organized lectures, discussions of music from the Andes, and seminars on car insurance, Armenian genocide, or psychological violence in children. The center was hardly more successful than the "free expression" wall. A board permanently on display enjoined people to— among other hollow phrases—"share solitude." (A sentiment perhaps designed to comfort the center's staff.)

Even as the second group of "target" customers remained deaf to the development corporation's seduction campaign, the bowels of the earth spewed forth—via the mouths of the Metro and RER suburban lines—masses of creatures who were as undesired (not to say undesirable) as they were unpredicted (not to say unpredictable): suburban ghettoites. Every day the underground hub was a site of passage for hundreds of thousands of these representatives of the middle and lower-middle classes who could not be counted upon to shop at Yves Saint-Laurent, wear Pinet shœs, or sport Guerlain perfume. And it proved impossible, despite deployment of the most ingenious artifices, to assimilate them with the "assimilated innovators" or "consistent pioneers." Yet they seemed amenable to spending part of their middling incomes at the Forum. They represented a daily pool of 700,000 potential customers—but the eggheads at the mixed public/ private corporation hadn't thought of them. So the suburbanites jogged the technocrats' memories.

Once the developers realized that the modern Faubourg Saint-Honoré (which they had conceived all alone) was stillborn, and that its minor-league version was not going to be a hit either, they got down to saving face and their shirts. They called on FNAC (a large book, record, and electronic goods chain), which first had been refused premises at the Forum, and whose management had bided its time until it could dictate its own terms. FNAC had initially been deemed too lowly to be included among the aristocrats of trade, but now the developers were counting on it and its noble business of selling books and records to serve as a flagship for the Forum des Halles, and they hoped that some of its customers would go shop in other mid-range stores. FNAC set its own rent.

It even became the model for the other retailers in the Forum. The president of their association was dazzled by a system in which most of FNAC's turnover came from selling electronic goods while most of its publicity and image-building came from public discussions with authors and other cultural events. As the president stated to *Express Magazine*, "When you want to go to bed with a woman, you don't say, 'Wanna go to bed with me?' You say, 'Would you like to come back to the house for a drink?'" FNAC played the role of "a drink back at the house," and once it moved in (and luxury-goods aristocrats moved out), it attracted retailers in synergy with it—Habitat with its household furnishings, Pier Import in the same niche, retailers of organic and natural products, sportswear, and "California-style" fancy items. Thus the boutiques on the upper level found tenants less glamorous but more permanent than the initial house-warmers.

As to the lower levels, they were abandoned (with the discretion suited to defeats) to the suburbanites disgorged from the deepest depths, to their small appetites and modest means. Cheap clothing and industrially-prepared fast food shared most of the available premises. They remain to this day the main concessions there, and have swarmed into the newer, second wing of the Forum, invisible from the outside but less crushed and less pathetic than those within the original wing. Yet still unworthy of the center of a city like Paris.

Unworthy is far too tame a word to describe the architecture framing the Forum. It would be a Herculean task to detail the feebleness, emptiness, and blandness of it, the total absence of ideas, aesthetics, ambition, spirit. And yet this total nonentity now enfolds the heart of Paris. A heart that no longer pumps any energy into the city. A grim plateau flanked by restaurants which, to the southwest, draw an "in" crowd that "thrills to *Vieux Paris*" as embodied by the vestiges of a few old cafés and restaurants once frequented by market porters. Restaurants to the north, meanwhile, specialize in "tourists-who-were-told-that-Les-Halles-was-authentic." They also attract a night crowd who, for want of better, knows that at least it will always find something open and, on occasion, edible. Singers and musicians panhandle in front of the outdoor terraces; they can be heard quite distinctly from the apartment of my friend Charlotte, on the top floor of a building flanking the Bourse de Commerce, facing Beaubourg (with Père-Lachaise cemetery visible in the far distance). One day in late spring when I was having a drink at her place after dinner, when night had not yet completely closed in, a Bob Dylan song wafted up from the pavement opposite the terraces.

"It's ten o'clock," said Charlotte.

"Pardon?"

"Ten o'clock. Dylan is always at 10:00 P.M. At ten-thirty there's *L'Accordéoniste* played, of all things, on the accordion. At eleven it's the turn of the violinist—jazz and Gypsy tunes. At eleven-thirty, another accordionist comes by. Every night, each arrives at the appointed hour, plays the same repertoire as the night before, and heads off. They leave a five-minute interval between acts. I've observed this daily ritual for the past two months. You'd think they punch timeclocks. I can't think of anything more depressing."

Depressing, drab, glum, dull, boring, banal—every one of these adjectives applies to what has replaced the old marketplace at Les Halles. But here again, such decline was far from inevitable. Baltard's pavilions might still be standing. They might house a large flower market and various semiwholesale or retail markets. Paris could have kept its "belly"—perhaps slimmer than the old potbelly, but that would be in keeping with the times. Customers would have come not only from neighboring *quartiers* but also from every part of the city, in search of quality, competitive prices, the fun of shopping there, and the beauty of the site—nothing is more popular today than markets. Theater, dance, and music groups could have moved into other pavilions—director Ariane Mnouchkine and choreographer Maurice Béjart had already indicated their interest, as did others. And Paris apparently lacks a major concert hall—who would believe that Paris was able to turn the Orsay train station into a museum yet couldn't get an auditorium out of Baltard's buildings? Even in the worst case, the acoustics wouldn't have been any poorer than those at the new Bastille Opera House.

Between the impoverishment of university libraries and the crush at the Bibliothèque Nationale, Paris has suffered from a dramatic lack of public reading facilities since the late 1960s. Why didn't anyone think of rectifying this shameful shortcoming by converting the pavilions and their vaulted cellars, perhaps complementing the library with a videotheque, cinematheque, and mediatheque? Because they wanted to build the icy, ponderous, repulsive new Bibliothèque Nationale de France?

City councilors regularly refer to the need to balance the respective weights of the east and west sides of town; but the question of putting life back into the center, the pivot between these forces, is never raised. The capital's elected officials might like to meditate on a few drastic facts which usually start them prattling, if not acting. In the 1st arrondissement, for example, there are now more parking spaces than schoolchildren. And one of the department stores in the heart of Paris decided to appeal to a younger clientele by firing all its salespeople who were "too old."

Paris is henceforth devoted to the ideology of the urban village. Yet even if, throughout its history, it has featured strongly individualized *quartiers*, aware of their specialness and ready to stress it, that attitude was transcended by the feeling of belonging to a common city—part real, part myth—whose center was seen by all as a kind of empyrean sphere where the city's virtues were enshrined: liberty, vital-

248

ity, diversity. A place where not even clocks had the power to regulate activities, where night could equal day (and sometimes outdo it), where the dark was less frightening than elsewhere. Where chance played its finest, and most varied, role. Where humanity could be seen in every light. As I said, this place was partly a myth, but the myth was believable. A belief shared by Parisians, provincials, and foreigners alike, galvanizing everyone's devotion to the city. By failing to nurture this myth and this reality after the departure of the market for Rungis, by becoming a *tabula rasa*, the center of Paris ceased to exist; and in losing its center the city lost the best of itself. I would add—even if the remark seems anecdotal or trivial—that Paris has lost the respect of its inhabitants: I know of no other developed city in the world where so many men piss outdoors, at all hours of the day and without the least shame. The banks of the Seine reek with urine as soon as temperatures become springlike—as do the grotesque gardens above the Forum, not to mention the platforms of God knows how many Metro stations and the corners of how many streets. (Although it should be admitted that you now have to pay for public conveniences.)

Deprived of their idealized city (in the sense that people talk of an idealized self), Parisians are prey to their worst drives, headed by vanity and complacency. I can't think of any period in its history when the capital offered so little to the rest of the world, when it was less open to cosmopolitan ideas, styles, and influences, when it was so provincial. Yet at the same time, I can't think of a period when its inhabitants were so complacently unaware of this provincialism. Flaubert's Monsieur Homais would be right at home here, making pompous prophesies in his "urban village" and only seeing things his own way. For the coming millennium, he is being offered a city in which small-town attitudes will prosper. The municipal transportation authority is thinking of replacing the major bus lines that crisscross the city and go from one *quartier* to another with lines that will spiral in snail form within the capital's villages.

And, even as Parisians consent to the collapse of their city, electioneering and political correctness in the name of decentralization (which merely results, moreover, in the creation of regional monarchies) have united to deprive the city of the means to recover its ambition, that is to say, first of all, to reclaim its ambitiousness and its heart. It may be that this Parisian daze will turn out to be just a bad moment in the city's history; but it may also point to its future, one like Venice. All that would remain of a city that welcomed so much humanity, gave birth to so many ideas, and created so much public and private freedom, would be magnificent tombstones waiting to be photographed. And the only living remnant of grand old Paris, a Parisian's Paris, would be the Seine.

Cet ouvrage a été réalisé par la
SOCIÉTÉ NOUVELLE FIRMIN-DIDOT
Mesnil-sur-l'Estrée
pour le compte des Éditions Flammarion
en octobre 1999

Imprimé en France
Dépôt légal : octobre 1999
Nº d'édition : FA366409 – Nº d'impression : 48123